D0848006

TURGENEV:
THE NOVELIST'S NOVELIST
A Study

TURGENEV:
THE NOVELIST'S NOVELIST
A Study

by

RICHARD FREEBORN

GREENWOOD PRESS, PUBLISHERS
WESTPORT, CONNECTICUT

Library of Congress Cataloging in Publication Data

Freeborn, Richard.
   Turgenev : the novelist's novelist, a study.

   Reprint of the ed. published by Oxford University
Press, London.
   Bibliography: p.
   Includes index.
   1. Turgenev, Ivan Sergeevich, 1818-1883--Criticism
and interpretation.
[PG3448.F7 1978]   891.7'3'3 [B]   77-18683
ISBN 0-313-20187-0

This reprint has been authorized by the Oxford University Press

Reprinted in 1978 by Greenwood Press, Inc.
51 Riverside Avenue
Westport, CT. 06880

Printed in the United States of America

10 9 8 7 6 5 4 3 2 1

'Turgenev is in a peculiar degree what I may call the novelist's novelist, an artistic influence extraordinarily valuable, and ineradicably established.'

'Ah, he was the real, but a thousand times the only—the only real beautiful genius!'

HENRY JAMES ON IVAN TURGENEV

PREFACE

In the transliteration of Russian words and names I have tried to be as simple as possible, using an approximate phonetic equivalent in English where there is no alphabetical equivalent (i.e. kh for Russian X, shch for Russian щ, etc.). Where the Russian letter 'e' stands in an initial position or is preceded by another vowel, I have inserted a 'y' (i.e. Yelena, Dostoyevsky). I have also used 'y' to express the Russian й and ы and, as is usual, ий and ый in a final position in attributives and proper names. The soft sign has been expressed by an apostrophe, although I have omitted this in such names as Gogol, Gorky, Ryazan. I have preferred, however, to use *Eugene Onegin* rather than *Yevgeny Onegin*.

In translating the Russian term *zapadnik* I have chosen to use Westernist, rather than Westerner or Westernizer, which are sometimes used. Westerner has an ambiguous meaning in English—meaning either one who adheres to Western beliefs or comes from the West—while Westernizer has an oddly old-fashioned ring. In using the term Westernist I have attempted to invoke only the one meaning as it applies to Turgenev—that is to say, as a Russian who adhered to Western beliefs and European principles.

In giving dates I have indicated when they refer to the Old Style (in the nineteenth century the Russian calendar was twelve days behind the Gregorian) by inserting O.S. in brackets. When Turgenev in his correspondence put two dates, I have usually offered both.

The extracts from Turgenev's work quoted in the text are in my own translation, based on definitive Soviet editions. I have translated myself in order to ensure what—I hope—is reasonable accuracy, though I do not wish to claim that my translations have any special merit. For this reason, I have not given specific references to the Russian sources of Turgenev's fiction, believing that these can easily be identified in the many English translations of Turgenev's fictional works which are now available. Source references are only given for his non-fictional works and for his correspondence. Places of publication of English, French and Russian works referred to in the notes are London, Paris and Moscow respectively unless otherwise indicated.

Finally, I must acknowledge a profound debt of gratitude to my colleague, Mr. J. S. G. Simmons, for his invaluable help in reading through my text with such care and in offering advice on bibliographical matters. I am also indebted to Mr. Gilbert Phelps for his assistance in identifying the source of a Henry James quotation.

R. F.

CONTENTS

INTRODUCTION

During his lifetime Turgenev acquired many reputations. He was a political figure whose views received approval and sympathy in some quarters, disdain and outright rejection in others, a man who regarded himself as a European in Russia and a Russian in Europe, a man who appointed himself as an unofficial intermediary between the culture of his birthright and the culture of his adoption, a man of extraordinary, innate contradictions, whose admiration of youth was paralleled by a hypochondriacal fear of death, whose aristocratic extraction was never to be completely overcome in his desire to be the enlightened humanitarian, a man, finally, who never married but devoted the greater part of his adult life to a seemingly unrequited passion for a married lady. Of one thing we may be certain in speaking of Turgenev: he never betrayed the least sign of 'bourgeois' conformity in the way he lived his life, despite his admiration for certain aspects of the 'bourgeois' West or his eight-year residence in the 'bourgeois' circumstances of Baden-Baden. His life and his many reputations were essentially products of a nineteenth century that still took its examples from the eighteenth. He believed in Man with a capital M, not the economic unit of proletarian man which Marx raised upon his revolutionary pedestal; he believed in the principles of 1789 and not the materialist principles of the Communist Manifesto; he believed in the eighteenth-century classical view of the Fates and not in the Nietzschean idea of free will. But for all this Turgenev remains a figure integral to the middle years of the nineteenth century in the sense that he could enjoy to the full that enlightened cosmopolitanism and free intercourse of cultures which was the privilege of the European aristocracy of that time—a privilege since jeopardized by economic change and the exaggerated twentieth-century concern for differentiation between nations. It was because Turgenev could travel so easily from cultural centre to cultural centre and feel himself as much at home in Berlin as in Moscow, or in Baden-Baden as on his estate at Spasskoye, that he acquired his many reputations and might be called, as Dostoyevsky called Herzen, a *gentilhomme russe et citoyen du monde*.[1]

[1] F. M. Dostoyevsky, *The Diary of a Writer* (1949), i. 5.

But the Turgenev whose name and fame have extended into the twentieth century and will endure longer still is the Ivan Turgenev who enjoyed an international reputation as a writer of novels. The other reputations, which were so ephemeral, have rightly waned. Nowadays Turgenev's name is respected as one of the half-dozen or so great Russian novelists of the nineteenth century, standing beside Tolstoy and Dostoyevsky, one whose influence is still to be felt in a variety of ways even in the literature of the present day. Translations of Turgenev's novels and stories are still widely read in the West, while his fame and popularity in the Soviet Union are undisputed. For an understanding of Turgenev's achievement, however, it is clearly necessary to attempt an assessment both of Turgenev's place in the literature of his own country and of those original features in his work as a novelist which contributed so much to its success. Turgenev's reputation in the West has been at the mercy of invidious comparisons with his two outstanding compatriots, Tolstoy and Dostoyevsky, and comparisons of this kind—justifiable in the sense that all three wrote their work in Russian—have often tended to leave out of account the fact that Turgenev was the forerunner, even in a sense the guide, of the other two writers. His achievement had a special character, both for Russian literature and for Europe, which was quite distinct from the achievement of other Russian novelists of repute, and the special character of this achievement is worthy of particular attention.

This study sets out to illuminate the distinctive features of what is sometimes referred to as the 'Turgenevan novel' and to examine the development that it underwent at Turgenev's hands. He was, in Henry James's estimate, both 'the novelist's novelist'[1] and 'the beautiful genius'.[2] With his knowledge of his art, he was—for his own age, at least, if not perhaps for the harsher world of the twentieth century —'the novelist's novelist'. Although this study is concerned primarily with his place in his own age, it also attempts to justify Henry James's estimate. It is salutary to be reminded that genius can be beautiful. Turgenev's genius is not open to question; it is that ill-used word 'beautiful' which provides a more fruitful subject of study.

[1] Henry James, *The House of Fiction: Essays on the Novel* (1957), 170.
[2] Quoted from Ford Madox Ford, *Mightier than the Sword* (1938), 190.

I

THE BEGINNINGS
YOUTH, PHILOSOPHY, POLITICS

TURGENEV wrote only one brief autobiographical sketch for publication during his lifetime. 'Frankly,' he wrote to a correspondent in 1869, 'any biographical publication has always seemed to be pretentious; but to refuse to write such a thing, generally to lend importance to it—that's even more pretentious. . . .'[1] Six years after that letter he wrote out an autobiographical sketch for publication in a journal called *The Russian Library*.

Ivan Sergeyevich T. [he wrote], was born on October 28, 1818, in the town of Oryol to Sergey Nikolayevich Turgenev and Varvara Petrovna Lutovinova —the second of three sons; the eldest of them, Nikolay, is still alive [in 1875], the youngest, Sergey, died in his sixteenth year. Turgenev's father served in the Yelizavetgrad cuirassier regiment which was quartered in Oryol. Retiring with the rank of Colonel, he settled on his wife's estate in the village of Spasskoye-Lutovinovo, which was ten versts from the town of Mtsensk in the Oryol province, and in 1822 he undertook with his entire family accompanied by servants—in two carriages and a wagon—a trip abroad, in the course of which I. S. almost perished, in the Swiss town of Berne, having lost hold of the railings which surrounded the pit in which the town's bears were kept; his father just managed to catch him by the leg. On their return to Spasskoye the Turgenev family settled down to country life, that squirearchal, slow, expansive and petty life, the very memory of which has already been almost forgotten by the present generation, with its usual round of tutors and teachers, Swiss and German, home-grown 'uncles' and serf nannies. At the beginning of 1827 the Turgenevs moved to Moscow where they bought a house on the Samotyok, and in 1833 I. S., being then only fifteen years of age, entered Moscow University, choosing the 'philological' faculty, as it was then called. . . . In 1834 Ivan Sergeyevich's father transferred him to the University of St. Petersburg so that he could share lodgings with his eldest brother who had entered the artillery of the Guards, and in that same year he died. I. S. left the university in 1837 as a graduate student, and in 1838 he set off to undertake

[1] Letter to K. K. Sluchevsky, 8 March 1869. Quoted from I. S. Turgenev. *Sochineniya* (1933), xii. 501.

further study in Berlin on the steamship *Nicholas I* which caught fire within sight of Travemuende. The amount of knowledge which he took with him from St. Petersburg University was not great: of all his professors only P. A. Pletnyov was capable of having any influence on his audience. In Berlin I. S. concerned himself primarily with Hegelian philosophy (under Werder), with philology and history. . . . I. S. spent two semesters in Berlin; together with him Granovsky and Stankevich also attended courses. In 1840, after a short visit to Russia and a trip to Italy, he again returned to Berlin and remained there for about a year, sharing lodgings with the famous M. A. Bakunin, not at that time occupied in politics. In 1841 he returned to Russia, entered in 1842 the Ministry of Internal Affairs under V. M. Dal', served very badly and inefficiently, and in 1843 retired from the service. In that year he began his literary career—he published a short poem *Parasha* without, however, adding his name, and also became acquainted with Belinsky. In the course of the two following years he continued to write verses and even poems, which neither deserved nor received any acclaim, and, going abroad at the end of 1846, he had practically decided to abandon or change his career; but the success of a short prose piece entitled *Khor' and Kalinych*, which he had left in the editorial office of the recently rejuvenated journal *The Contemporary* brought him back to literary pursuits. Since then they have not ceased—and last year [1874] there appeared the fifth edition of his collected works. A brief pause in his literary activities occurred only in 1852 when, on account of the publication of his article on the death of Gogol, or, to be more precise, due to the appearance of the separate edition of *A Sportsman's Sketches*, I. S. was imprisoned for a month and later sent to his estate, from which he only returned in 1854. Since 1861 I. S. has lived for the greater part abroad.[1]

As one might expect, this is Turgenev giving his official view of himself, disavowing, in the manner of Nekrasov, his squirearchal or gentry background, exalting the importance of learning, emphasizing his association with the leading figures of the time—such as Granovsky, Stankevich, Belinsky, and Bakunin—and representing himself as a writer who has suffered official persecution in the cause of literature. This autobiographical sketch must be thought of as being addressed, as was so much of Turgenev's work, to the younger generation. In this case, its audience would be the generation of the populists of the 1870's, such young people as Marianna and Nezhdanov of *Virgin Soil* or the slightly older 'younger generation' of the radicals of the sixties, for whom Turgenev, the man of the forties, was already 'an archaic survival'—as Bazarov called Pavel Petrovich Kirsanov, the representative of the 'fathers' in *Fathers and Children*—and in whose eyes

[1] I. S. Turgenev, *Sobraniye sochineniy* (1956), xi. 417-19.

Turgenev always, sometimes unnecessarily, felt the need to justify himself. This autobiography, therefore, is interesting as much for what it omits as for what it says. It relates the bare facts of Turgenev's life up to the second half of the 1840's, during the period when Turgenev still regarded himself as being youthful. To be more precise, this is really an autobiographical sketch of Turgenev's life up to 1848, that fateful year when the forties, the decade of high ideals and grand illusions, came to an end with the death of Belinsky and the Paris revolution, shortly to be followed by the Petrashevsky affair (that was to send Dostoyevsky into a ten-year exile).

Turgenev was born, as he says, on October 28 (O.S.), 1818 in the town of Oryol. The marriage of Varvara Lutovinova and Sergey Nikolayevich Turgenev was scarcely more than an uneasy partnership. Varvara Lutovinova was considerably richer and six years older than her husband, and she was endowed with a domineering character. It is Turgenev's father who appears to be the active partner of the marriage in the autobiographical sketch, whereas it was in fact his mother who proposed and disposed in the Turgenev household with a wanton disregard of her children's or her servants' feelings. Turgenev's laconic reference to the 'slow, expansive and petty life' on the Spasskoye estate hides the cruel truth about his boyhood years. His mother was, in his own words, a 'capricious and power-loving woman, who alone gave us—and sometimes even took from us—our means of survival'.[1] Her rule was draconian and her idea of justice entirely suited to her position as the sole authority in the household. Punishment was meted out to serfs, children, and tutors with an imperious arbitrariness; and Turgenev himself suffered no less than the others. The extent to which such harsh experiences may have affected Turgenev's character is matter only for speculation. He emerged from those early years at Spasskoye surprisingly without bitterness. They were, after all, a mixture of Oblomov's dream and Ostrovsky's 'dark kingdom', of the feudal idyll and the feudal hell. Turgenev was to make use of the idyll on many occasions in portraying the country background of his novels, but at the same time Spasskoye taught him that the idyll was simply a mirage based on a corrupt system of land-tenure and the moral injustice of serfdom.

In 1827, two years after the Decembrist rising, the Turgenev family moved to Moscow. The Decembrist rising has been aptly described as

[1] Letter to S. A. Vengerov, 19 June (O.S.) 1874. I. S. Turgenev, *Sobr. soch.* (1958), xii. 460.

the attempt of the Russian nobleman to make a revolution to lose his rights. In this sense, it was a moral revolution in the name of the emancipation of the serfs and constitutional rights against the immorality of the Tsarist autocracy. The moral example of this rising, rather than the diverse political aims and doctrines of its participants and adherents, was what caught the imagination of the younger generation of the upper-class intelligentsia to which Turgenev belonged. Turgenev as a boy may have shown 'republican' tendencies, but the Turgenev of nine years of age who went to the Weidenhammer school with his brother Nikolay and two years later to the Armenian institute was never wittingly educated in the ideals of either 1789 or the Decembrist rising of 1825. Idealistic, however, he certainly was. The first strong literary influence of his life, so he tells us in his *Literary Reminiscences*, was Zagoskin's novel, *Yury Miloslavsky*, the melo-dramatic but awe-inspiring contents of which were narrated to him by one of the masters at the Weidenhammer school.[1] Yet Zagoskin himself, who used to visit the Turgenev house, presented, by virtue of his muscular and ungainly physique, such a contrast to the idealistic content of his novel that he had little appeal for the young Turgenev. Moreover, Turgenev's adolescence was spent in the shadow of Idealism. The cult of Schelling had found adherents among the young students of Moscow University at the beginning of the thirties and, though Turgenev was too young to participate in the university circles of those years, it is probable that he also felt the influence of the cult by way of the tutor, Klyushnikov, who prepared him for the university entrance examinations. But the Schellingian cult was not an isolated phenomenon. It was accompanied by the first inklings of a new political awareness after the tragedy of 1825 and an increased interest in the meaning of nationality (*narodnost'*). By the time Turgenev had moved to St. Petersburg University in 1834 Belinsky, the critic, who was later to have such an influence on him, had already published his first important critical article, *Literary Reflections*, in which he interpreted the problem of a national literature in strictly Schellingian terms. In the same way, Herzen, also later to be a close friend of Turgenev though never as close as Belinsky, had already begun to preoccupy himself with social and political questions. Schelling, politics, nationality—these, particularly the last, were the catch-words of the young Russian intelligentsia of the thirties. But for Turgenev to appreciate the spirit of the times properly he had to plunge into what he called

---

[1] *Literaturniye i zhiteyskiye vospominaniya* in *Sobr. soch.* (1956), x. 331-3.

'the German Sea'. He explains what he means by this in the opening to his *Literary Reminiscences*:

Having completed the course in the philological faculty of St. Petersburg University in 1837, I set off in the spring of 1838 to complete my studies in Berlin. I was 19 years old; I had dreamed of this trip for a long time. I was convinced that in Russia it was only possible to acquire a certain amount of provisional knowledge, but that the source of true knowledge was to be found abroad. There was not one among the number of teachers in St. Petersburg University at that time who could shake my conviction; besides, they were also convinced of it; the Mininstry of Education, headed by Count Uvarov, also had the same opinion, in sending young men abroad to German universities at the Ministry's expense. . . . This aspiration of young men—my contemporaries—for foreign parts was reminiscent of the way the Slavs looked for leaders among the Varangians from across the seas. Each of us felt exactly the same, that his *land* (I refer not to fatherland as such, but to the moral and intellectual heritage of each one of us) was great and bountiful, but in disorder. For myself I can say that I personally realised all the disadvantages of such an uprooting from my native soil, of such a violent disruption of all the links and threads that bound me to the life in which I had grown up . . . but there was nothing to be done about it. That life, that milieu and especially that stratum, if one can so express it, to which I belonged—the land-owning stratum, the serf-owning stratum—did not represent anything capable of holding me back. On the contrary, practically everything that I saw about me caused me to feel embarrassment and dissatisfaction and, finally, disgust. I could not hesitate for long. I had either to conform and set off meekly along the common rut, the beaten track; or I could turn my back once and for all, put far behind me 'all and everything', even at the risk of losing much that was dear and close to my heart. And that's what I did. . . . I flung myself head first into 'the German sea' which was destined to cleanse and renew me, and when I finally emerged from its waves I was a 'Westernist' and that I have remained ever since.[1]

Why a 'Westernist'? One may appreciate that there should be a nationalist party in the Russia of this time, but to the Western mind it may seem odd that a Russian should like to think of himself as an advocate of the West, should, what is more, be proud to be known as a 'Westernist' as opposed to a 'Slavophil' or representative of the nationalist faction. Westernism and Slavophilism, however, were not as mutually exclusive as are political parties in the West today. Westernism and Slavophilism were primarily states and attitudes of mind, the former favouring not a vague Western cosmopolitanism but European principles of enlightenment and social justice, the latter advocating

[1] Ibid., 260-1.

a return to the doctrines of the Orthodox Church and a somewhat romantic interpretation of the indigenous culture of the Russian peasantry. Both had common ground in their desire to promote a better future for Russia; both were equally sincere in their patriotism, in their love of Russia and its people. Yet states or attitudes of mind, although not strictly speaking organized into distinct political movements, can be just as mutually antagonistic and given to polemics. The forum for the airing of the different views was initially the university circles and the salons; later the quarrels were carried into journalism. These quarrels developed chiefly over the problem of interpreting the reforms that had been instituted by Peter I at the beginning of the eighteenth century. To the Westernists Peter I, with his introduction of Western ideas, his reform of the administration along Western lines and his insistence on the need for science, was a hero who had shown the path that Russia should take in the future. To the Slavophils Peter I was anathema, for he had undermined the patriarchal principles of the old Muscovy and destroyed the former unity existing between the Tsar and his people, that spiritual bond which was more valuable to the religious Slavophils than any Western principle of government. Politically, the Westernists were liberals, though there as many shades of liberalism as there were Westernists, while the Slavophils claimed to be apolitical, though in their wholehearted support for the autocracy—a support by no means as wholeheartedly reciprocated as they might have wished—they were clearly conservative in their political bias. In this connexion Turgenev goes on to say, and in so doing defines his Westernist standpoint:

I would not think of blaming those of my contemporaries who achieved that freedom and awareness towards which I aspired by another or less negative path. . . . I only want to say that *I* saw no other path before me. I could not breathe the same air or remain close to what I hated so much; for this I lacked, possibly, the necessary endurance and strength of character. I had to get far away from my enemy so that I could fall upon him all the more powerfully from a distance. In my eyes this enemy took a definite form and bore a particular name: this enemy was—serfdom. Under this heading I gathered and concentrated everything against which I had decided to fight to the bitter end, with which I had sworn never to come to terms. . . . This was my Hannibal's oath; and I was not the only one to make such an oath at that time. I went to the West in order the better to fulfil it. And I do not think my Westernism deprived me of all feeling towards Russian life, of all understanding of its peculiarities and needs. . . . I will also say that I have never recognised that unassailable barrier which other scrupulous, even zealous, but poorly informed, patriots persistently want to make between Russia and Western Europe, that Europe with which we are so closely linked by race, language and faith. Does not our Slavonic race—in the eyes of the philologist or the ethnographer—constitute one of the important branches of the Indo-Germanic peoples? And if it is impossible to deny the influence of Greece on Rome and their combined influence on the Germano-Romanic world, then on what grounds can one deny the influence of this—whatever you like to call it—kindred, homogeneous world on us? Surely we are not so lacking in indigenous qualities, so weak, that we have to be frightened of every outside influence and wave it away from us in childish horror for fear that it might taint us? I do not think so: on the contrary, I think that even if you washed us over and over again you would never be able to rid us of our essentially Russian nature.[1]

In these extracts from Turgenev's *Literary Reminiscences*, written in 1868 at a remove of thirty years from the time when he first went to Germany, one may naturally detect more than a simple outline of motives. He is here attempting—in rather sharp, hurt tones—to vindicate himself in the face of hostile charges of lacking patriotism, of being divorced from Russia, of fawning before the West, which were levelled at him during the sixties. But, these considerations apart, this plunge into 'the German sea' was simply Turgenev's way of coming to terms with Russia and with himself. Annenkov notes this when he says:

Europe was for him the land of regeneration; the roots of all his aspirations, the bases for the nurturing of his will and character and the development of his ideas were grounded in her soil. . . . It was not an absence of nationalist sympathies and a haughty indifference to the structure of Russian life which made Europe a necessity for him, but the fact that in Europe social life flowed more freely, swallowing up empty strivings, that in Europe he felt himself to be simpler, more sensible, more true to himself and freer from worthless temptations than when he stood face to face with the reality of Russia.[2]

The voyage, then, to Germany in 1838 was a very important moment in Turgenev's life. He was making an escape from a Russia which had come to repel him for personal as well as for reasons of principle; and in the West the nineteen-year-old Turgenev was to find new dedication and new vigour.

The most important thing that Turgenev was to find in the West was friendship with Stankevich. 'Stankevich', Turgenev wrote of him, 'had such an influence on others because he had no thought for himself.

[1] Ibid., 261-2.
[2] P. V. Annenkov, *Vospominaniya i kriticheskiye ocherki* (SPB., 1881), 191.

because he was sincerely interested in other people and, as though he himself did not notice it, attracted everyone to follow him into the sphere of the Ideal.'[1] This was not only the Ideal of Hegel or Schelling, but that interpretation of the Ideal offered by the young philosopher, Werder, whose courses Turgenev attended in Berlin. For Werder, philosophy was service of the divinity, religious edification, not in the passive sense, but of a kind that might elevate man towards humanitarian ideals and nurture in his heart a love of liberty. Turgenev was undoubtedly enthralled by this teaching. His interest in philosophical questions was paramount at this time, even though they implied political issues. His copies of the works of Hegel were scored with notes, and later, upon his return to Russia, he was to offer papers for an M.A. degree in philosophy at St. Petersburg University. But Turgenev was always more interested in human beings than in ideas; the ideas were important only so far as they shed light on the inner life of the individual. It is for this reason that the figure of Stankevich is so important in Turgenev's development during these years. Naturally inclined to be idealistic, attracted by idealistic philosophies, in his relations with friends he quickly showed a tendency to idolize and hero-worship. Stankevich was by no means an unworthy object of the young Turgenev's admiration. He embodied in his person so many of those high ideals which Turgenev had learned to reverence through his philosophical studies: a fervent belief in truth, a total dedication to the Ideal, a natural nobility. But more than these, probably, Stankevich embodied that ideal of altruistic service to a greater cause—the cause of enlightenment and humanity. It was not, however, until 1840, while in Rome, that Turgenev was to enter into a close relationship with his friend. It was in his relationship with Stankevich that Turgenev underwent his 'regeneration', that he became whole, reconciled, appreciative of nature and art, aware of himself; it was also in connexion with this relationship that Turgenev was to have personal experience of the fleetingness of life, the 'quarter of an hour' quality of happiness, which was later to supply the philosophical basis of his fiction. His letter to Granovsky on the occasion of Stankevich's death is sufficiently eloquent evidence of the shock he suffered:

We have suffered a great misfortune, Granovsky. I can scarcely gather the strength to write. We have lost a man whom we loved, in whom we believed, who was our pride and our hope. . . . On June 24 Stankevich died in Novi. I could, I ought to finish the letter here. What is there for me to say, what use

[1] *Soch.* (1933), xii. 246.

are my words now to you? I am continuing the letter not so much for you, as for myself: I got to know him in Rome; I saw him every day and began to appreciate his lucid mind, his warm heart, all the charm of his personality. . . . But the shadow of impending death was already upon him. . . .

We talked frequently of death: he recognised it as the limit of thought and, so it seemed to me, secretly shuddered. Death has a profound significance if it springs—as was the case—from the heart of a full, growing life: to an old man death is reconciliation; but for us and for him it is the law of fate. Why did he have to die? He acknowledged and loved so profoundly, so sincerely, the sacred quality of life; despite his illness [tuberculosis], he delighted in ideas, in action, in love; he was preparing to dedicate himself to working for Russia. . . .

Stankevich was, in fact, for Turgenev, the embodiment of that notion of philosophy as service, altruistic dedication, religious devotion which their mutual teacher, Werder, had propagated. In the same letter he mentions Werder's reaction to the news of Stankevich's death. '*Ich fühle es*,' the German said. '*Ich bin auf dem halben Wege meines Lebens: meine besten Schüler, meine Jünger sterben, ob ich überlebe sie.*' But Turgenev concludes his letter in another vein:

I look around me, I seek—but in vain. Who of our generation can replace our loss? Who is there worthy to take from this man who has died the gospel of his great ideas, to preserve his influence, to follow in his path, in his spirit, with his strength? . . . Oh, if only something could force me to doubt the future, I would now, having outlived Stankevich, part with my last hope. Why shouldn't another have died, thousands of others, myself for instance? When will the time come when a more mature spirit will be a sure condition of superior physical development and our life itself the condition and fruit of happiness of the creator, and how is it that on earth beauty can perish or suffer? Up till now it has seemed that ideas were a blasphemy and punishment inevitably awaited everything that was more than the blessed mediocrity. Or is the envy of God aroused, as was the envy of the Greek gods? Or must we believe that everything beautiful and sacred, that love and ideas are merely the cold irony of Jehovah? What then is our life? But no—we must not lose heart and give in. Let us gather together, join hands, close our ranks: one of us has fallen, perhaps the best. But others are arising, and will arise, the hand of God never ceases to sow in the soul the seeds of great aspirations, and sooner or later light will banish darkness.

But for us who knew him his loss is irreparable. Was it not Rachel who said: 'Wäre noch nie jünger Mann gestorben, hätte man nie Wehmut gekannt.'[1] From the heart of the creator there flows both joy and grief. Freude

[1] Rachel refers to Rachel Varnhagen von Ense (1771-1833).

und Leid: often they sound the same and fuse together: one is not complete without the other. Now it is the turn of grief . . .[1]

This letter summarizes the feelings of Turgenev as he emerged from 'the German sea'; this was the knowledge that he acquired in the West. First of all there is the idea of death as the law of fate and, more specifically, as the fate which awaits those who strive to dedicate themselves to Russia. It is just such a fate that awaits Rudin, Bazarov, and Nezhdanov in Turgenev's novels. Or there is the mention of the loss suffered by his own generation in Stankevich's death, and this idea is one of great importance in understanding Turgenev's attitude towards the Russian intelligentsia. Numerically the Russian intelligentsia in the nineteenth century was incredibly and tragically small by comparison with the equivalent intellectual élite in the West, and its smallness made it unusually influential and extraordinarily valuable. Each individual member of the Russian intelligentsia, therefore, was proportionately more valuable, and often proportionately more brilliant, than his equivalent in the West. In this letter Turgenev expresses his jealously protective feeling towards the intelligentsia. It was as a result of this feeling that Turgenev was to become the chronicler of the Russian intelligentsia in his novels; this was to be the way in which he followed in Stankevich's path and performed his service to Russia. But the letter, in the passion with which it is written, also touches on those philosophical issues which are later to crystallize into Turgenev's philosophy of life. How is it, he asks, that beauty can perish or suffer? Has the envy of God been aroused? Or must we believe that everything beautiful and sacred, that love and ideas are merely the cold irony of Jehovah? In the letter they are merely questions, but they are the questions which will later be posed in all his novels, leading to that final question which must inevitably be asked: What then is our life? Although there is no overt pessimism in these questions, the answers that Turgenev is later to give in his novels will be profoundly and bitterly pessimistic. Life will become for him 'a tragic comedy' in which the human will is at the mercy of powers vastly superior to it. Even so, in the supreme objectivity of his realistic view, Turgenev will always compound his novels of those things which he mentions in his letter—of love and ideas, of joy and grief—and it is in the fine balance between these opposed elements that the secret of his art as a novelist is to be found.

[1] *Sobr. soch.* (1958), xii. 15-18.

He was to take all these things back with him to Russia. Chief amongst them was the image of his dead friend, Stankevich, and the ideals which he embodied. He was also to have gained the friendship of Bakunin who was shortly to abandon Hegelianism in favour of revolution. As Turgenev's friendships changed, so his interests and ideas changed. The era of romanticism and the Ideal was passing and Turgenev was to return to a Russia where intellectual preoccupations had undergone a significant change as well.

II

The Turgenev who left Berlin in May, 1841, after completing his course of studies, was very like the young Lensky of Pushkin's *Eugene Onegin*. He, like Lensky, had made Goethe and Schiller his masters; he also was the romantic youth awaiting his first initiation. The initiation was soon accomplished. Shortly after his arrival in Russia he began a liaison with a peasant woman, A. E. Ivanova, by whom he was to have a daughter in the following year (1842). Although the child was illegitimate, it was regarded as a fact of little consequence— there are several such liaisons in Turgenev's fiction, notably the relationship between Nikolay Petrovich Kirsanov and Fenichka in *Fathers and Children*—and Turgenev's attitude towards his daughter was to be one of bland indifference, modified occasionally by a rather unnecessary parade of paternity to which he was temperamentally unsuited and which was embarrassing for his daughter as she grew older. More in character was his brief affair with Bakunin's sister, Tat'yana, during the winter of 1841-42. It came to be known as the 'Pryamukhino' affair—platonic but nevertheless intense—and it served to rid Turgenev of his youthful romanticism. Shortly after the affair ended, he sat for his M.A. degree in philosophy, travelled to Dresden and Berlin, and then, upon returning from Berlin towards the end of 1842, set up permanent residence in St. Petersburg with the aim of entering the Civil Service.

The next year was to be crucial. It was notable for three events which were to have a profound and lasting influence on the course of his life: the publication of his poem *Parasha*, his meeting with Belinsky and his first acquaintanceship with Pauline Viardot. The publication of his poem and the favourable review which it received from Belinsky were to initiate his literary career. Despite the doubts, hesitations, and changes of mind that were to be the invariable accompaniment of his creative development, he was now a writer and a writer he would remain for the rest of his life. The direction, however, that his work was to take was the result, very largely, of his first meeting with Belinsky in February of that year. Goethe and Schiller, Hegelianism, the Ideal were not sufficient; under Belinsky's tutelage they were to be replaced by other and more concrete ideals. Yet Turgenev's reverence for beauty and the equally important accompanying notion that happiness was never to be fully attained, love never fully requited, found their expression in a relationship of a different kind: his lifelong —and, by most accounts, platonic—devotion to the singer, Pauline Viardot. It seems that the propriety of this relationship was never to be called in question, nor was it noticeably resented by the husband, Louis Viardot. Turgenev was to be her devoted 'friend' for the forty years that remained to him. Pauline Viardot, with her beautiful voice and her attractive character, was to represent for Turgenev the glamour of things European, the epitome of civilization and culture and a living symbol of the free flight of music, detached and remote from terrestrial cares, which was to be the poetic ideal of his art. He could never escape from the charm of Pauline Viardot. He was to trail across Europe after her; practically all his future travels and places of domicile were the result of his infatuation for her; he was to correspond with her, live next door to her, become a recognized part of her life; finally he was to die in her arms.

By 1843 the mood prevailing among the Russian intelligentsia had changed. The romanticism of the previous decade with its Byronism, its admiration for Schelling, its attempts to define the meaning of *narodnost'*, its first tentative steps towards a new political awareness, had been replaced by a mood of increasing realism. Poetry had been displaced by prose as the most important medium of literary expression; Schelling had been displaced by Feuerbach and the works of French socialist writers such as Proudhon, Fourier, and Louis Blanc. The problem of nationality had been modified; it had become the problem of social reorganization and social ideals that was to preoccupy the Russian intelligentsia throughout the nineteenth century and the beginning of the twentieth, until the revolution of 1917 was to put an end to it.

No man is more representative of the forties than Vissarion Belinsky. He was not of squirearchal or gentry extraction. This single fact— putting aside for the moment the question of his sensitivity and integrity as a critic—lent him an unusual moral stature. In the first place, he had no rights to lose, as had the Decembrists. He was not in their tradition, being not a member of the upper class of the gentry but the son of a doctor; in this sense he was 'plebeian' or 'classless' or what at that time was called a *raznochinets*. Secondly, he had enjoyed few of the privileges of education and cultural heritage that members of the upper class were able to enjoy. He was very largely self-taught and depended for a great deal of his information about the ideas current in the West on what his friends could tell him, since he had only a slight knowledge of any language save his native Russian. His critical articles all betray the indiscipline of the autodidact and the reverence for ideas which is often characteristic of the man who has never studied ideas at their source. But for these deficiencies of education and knowledge he compensated with a devotion to his self-appointed task as the 'discoverer' and publicist of Russian literature that had no precedent. No one before Belinsky had understood the importance of literature as a social force. Belinsky himself had not sprung fully armed for his task from the head of Zeus: between 1834 and 1840 he had struggled, as his articles and letters bear witness, to discover for himself and his generation a new ethic and a new faith that could supplant the threadbare, ritualistic doctrines of Orthodoxy and the reactionary principles upon which the autocracy was based. By the beginning of the forties he had passed through phases of addiction to Schelling, Fichte, and Hegel and had finally discovered the ideas of Feuerbach and the French socialists. Socialism now became for him the be-all and end-all of human endeavour, while literature, in conformity with it, had to become a medium of social censure, a forum for criticizing the evils of feudalism and an ideological weapon in the struggle against reaction. Realism was now Belinsky's catch-word, but a realism that had to be critical of the existing reality. Partly unconsciously, it seems, out of his desire to see change—Dostoyevsky called him the most hurried man in Russia—and out of his abhorrence of the corruption, the inhumanity and the social injustices that he saw around him, he became the champion not only of a national literature but also of a tendentious literature. For this Belinsky has been blamed and applauded. Yet it is no more than the usual legacy of a man, such as he was, who had the ferocity of one indubitably convinced that he knew the truth.

Belinsky became the spokesman of the Westernists during the forties when the two ideological attitudes of Westernism and Slavophilism became finally differentiated. Turgenev, as he states in his *Literary Reminiscences*, returned to Russia after his immersion in the German

sea already a Westernist—by instinct and inclination, at least, if not
by political orientation. From Belinsky he was to acquire that political
orientation which was to characterize him as a novelist and a chronicler
of Russian society. Yet, as was the case with Stankevich, Turgenev
was clearly more attracted to Belinsky, the man, than to Belinsky, the
ideologue. For Turgenev Belinsky meant primarily 'ein guter Mann'
in the sense that Goethe used the expression,

> Ein guter Mann in seinem dunklen Drange
> Ist sich des rechten Weges wohl bewusst. . . .[1]

as of a man who even in his vague aspiration after truth instinctively
chooses the right path. Moreover, he was by nature a man who stood
at the centre of Russian society, as one of an intermediate class between
the land-owning gentry and the landless peasants, close to the heart of
the nation and embodying its inferior as well as its superior qualities.
In the same way, his political feelings, though very forthright, remained largely based on instinctive sympathies and antipathies.
Turgenev wrote of him in his *Literary Reminiscences*:

Belinsky was just as much of an idealist as he was a social critic; he criticised
in the name of an ideal. This ideal was of a very definite and homogeneous
character, although it was called and is still called by different names: science,
progress, humanity, civilisation—finally, the West. Well-intentioned people,
but not sympathisers, even use the word: revolution. But it is not a matter of
names so much as of essence. . . . Belinsky devoted himself entirely to the
service of this ideal; in all his sympathies and all his activity he belonged to the
camp of the Westernists, as their opponents called them. He was a Westernist
not only because he recognised the superiority of Western science, Western
art, Western social systems, but also because he was profoundly convinced of
the need for Russia to acquire everything that had been produced by the West
in order that she might develop her own powers and her own importance. . . .
The acceptance of the results of the Western way of life, the application of them
to our own life, taking into account the peculiarities of race, history and climate
—in other words, by being quite open and critical towards them—that was the
way in which we could, in his opinion, finally achieve something distinctively
Russian, an idea which he cherished considerably more than is generally
believed. . . . Indeed, Belinsky loved Russia; but he also passionately loved
enlightenment and freedom: to unite these, for him, noblest of interests—that
was the whole meaning of his work, that was what he strove for.[2]

Love of Russia coupled with an equally fervent love of Western
principles of enlightenment and freedom—this was what Belinsky

---

[1] *Lit. i zhit. vosp.*, 279.   [2] Ibid., 292-3.

bequeathed to his younger contemporary. This was the only faith Turgenev ever had, absorbing and transcending all other religious or philosophical beliefs, and he learned it from Belinsky. Between Turgenev and Belinsky there was something of a son-father relationship. Turgenev accepted the advice and guidance of Belinsky, both as literary mentor and as social ideologue, much in the way that he might accept the advice of a father—with deference to greater experience and maturity, though with the natural reservations of a younger man; while Belinsky tended to treat him as a precocious progeny whom he would have liked to turn into a blind disciple. Belinsky recognized Turgenev's literary talent, though he only began to give it his approval when it showed signs of following his ideas. Turgenev admired the man and to that extent accepted the ideas—the finest memento of this admiration is the dedication of *Fathers and Children*—but his Westernism was to be more liberal, less passionate, not so completely instinctive, more reasoned and less radical than the Westernism of his teacher.

But Belinsky was simply the guide. Turgenev was spurred on to engage in literary activity during the forties as much as anything by the need for money which his despotic skinflint of a mother withheld from him. Annenkov notes that

until he obtained his inheritance in 1850 he participated in the normal life of his rich friends by subsisting on loans obtained against his future expectations and through money advanced him by editors for works as yet unwritten—in a word, he led the life of a bohemian of noble extraction, a life of aristocratic beggary, just like all the golden youth of that time.[1]

Turgenev, in fact, who was never naturally endowed with an excess of energy, was obliged to undertake a variety of literary activities, from the writing of poems and stories to such hack-work as reviewing and translating. But he never experienced the kind of penury that some of his literary contemporaries, such as Nekrasov and Dostoyevsky, had to undergo. Turgenev still had enough money to remain the urbane socialite with all the appearance of one of independent means. He remained also outside the different literary coteries—again it is Annenkov who notes this[2]—as an outside observer of the social scene. Even with his literary work for the most progressive journal of the time, *The Contemporary*, the platform for Belinsky's radical publicism at the end of his life, he still contrived to remain as far as possible a free agent,

---

[1] P. V. Annenkov, *Literaturniye vospominaniya* (SPB., 1909), 484.
[2] Ibid., 476-7.

for in his case it was always artistic considerations that were to pre-
dominate. He could not observe his contemporaries without that
freedom of manœuvre essential to all artists who are more concerned
to make man real than make him better. Similarly, though he came to
be regarded as 'a man of the forties'—meaning by this his adherence
to the socio-political and literary ideals of Belinsky—he retained for
himself an ideological freedom of manœuvre which to many may have
seemed evidence of a lack of conviction, but which is better interpreted simply as evidence of the fact that he felt a healthy scepticism
towards every kind of ideological system.

The forties were climaxed by the events of 1848, by which time
Turgenev was already beginning to enjoy considerable fame as the
author of *A Sportsman's Sketches*. He was also, even at this early stage
in his career, tending to regard himself as one whom life had passed by.
This mood, to which Turgenev succumbed easily and for slight reason,
was aggravated by the death of Belinsky and, what is more important,
by the failure of the Paris revolution. All his Westernist sympathies
had led him to hope that 1848 would see the realization of the ideals
of 1789; but it was the *bourgeoisie* that triumphed and destroyed
Turgenev's initial hopes of the communes. His cool detachment,
however, prevented him from experiencing the profound shock of
disillusionment that his friend, Herzen, was to feel. Turgenev did not
reject the West as no longer capable of achieving those principles of
enlightenment and freedom which had inspired Belinsky. He did not
reject the West as did Herzen. But he followed Herzen to the extent
that he began to reappraise his attitude towards Russia, realizing that
Russia itself, despite its backwardness, might have spiritual virtues
which the West, in its bourgeois craving after money, had overlooked
and forgotten. It was an elegiac mood that accompanied this reappraisal, and the mood is reflected in the later *Sketches* after 1848 and
permeates to a greater or lesser extent all his subsequent fiction.

In 1849 his letters to Pauline Viardot have the appearance of being
written by a tired man who has retreated from the social hurly-burly
and is content to spend his time in contemplation of nature and
reading. In 1850 his mother died, and the estate of Spasskoye, in
addition to his father's estate of Turgenevo which he had inherited
earlier, became his property. His days of 'aristocratic beggary' were
now over. Even so, the prevalent mood of despondency remained.
There was an external cause for it in the increasingly oppressive nature
of the measures taken by the Tsarist government. After 1848 Russia

had become a citadel of reaction where every form of cultural initiative was suspect. Turgenev was to experience this oppression at first hand when he was arrested in 1852 for the publication of his obituary notice on Gogol. That arrest and the subsequent enforced exile to his estate at Spasskoye, which was not revoked until towards the end of 1853, had the reverse of the effect intended by the government. It was the official accolade that gave him his respectability as a writer, for it made Turgenev, the least likely of martyrs by nature, a martyr in the cause of literature. But for our purposes this act of victimization in 1852 represents the end of the beginning in Turgenev's development; after this Turgenev is to become preoccupied with the mature work upon which his fame rests—his novels—although his heart was always to remain in the forties.

2

THE LITERARY APPRENTICESHIP
PUSHKIN—*A SPORTSMAN'S SKETCHES*

TURGENEV underwent his literary apprenticeship in the forties, but in any discussion of his literary development it is necessary to begin a decade earlier. In fact, in any study of the major Russian writers of the nineteenth century one has to begin with Pushkin. Pushkin was an artistic example and a literary determinant of the utmost value. His many merits cannot be described in so many words, but his influence is undeniable, and his influence on Turgenev is particularly important because it was from Pushkin that Turgenev was to take his literary example, especially in the case of the novel. Before Pushkin there was no Russian literature to speak of and there was certainly no indigenous Russian novel. It is probably in respect of the novel that Pushkin made his greatest contribution to the development of nineteenth-century Russian literature, since it was in the novel—specifically in the *realistic* novel—that nineteenth-century Russian literature was to be so outstanding.

In 1846, in a review of *The Death of Lyapunov*, a play by Gedeonov, who was a rival for Pauline Viardot's affections—and this, among other things, accounts for the unfavourable tone of the review—Turgenev offered a brief summary of the kind of development that had occurred in Russian literature during the first half of the nineteenth century:

> The history of art and literature in Russia is remarkable for its special dual growth. We began with imitation of foreign models; writers with a purely superficial talent, garrulous and prolific, presented in their works, which were entirely devoid of any living connection with the people, nothing more than reflections of other people's talents and other people's ideas. . . . Meanwhile, a revolution was quietly occurring in society; the foreign elements were being remoulded, were being assimilated into our blood-stream; the receptive Russian nature, just as if it had been awaiting this influence, developed and grew not day by day but hour by hour, and developed along its own path. . . .[1]

1 *Sobr. soch.* (1956), xi. 56.

In the context of the review Turgenev is referring to the importance of Gogol and in this he is following Belinsky (the review was in fact first thought to have been written by Belinsky). But in the emphasis which he lays upon the increasing realism and the extraordinary rapid development of Russian literature Turgenev is remarking something that is common to Russian literature as a whole during the nineteenth century and is particularly true of the novel. In 1830, for instance, Russian literature could boast of no novel of importance, whereas in 1880 Russian literature could boast of a tradition of the realistic novel equal to, if not superior to, that of any other European literature. For the beginnings of this extraordinarily rapid growth one has to look to Pushkin. Before Pushkin, in the work of Karamzin (*Poor Liza, A Knight of Our Time*) at the turn of the century or in the later work of such writers as Polevoy, Marlinsky, Vel'tman and Zagoskin, certain tentative beginnings had been made. Their work, meeting the demand for pseudo-historical novels on the lines of Walter Scott or romances on the French model, had the effect of gradually awakening the Russian reader to the importance of literature as an educative and social force. No one could have called the work of these writers—with the exception of Karamzin's short prose works—specifically Russian. Despite the fact that the settings and the names might be Russian, their works were imitative of models in Western European literature. To this extent their stories were quite simply not 'real', not directly related to the experience of the Russian reader. Yet this consideration of 'reality' is very important, for the Russian novel as we know it is the Russian *realistic* novel which set out to portray, and by inference to expose, the realities of Russian social life, its virtues and its vices. The first work of this kind to appear was Pushkin's *Eugene Onegin*, completed in 1831.

The work was an oddity in formal terms, being a 'novel in verse', as Pushkin subtitled it, and it had no successors in this particular genre. However, it was a work which presented to the Russian reader a picture of his own society in unmistakable clarity and detail, and it illuminated one of the most important problems of the day: the problem of the 'superfluous man'. In concentrating on this problem Pushkin was drawing an important distinction between the 'imitative' elements in Russian society and the elements in Russian society which might be called 'indigenous', represented in the novel by the contrast between the metropolitan civilization of St. Petersburg and the traditional life of the Russian countryside, though this contrast is chiefly apparent in the relationship between hero and heroine. Pushkin's hero, Onegin, was a 'superfluous man', a product of those Western influences which had penetrated Russian society after the Napoleonic campaign. He was Byronic, both in inspiration and in manner, but he was a Russian Byronic hero who adopted the pose of Byronism as a form of protest against prevalent conditions. It is in the social sense that he must be regarded as 'superfluous'—as a man who by virtue of his upbringing, his undisciplined and tragically inadequate education and the adoption of the Western pose of Byronism in Russian circumstances finds himself indifferent to those circumstances, intolerable of their norms and proprieties and, as a consequence, 'superfluous' in the social conditions of his time. Naturally, there is here an implied criticism of Russian society itself. This 'superfluous man' is not unintelligent or without talent. Indeed, he represents new ideas, however poorly assimilated they may be, and a new social force, a new generation with new aspirations. Such aspirations, however, have been stifled by society, with the result that the 'superfluous man' has become a divided character, in which the head and the heart are mutually antagonistic; he betrays signs of disillusionment and emotional indifference, a mind that prides itself on cynicism and a precosity that cloaks itself in haughtiness. Such are the inner symptoms of the 'superfluous man', the living embodiment of the sickness at the heart of Russian society, which Pushkin exposes in his psychological portrait of Eugene Onegin, and in so doing he created a prototype figure for several generations of similar heroes in the Russian realistic novel. But of equal importance is the figure of the heroine, Tat'yana, whose emotional spontaneity and 'naturalness' are contrasted with the egotistical preoccupations of Onegin. It is in the relationship between Tat'yana and Onegin that the contrasting issues in the fiction—the opposition of imitative and indigenous, of town and country, of new and old—are not only made clear, but interact upon each other, revealing the social, psychological and—what is most important—the moral dilemma at the root both of Russian society and of all human relationships in general.

This relationship establishes a formula which is to be followed by several subsequent Russian novelists, though especially by Turgenev. The relationship only begins when the hero finds himself in a milieu that is unfamiliar to him, either through long dissociation or simply because he has had no previous knowledge of it, and the result is that the hero appears in this milieu as a relative stranger, whose very strangeness and newness are a source of fascination to the heroine. The contrast afforded by the presence of the hero in this strange milieu is at once both social and psychological. His social attributes contrast with the social characteristics of the strange milieu and his psychological attributes contrast with the psychological characteristics of the heroine, who is always an integral part of the milieu in which he finds himself. When the heroine falls in love with him, as is usually the case, the love is represented as a challenge to his character, which he can either accept or fail to live up to, and the extent to which he succeeds or fails reveals the extent of his moral worth.

In Pushkin's novel Tat'yana falls in love with the stranger-hero, Onegin, imagining him to be the very image of the romantic heroes whom she had learned to admire from her reading, but he coldly dismisses her challenge and lectures her on the need to control her youthful feelings. Haughtily disdainful of her love for him and scornful of the provincial society in which he finds himself at her nameday ball, he asserts his egoism by deliberately paying his attentions to her sister, Ol'ga. This immediately provokes the young romantic, Lensky, who is in love with Ol'ga, and he challenges Onegin to a duel. Onegin has no wish to fight a duel with his romantic young friend, but honour must be satisfied. As a result of the duel Lensky is killed and Onegin leaves the district. After lengthy travels Onegin eventually returns to St. Petersburg, the world that is familiar to him, where he once more meets Tat'yana, who is now married, and he falls desperately in love with her. But it is already too late: she has vowed to remain faithful to her husband. On this note the superficial action of the novel ends, leaving the moral in the air for many other Russian writers to grasp and make into a recurring theme in Russian literature. This recurring theme is one of happiness, its meaning and the extent to which it is imperilled either by human necessity or by superhuman agencies which rule over man's destiny. In Pushkin's novel there is a law of fate which orders the destinies of his hero and heroine. Their mutual happiness may have been precluded at the beginning of their relationship by the mutual disparity in social background and psychological attributes which divided them, but in their final meeting they face each other as equals—Onegin stripped of his social *hauteur* and his Byronic pretence, Tat'yana of her earlier naivety and her illusions about him. It is only the law of fate that now seems to divide them. The unspoken moral of the novel is simply that the relationship is doomed, that neither hero nor heroine is fated to enjoy happiness.

CT

It seems that the social disparity which divides them, the differences in psychological attitude revealed during the course of the relationship, the moral calumny visited on Onegin by the killing of his best friend and the marital responsibility which Tat'yana has incurred in her marriage to the old general have the nature of inevitable laws which blend to circumscribe their lives in their final tragic meeting.

The 'realism' of this novel is not due simply to the fact that it presents a 'realistic'—that is to say, recognizable—picture of Russian life. Its 'realism' also resides in the emphasis laid upon psychological analysis and contrast in the characterization of the hero and the heroine. Finally, the impression of 'realism' is due as much as anything to the objective, uncommitted attitude of Pushkin towards his fiction. By presenting his fiction in this realistic manner Pushkin is both implying social criticism, without overtly offering any comment that could be offensive to the censorship, and professing a realistic view of life in which fate is as much of a reality as any other aspect of life. The action of the novel is set down much in the form of a documentary record, for which, as it were, Pushkin scarcely regards himself as being responsible. He is only the dispassionate chronicler, relating all the necessary facts culled from the lives of his hero and heroine with the required deference and Olympian magnanimity. The ribald, wry, slightly ironical passages of commentary that accompany the action of the novel do not, in fact, impair the objectivity of the way it is presented. They lend the work an air of topicality, of immediate reference to the period being described. This very topicality is to be a great feature of the Russian nineteenth-century realistic novel. On the example of Pushkin's *Eugene Onegin*, the Russian realistic novel was to become a fusion of *belles-lettres* and journalism, of art and social criticism, which was to comprise a committed literature of a far more pointed, dedicated variety than its equivalent in Western Europe.

Turgenev's novels owe much to the pattern established by *Eugene Onegin*. But when Turgenev began writing, Pushkin's reputation, so strong in the twenties, was already beginning to decline. In the thirties Turgenev became heir to the Byronic romanticism of the decade, expressed most fully in the poetry of Pushkin's successor, Lermontov. Turgenev's first known literary work dates from 1834 when he was sixteen years old. In December of this year he completed a poetical drama, *Steno*, modelled on Byron's *Manfred*. It is a work of little intrinsic merit, though it naturally claims our attention as the first surviving work and because it contains portents of his later development. The hero, Steno, is a typical product of the romanticism of the period, the intellectual crossed in love who loses faith in life and yearns for death as a means of escape from his spiritual torment. He is represented as a man divided against himself, whose heart has been oppressed and atrophied by experience of life and whose mind, always searching to discover a meaning to existence, works in a vacuum, unwilling to admit anything beyond itself. If the *leit-motif* of the dramatic monologues put into his mouth is primarily despairing and cynical, there is the compensating factor that he is portrayed as one who is not afraid to exercise his intellect nor afraid to assert his human rights in face of life's apparent purposelessness. In this respect he is in embryo the first of Turgenev's 'superfluous men', to be compared, if only as a result of the Byronic inspiration common to both, and not in any realistic social sense, with the Pushkinian model. Similarly, the formula which is to form the basis for so many of Turgenev's studies of this type of intellectual hero is expressed here for the first time in the contrast which is drawn between Steno, the intellectual divided against himself, and the girl, Dzhuliya (Julia), whose simple expression of emotion in her love for him is a challenge to his complicated heartsearchings. It is in the monologues that the interest of the work resides; they betray a concern for philosophical questions, for the meaning of life and man's attitude to God, which is striking evidence of Turgenev's intellectual maturity. But the melodramatic story betrays the fact that this is a romantic work written by an impressionable author of tender years. Dzhuliya, having befriended Steno and fallen in love with him, eventually dies of love with the hero's name upon her lips. Steno's fate is no less disquieting. Unable to reconcile himself to the sincere love that has been offered him, he seizes a loaded pistol and shoots himself before retribution, in the shape of Dzhuliya's brother, can overtake him.

Steno was not an isolated work in this early period. In 1835 he wrote an unfinished poem called *The Old Man's Story*. In 1836 he translated parts of *Othello* and *King Lear* (with which he was very dissatisfied and later destroyed) and he also translated *Manfred*, but as he remarked in a letter to his friend, Nikitenko: 'I am quite unfitted to be a translator.'[1] It was in this same year that he published a lengthy review of a book by A. Muravyov on Russia's holy places in the journal of the Ministry of Education. In 1837, before leaving for Germany, he was preoccupied with a large work to be entitled *Our Age*. In addition, he admitted to

[1] Letter to A. V. Nikitenko, 26 March/7 April 1837, in *Sobr. soch.* (1958), xii. 12.

having written about a hundred short poems and three other works—
Calm at Sea, *Phantasmagoria on a Summer Night* and *Dream*. Of all these
only *Steno* and one or two short poems have survived.

Between 1838 and 1843 several of his poems appeared in *The
Contemporary* and *Annals of the Fatherland* and he busied himself with
other short poems, some short dramas, and a longer work, *The
Temptation of St. Anthony*. All his poems betray a remarkable poetic
competence and an obvious lyrical vein. He drew on his knowledge
of Shakespeare and Goethe, especially the latter, for some of his
themes, but these poems are chiefly revealing for their lucid, classical
form, despite the romantic tinges in their subject-matter, and in this
they owe much to Pushkin's example. But such poems are necessarily
slight and often very personal in their content. It is with the publication
of *Parasha* in 1843 that Turgenev's work shows signs of a new maturity.

Parasha, 'A Story in Verse', as it is subtitled, composed of sixty-
nine stanzas, is important for the extent to which it falls directly into
the Russian tradition. It owes much to Pushkin, betraying the influence of *Eugene Onegin* in its evocation of the Russian scene, in its
portrayal of the hero and heroine, especially the latter, and in its
lighthearted, fluent manner. Its story is so slight as scarcely to bear
examination: Parasha, the heroine, typical of the many provincial
young ladies who are to be encountered in fictional works of the time
and obviously modelled on Pushkin's Tat'yana, falls in love with a
certain Viktor Alekseich and finally marries him. It is the background
scene, the bantering commentary and the characterization which supply
the interest of the work. Here Turgenev reveals himself, if only
sketchily and in certain set passages, as an incomparable master of
nature description. However, it is Parasha herself who is of greatest
interest, for here for the first time in Turgenev's work we find a full-
length portrait of a heroine, artless but capable of deep emotion,
innocent but not insipid, awakened to life through her love but not
sentimentalized, who is to be the archetype of so many future Turgenevan studies. She is the unified personality, responsive to her
natural feelings and inclinations, to whom is contrasted the figure of
Viktor Alekseich, the haughty and indifferent hero, reminiscent of the
disillusioned heroes of Byron, though of more markedly Russian
derivation and character.

Although in its theme and form *Parasha* is largely derivative in
inspiration, for Turgenev's development as a writer it is significant
because it marks his first attempt to come to terms with the Russian

scene. *Steno* had been set in Italy, although it might have been set anywhere. The same can be said of *The Conversation* (1844), a dialogue in verse, which, like *Parasha*, was also highly praised by Belinsky. It is notable for the way in which the question of the romantic hero's disillusionment and lack of will is given an unmistakable social slant in the young man's censure upon his own generation. This shows the direction in which Turgenev's thought is moving, but neither *Steno* nor *The Conversation* betray any attempt at depicting the particular malaise of Turgenev's generation—the atrophying of the passions and the will, the morbid preoccupation with 'ego' and intellect, which are the marks of a divided personality—in the circumstances of Russian society. These works define and analyse this malaise in general terms. It is only in *Parasha*, particularly in the figure of the hero, Viktor Alekseich, that Turgenev attempts to define this malaise in social terms.

Subsequently this sociological slant, clearly inspired by the teaching of Belinsky, was to form the basis of all Turgenev's character studies in this type of disillusioned, divided intellectual. Much later he was to give it a universal inference in his comparison between the types of Hamlet and Don Quixote (in his lecture of 1860). Evidence, however, of the increasing maturity of Turgenev's thought on this subject is to be seen in his review of Vronchenko's translation of Goethe's *Faust* (*Annals of the Fatherland*, February 1845), where he writes:

We have called *Faust* an egotistical work. . . . But could it be otherwise? Goethe, the champion of all that is human and terrestrial, the enemy of every spurious ideal and everything supernatural, was the first to defend the rights —not of man in general, no—but of individual, passionate, limited man; he showed that an indestructible force is secreted in him, that he can live without any external support, and that with all the insolubility of his personal doubts, with all the poverty of his beliefs and convictions, man still has the right and the opportunity to be happy and not to be ashamed of his happiness.[1]

Although this refers to Goethe's view of man, it might also refer to the view of the problem held by Turgenev himself. He was also to become champion of 'individual, passionate, limited man' who has 'the right and the opportunity to be happy and not be ashamed of his happiness'. But Turgenev's view, as he explains a sentence later, has undergone the modification demanded of it by the sociological ideas of the time. 'For we know', he writes, 'that human development

[1] *Sobr. soch.* (1956), xi. 33.

cannot stop at such a result; we know that the cornerstone for man is not man himself, as an indivisible unit, but humanity, society, which has its own eternal, unshakable laws. . . .'[1] Two distinct problems are discernible here. There is the problem of man with his right to individual happiness and the larger issue of humanity and society with their own eternal laws. The inference of this opposition of man and society, of the indivisible unit and the greater law of humanity, is to be projected into the contrast between egoism and altruism which is at the root of practically all the relationships in Turgenev's novels. Man, the egotistical being, has to abandon his purely egotistical rights in order to be of service to the higher laws of humanity and society. It is in this connection that Turgenev offers a striking conclusion:

. . . any 'reconciliation' of Faust outside the sphere of human activity is unnatural, but of any other kind of reconciliation we can at present only dream. . . . We will be told: such a conclusion is joyless; but, firstly, we are not concerned about the pleasantness but about the truth of our views; secondly, those who argue that unresolved doubts leave behind them an appalling emptiness in the human soul have never sincerely and passionately surrendered themselves to a secret struggle with their inner selves; if they had done, they would know that on the ruins of systems and theories there remains one thing, indestructible and imperishable: our human I, which is immortal, because it, it alone, can destroy itself. . . . So let Faust remain incomplete, fragmentary, like the time of which it is an expression—a time for which the sufferings and joys of Faust were the highest sufferings and joys, while the irony of Mephistopheles was the most pitiless irony! It is in the incompleteness of this tragedy that its greatness lies. In the life of every one of us there is an epoch when Faust seems to us the most remarkable achievement of the human intellect, when it satisfies all our demands to the full; but there comes another time when without ceasing to recognise Faust as a great and beautiful work, we journey forwards following others, perhaps lesser talents, but the strongest of characters, towards another aim. . . . We repeat that, as a poet, Goethe had no equal; but it is not only poets that we need now. . . .[2]

In this conclusion Turgenev touches on several issues that are to have a prominent part in his later career as a realistic writer. Man for Turgenev will always be the apotheosis of reality, its single criterion, and there will be no 'reconciliation' of man outside reality. 'Our human I,' as he

---

1 *Sobr. soch.* (1956), xi. 33.

2 Ibid., 35-6. For an extended study of Turgenev's attitude to *Faust* and of this article on Vronchenko's translation in particular, see Dr. Katharina Schütz, *Das Goethebild Turgeniews* (Bern, 1952).

says, is 'immortal, because it, it alone, can destroy itself . . .' and there
is to be no other kind of immortality for man in Turgenev's fiction.
This totally realistic and unsentimental view has to be accepted without
reservations, for Turgenev does not offer any palliatives to the human
soul that are not consistent with the reality of man's existence. Such a
conclusion may be 'joyless'—we may like to think of it as pessimistic
—but, as Turgenev notes, he is concerned only with truth. Accepting
this and the great importance which Turgenev ascribes to *Faust* and
its creator, whose influence is to be felt throughout Turgenev's work,
it is the 'other aim' which must also be taken into account. This other
aim is his concern not simply for 'our human I'—though single man,
alone, isolated, denying God and any convictions save those which
he can justify to himself as a rational being, will always be at the centre
of Turgenev's fiction—but the social context and the social purpose of
the intellectual of his day. This is to be Turgenev's main aim in the
future.

This concern for man, 'the indivisible unit', 'our human *I*', coincides
with Turgenev's real forte as a writer, which was portraiture. All the
other components of his fiction were made subservient to the aim of
providing a portrait of one or another person. As an aid to such
portraiture Turgenev made use of the Pushkinian formula of contrast
between hero and heroine—as, for example, in such early works as
Steno and *Parasha*—in which the role of the heroine was that of a
yardstick of all that is natural and emotionally unaffected, against
which the hero's falseness was to be judged. But in several of the stories
which he published at the beginning of his career the problem of
portraiture itself is the main feature. In *Andrey Kolosov*, for instance, the
first story in prose that Turgenev published (1844), the contrast is
drawn between the emotional 'realism' of the central figure, Andrey
Kolosov, and the emotional 'romanticism' of the narrator of the story.
Kolosov fell in love with a girl, afterwards ceased to love her and
abandoned her. The moral is drawn by the narrator:

'This has happened to everyone,' [he remarks] '. . . but which one of us has
been able to break with the past at the right moment? . . . Gentlemen, the
man who parts with a woman, his former love, at that bitter and all-important
moment when he unwillingly acknowledges that his heart is no longer entirely
consumed by love for her, such a man, believe me, understands the sacred
nature of love better and more profoundly than all those petty people who from
boredom and weakness continue to play on the broken strings of their drooping
and sensitive hearts.'

Here is one of the most important themes in Turgenev's work, already presented with the realism of manner and psychological percipience which are to be characteristic of Turgenev's later studies. And just like Steno, or like the narrator of *Andrey Kolosov*, so many of Turgenev's later heroes are to play on the broken strings of their drooping and sensitive hearts with a morbid, introspective relish. But Turgenev is often to accompany this kind of portrait with a tone of satire and implicit censure. It is the un-Byronic, the 'natural' hero who is to gain Turgenev's approval in such essays in contrasting portraiture as *The Duellist* (1846) or *Khor' and Kalinych* (1847), the first of his *A Sportsman's Sketches*. The tendency in all his stories of the mid-forties can be seen as a movement away from preoccupation with romanticism, whether it be the romanticism of the hero-figure or the melodramatic terms in which such stories as *The Duellist* or *Three Portraits* are couched, towards a naturalness in both characterization and form. As one might expect, the influence of Gogol is to be detected in this trend towards greater realism, to be seen especially clearly in *Petushkov* (1847). The major influence, however, though not of a literary variety but just as important, was Belinsky.

Apart from all other political considerations, Belinsky insisted on the sacred importance of the individual. Although he thought of the individual as primarily valuable for his intelligence and thus always upheld the importance of the Russian intelligentsia, his thinking was pervaded by a spirit of Christian humanism—best expressed in his famous *Letter to Gogol* of 1847—which viewed all men as equal. It was this that made him pay particular attention to the social untouchables in Russia, the oppressed city-dwellers such as those depicted in Gogol's *The Greatcoat* or in Dostoyevsky's *Poor Folk* and the peasants, first depicted in the forties by Grigorovich in his *Anton the Unfortunate* and *The Village*, works which Belinsky seriously overestimated simply because he was so anxious to see Russian literature live up to the humanistic ideal that he had conceived for it. Moreover, serfdom was an injustice, and Russian literature had therefore to expose it, in Belinsky's opinion. The influence of Belinsky's humanism could not fail to have its effect on Turgenev and it was to be this influence of the spirit of the forties, as fostered by Belinsky, which inspired him to write the work that first brought him literary fame, *A Sportsman's Sketches*. Here Turgenev, the painter of portraits, reached maturity. Between 1847 and 1851 twenty-one such *Sketches* appeared in *The Contemporary*—*Sketches* which mirrored the new mood of social awareness and responsibility which *The Contemporary* had been designed by Belinsky to create. It was not a new Turgenev who emerged in these works, simply a Turgenev who was applying his artistic talents as a painter of portraits to a purposeful social end. Here the other aim, of which he spoke in his review of Goethe's *Faust*, comes into its own, and the aim consisted in presenting to educated, upper-class Russian society portraits from rural life, especially life among the peasants, just as Gogol and Dostoyevsky had provided pictures from urban life or George Sand had provided pictures from rural life in France or, more aptly, Harriet Beecher Stowe pictures of negro slavery in America.

This does not mean that the purposefulness or tendentiousness of Turgenev's portraits was accompanied by an excessive beating on the old sociological drums. The beating is very muted—considerations of censorship, apart from anything else, were bound to make it so. These *Sketches* are simply an album of pictures from Russian rural life, unified very loosely by the presence of a common narrator, the *Sportsman*. In the majority of cases they are brief episodes taken from the narrator's experience and the narrator's part in the narrative is scarcely more than that of observer. It is, in fact, only the compassionate, frank observation which suggests that these are pictures having the social purpose of exposing the injustice of serfdom. Overt tendentiousness is to be detected more readily in those *Sketches* which portray the land-owning classes. Turgenev's squirearchal background naturally cast him in the role of critic of the gentry and their tyrannical disregard of their peasants' lives. But several of the *Sketches* which are set among the land-owning classes have definite story interest (*Pyotr Petrovich Karatayev, My Neighbour Radilov, The Provincial Apothecary*, for instance) and are frequently little more than love-stories with a rural background that have nothing substantially important to tell us of the problem of serfdom. In other words, *A Sportsman's Sketches* is by no means a homogeneous work, being diverse and experimental in form as in content, although it is the studies of peasant life which give its unity of theme and its importance as a sociological document.

In examining this theme one may draw certain conclusions about Turgenev's development as a writer between 1847 and 1851. Accepting that it is the observation which is the most important feature of those *Sketches* that deal with peasant life, and that such observation derives as much from Turgenev's personal experience as from the experience which he may impute to his narrator, then one can trace the way in which Turgenev's attitude to the content of his fiction and his literary method undergo significant changes, maturing and deepening as his understanding of the Russian scene and of human nature grows more profound. The first *Sketch* betrays a frankly Westernist approach to the peasants. Khor' and Kalinych are recognizable types, equatable with the European literary types of Don Quixote and Hamlet. In his original version of the *Sketch* Turgenev compared them rather grandiloquently to Goethe and Schiller.[1] But the inference of this method is clear. Turgenev was attempting to humanize his peasants, to project their images on the public mind in universal terms and thus to make them more acceptable. The result may have produced 'idealized' portraits, figures who are observed and wondered at rather than profoundly understood and appreciated, but there is no denying that this method was effective in its sociological intent. The same proselytizing, Westernist approach can be seen in the contrast between the natural, universally human characteristics of the peasants and the 'inhumanity' which is suggested in the portraits of the land-owners in such stories of 1847 and 1848 as *Yermolay and the Miller's Wife*, *L'gov*, *The Bailiff* and *Raspberry Water*. The influence of Belinsky's ideas on the importance of the individual and his rights lies behind the morality of these pictures from peasant life, and it is significant that *The Bailiff*, the most outspoken of these, was written while Turgenev was at Salzbrunn with Belinsky in July 1847. But in 1848 a change occurs. The spirit of the forties had begun to die; Turgenev's earlier buoyant Westernism could not survive the shock of Belinsky's death and the failure of the Paris Revolution. In 1849 he does not publish any *Sketches* dealing with the peasantry. Instead, he returns to the problem of the 'superfluous man', in this case the faded, provincial *Hamlet of Shchigrovsky Province*, offering a touching but merciless exposure of this man's inadequacy and spinelessness. It is followed in the next year by a further examination of the same type (although this study was not included among his *Sketches*) in the figure of Chulkaturin in *The Diary of a Superfluous Man*. In both cases it is the lack of will, the humiliating self-pity and emotional weakness of such intellectuals which are emphasized, although these portraits are marked by a profounder psychological insight into

---

[1] Annenkov notes: 'He enjoyed any kind of discussion of his works, listened to it with the submissiveness of a schoolboy and displayed a willingness to make changes. One remark about the inappropriateness of the comparison which he had made between Khor' and Kalinych and Goethe and Schiller was sufficient to ensure that the comparison remained only in the pages of *The Contemporary* of 1847 where it first appeared and was not transferred to subsequent editions.' P. V. Annenkov, *Lit. vosp.* (SPB., 1909), 480.

the complexity and extent of their spiritual dilemma. It is this greater maturity of understanding and outlook that is also to become apparent in Turgenev's subsequent studies of peasant life. In 1850, for instance, two *Sketches* appear—*The Singers* and *The Meeting*—which deal exclusively with the peasants and not with the peasant-master relationship. Turgenev's attitude has obviously undergone an important change. The peasants are no longer studied as object lessons in a tendentious tract; they are studied as people possessing a culture and interests which are worthy of attention for their own sake. *The Singers* is a brilliant genre-picture of a singing competition between local peasant bards. The detailed observation of background and character, the astonishing manner in which the effect of the singing is conveyed without unnecessary grandiloquence or bathos and the frank depiction of the ensuing revelry make the work a snapshot from life that needs no sociological embellishment for it to be effective both as literature and as propaganda for the peasant cause. *The Meeting* is less striking artistically, although it is of interest for two reasons: firstly, in that it is an isolated attempt among these studies of the peasantry to illustrate a love-relationship. Turgenev had usually restricted himself to the role of observer in portraying the peasants, in the sense, at least, that he had never attempted to describe any kind of emotional relationship between them (although he had not hesitated to use love-stories as the basis for several of his *Sketches* with upper-class settings). Secondly, *The Meeting* illustrates a device of which Turgenev is to make considerable use in his novels: the use of the natural scene to highlight the emotions of the figures in the foreground (in this case, of the peasant girl's feelings as she awaits the arrival of her beloved and then witnesses his departure). In 1851 two more *Sketches* of this kind—*Bezhin Meadow* and *Kas'yan from Krasivaya Mech'*—make their appearance. Indeed, these two *Sketches* are among the finest that he wrote, betraying all the careful observation of his earlier ones but with an increased understanding of, and sympathy for, the peasants as Russians and as individuals, as human types with specific national characteristics and not as generalized types—as were Khor' and Kalinych, for example— endowed with literary or other traits to make them universally acceptable. There is a 'humanity' about the portraits of the peasant boys in *Bezhin Meadow* or the picture of the peasant-philosopher, Kas'yan, which raises these works into minor masterpieces. But this change of attitude in these later *Sketches* should not be taken as indicating any change of heart on Turgenev's part. These works may have appealed to the Slavophils and may give the impression that Turgenev has modified his Westernist views, although it was not so much a modifying of his views as a maturing of his talent and his profounder understanding of the Russian scene after 1848 that gave rise to such a change and set the seal on his fame as a champion of the serfs.

Between 1843 and 1852 Turgenev had revealed himself, firstly, as an incomparable painter of portraits and, secondly, as a master of the love-story. During this period, however, these talents are separate, two distinct veins running side by side through his work but never combining with any marked success. His most outstanding work of the period is, naturally, the portraits of individual peasants or episodes from peasant life which he offers us in his *Sketches*. In considering Turgenev's subsequent development as a writer, however, it is such stories as *Hamlet of Shchigrovsky Province* or *The Diary of a Superfluous Man*, in which an emotional relationship is studied, that are of greater interest, although even in these cases the element of pure portraiture ultimately outweighs the importance of these works as love-stories. It is in a different medium that Turgenev first succeeded in combining his talent as a portraitist with his talent as an analyst of the subtleties of feeling involved in the relationship between hero and heroine. This was his 'Comedy in Five Acts', *A Month in the Country* (1850), and the only full-length play that he wrote.

Apart from the stock device of comedy which demands that the characters should be intentionally ignorant of, should intentionally misunderstand or should intentionally overlook, the motives and feelings of other characters—and there is a great deal of this in *A Month in the Country*—this work is a comedy only in the Chekhovian sense. In fact, it was to form the basis of Chekhov's dramaturgy. The two main relationships in the play are essentially serious. The relationship, in the first instance, between Rakitin and the heroine, Natal'ya Petrovna Islayeva, is commonly supposed to be an oblique reflection of the kind of relations which existed between Turgenev and Pauline Viardot at this time. Rakitin is in love with Natal'ya Petrovna, but his love is not reciprocated. In the words of the narrator of *Andrey Kolosov*, he is one of those who 'continue to play on the broken strings of their drooping and sensitive hearts' long after there is any need to do so. Over a period of four years Rakitin has indulged this melancholy passion for Natal'ya Petrovna and their talk has become, as she puts it, like 'weaving fine lace'. This emotional lace-making, so claustrophobic and so relentlessly analysed by Turgenev, forms the basis of their relationship. What Natal'ya Petrovna looks for, however, is 'a glass of cold water on a hot day'—a passionate involvement that will recapture the ardour of her youth. She is to experience this in her feelings for the young tutor, Belyayev, and it is this second relationship which provides the central theme of the play. Since her feelings for Belyayev are just as incommunicable in the last resort and just as likely to remain unreciprocated as Rakitin's love for her, the result is an ironic commentary on the absurdity of human passions. The consequences are just as ironically tragic and pathetically comic as they are in the plays of Chekhov. But it is the nuances of dialogue, the incongruities of personal relationship and the characteristic, atmospheric flavour, which distinguish the work. Turgenev's experience from writing this five-act comedy was to prove invaluable to him in matters of construction and dialogue when he came to write his novels.

By the time of his arrest for his obituary notice on Gogol in 1852, Turgenev had reached a turning point in his career. In the eyes of the reading public he had acquired fame; in the eyes of officialdom—notoriety. But seen in the perspective of his life as a whole, until this moment he had simply been undergoing the apprenticeship which was to lead to his work as a novelist. Viewed in this light, *A Sportsman's Sketches* are no more nor less than the notebook of the future novelist, the trial sketches for the larger and more complex portraits, while *A Month in the Country* is the essay in theatrical construction which was to be such an important feature of the form of so many of his novels. Turgenev was already aware of the need to abandon what he called his 'old manner'.[1] But what form was his new manner to take? The choice was to be governed largely by the state of the Russian novel at this time.

Pushkin in his *Eugene Onegin* had established the pattern of future developments in the novel, but his novel was in verse and the tradition of the Russian novel was to be a prose tradition. Pushkin, in such short prose works as he wrote before his death in 1837, pared down the language and refined it to serve as an efficient vehicle for narrative devoid of unnecessary embellishment. His two successors—Lermontov and Gogol—were to adopt a less disciplined or classical approach to the question of prose language. The former was primarily a poet and his greatest contribution to the development of the prose language is limited to *A Hero of Our Time* which appeared in its completed form

[1] Letter to K. S. Aksakov, 16 October (O.S.) 1852. *Sobr. soch.* (1958), xii. 120.

in 1840. Lermontov's prose is a remarkable blend of the poetic and the prosaic, extremely supple and lucid, capable at once of sustaining lyrical flow and colloquial nuance without the least strain. But in point of form *A Hero of Our Time* is more of interest as a vehicle for the characterization of the hero, Pechorin, than as a novel. It is a concatenation of stories, an amalgam of different genres in the short-story form—the travelogue, the 'atmospheric' *conte* (*Taman*'), the diary form (*Princess Mary*)—and its content reflects the influence of such European writers as Constant and de Musset. The resulting portrait is another variation on the type of 'superfluous man' on the Byronic pattern, but the psychological characterization is more penetrating than was Pushkin's in *Eugene Onegin*. If *Eugene Onegin* was a documentary record, then *A Hero of Our Time* is a psychological casebook which points the way to the manner of Dostoyevsky. Gogol's contribution to the development of the Russian novel, on the other hand, had greater originality and greater enduring influence than Lermontov's. His *Dead Souls*, the first part of which appeared in 1842, bears little relationship to European literary tradition except in the sense that its picaresque form shows traces of the influence of Cervantes. It is a work so idiosyncratic and rich, so undisciplined and diffuse, such a mixture of *Kleinmalerei* and high-flown eloquence that interpretations of it have been as capricious and miscellaneous as its variegated elements. In its language and its characterization it marks a departure from all previous styles: the ornate richness of Gogol's devious sentence-structure, his protracted metaphors, his proneness to digression in the narrative are paralleled by the infinite variety of unrelated facts which he uses as embellishments to characterization. Yet it is a work poured out 'all of a piece' despite its profuseness; it is 'a poem', as Gogol called it, which is unmistakably stamped with all the intricacies and crudities of his personality. But, most important, it is the first generically Russian prose novel. It is at one and the same time a personal statement by Gogol and a social indictment, a satire on Russia's present and a profession of faith in Russia's future. With the appearance of the first part of *Dead Souls* Russian prose literature achieved maturity.

The works by Lermontov and Gogol initiated a decade of prose literature that was to see the emergence of such important writers as Dostoyevsky, Herzen, Goncharov, and Grigorovich—in addition, of course, to Turgenev. Of these only Herzen and Goncharov wrote what can, strictly speaking, be called novels. Dostoyevsky began his career in 1846 with the publication of his *Poor Folk* in Nekrasov's *Petersburg Almanac* and thereafter published such stories as *The Double*, *Mr. Prokharchin*, and *The Landlady*, but his only attempt at a novel was the curious, fragmentary *Netochka the Unnamed* and it was only after his return from exile in 1859 that his large novels were to appear. Similarly, Grigorovich wrote what can only be termed stories during this period, of which his studies of peasant life are the most famous. But Herzen's *Who is Guilty?* and Goncharov's *An Ordinary Story*, which appeared together in completed form in 1847, are both novels. Belinsky immediately recognized this and singled them out for comment and comparison as examples of the way in which 'the novel and the story (*povest'*)[1] give complete freedom to the writer as regards the predominant features of his talent, character, tastes, tendencies, and so on'.[2] Herzen's novel is a further study in the 'superfluous man', but its interrogative title indicates that it is more overtly publicistic and less exclusively literary than the previous studies. It is the social and the political problem, rather than the psychological problem, of the 'superfluous man' which is examined here. For this reason Herzen's novel cannot claim the purely literary merit which is a feature of Goncharov's *An Ordinary Story*. This latter work harks back to the pattern of *Eugene Onegin* in some respects, particularly in its emphasis upon the love-story, but its primary interest lies in its contrast between the rural and the urban scene, between the romantic ideas of the young nephew and the hard common sense of the uncle—an interplay of contrasts which is to preoccupy Goncharov in all his novels. Neither of these novels, however, can be regarded as good examples of artistic form. They give the impression of being media for the portrayal of different types of person and their concomitant problems with little attempt at the development of a consecutive plot or intrigue. The major feature, in fact, of the best work during the forties is portraiture rather than plot, so that the Russian novels to appear during the forties resemble extended short stories designed to provide extended portraits rather than novels designed—as Dickens's novels, for instance, which were rapidly becoming popular—to develop a particular intrigue. Moreover, there is an undisciplined and experimental air about all these novels; they represent the very beginnings of a tradition.

[1] There is no direct English equivalent of this word. It describes a work that stands midway between a short story and a novel, corresponding to what the Germans call a *Novelle*. I have preferred to translate it simply as 'story'.

[2] V. G. Belinsky, 'Vzglyad na russkuyu literaturu 1847 goda; stat'ya vtoraya', *Sobr. soch.* (1948), iii. 120.

But, for all their inadequacies, the novels of the forties have a character and flavour which are unmistakably Russian. By the time he was writing in 1846, Turgenev could rightly claim that the foreign elements had been remoulded and assimilated into the blood stream of Russian literature. This meant that there was a basis upon which to build. It now remained for Turgenev himself to turn the Russian novel into a work of art.

3

TURGENEV'S APPROACH TO THE NOVEL

AT the end of 1851, in a review of a long four-part novel by Yevgeniya Tur, Turgenev ruminated on the types of talent and the types of novel which had made their appearance in recent times. On the question of the types of novel he has the following amusing and perceptive comments to make:

A novel—a novel in four parts! You know, don't you, that apart from a woman no one in Russia in our time is capable of facing up to such a difficult and, in any circumstances, lengthy undertaking? Indeed, what can one fill four volumes with? The historical, the Walter-Scott type of novel—that expansive, solid edifice, with its unshakable foundations embedded in the soil of the nation, with its extensive introductions in the form of porticoes, with its reception rooms and dark corridors for ease of communication—this type of novel is practically impossible in our time: it has outlived its generation, it is not contemporary. . . . There remain two other types of novel which are closer to each other than may seem the case at the first glance—novels which, to avoid different interpretations which are not everywhere applicable, we shall call after the names of their chief representatives: the George Sand and the Dickensian. Such novels are possible among us and will, it seems, be adopted; but it is pertinent to ask now whether the basic elements of our social life have revealed themselves to the extent of demanding quadripartite dimensions in the novel that is to reproduce them? The success in recent times of various types of essay and sketch seems to prove the opposite.[1]

Turgenev's pessimism about the state of Russia's social development at this time is understandable. After the vigorous publicistic journalism of the forties, governmental reaction and oppression had become the order of the day in the fifties. And when the journals, the only organs of public expression in Russia at that time, were subject to reactionary pressures, so the social life of Russia suffered accordingly. But this was to be only a temporary relaxation in that extremely rapid 'hour by hour' development of Russian society that Turgenev, following

[1] From a review (*Plemyannitsa*: roman, soch. Yevgenii Tur. 4 chasti, Moskva, 1851) first published in *The Contemporary*, 1852, No. 1. *Sobr. soch.* (1956), xi. 121-2. Passages originally excised by the censor have been reinstated.

Belinsky, had noted in 1846—a period when the ideas acquired so hastily during the forties could be assimilated and fertilized, so that Turgenev's fears about Russian society, though justified on the face of it, were not to prevent him from making his own attempt at a novel. The question of the type of novel, however, still remained open.

In April 1851 Turgenev had written to a correspondent, saying that he intended to devote himself to a 'large work which I shall write *con amore* and at my leisure—without any *arrière-pensées* about the censorship'.[1] Such leisure was to be afforded him in the following year after his arrest and exile to Spasskoye. At that time he had informed Pauline Viardot that his enforced residence in the country would permit him to devote himself to his 'novel' with greater freedom, as he would now—perforce of circumstances—have neither the opportunity nor the need to consider the demands of the censorship.[2] He entitled his novel *Two Generations*, and by the beginning of March 1853 he had completed the first part of it (consisting of 'about five hundred pages', as he informed his friend, Annenkov[3]). Clearly Turgenev regarded the 'novel' as a work that would have to have large dimensions. The task of composing such a 'large work' was arduous and, as it turned out, beyond his powers at this time. By the end of 1853 he seems to have abandoned the struggle, although as late as the summer of 1855 he mentioned in a letter to Sergey Aksakov that he was once more preparing to work at his novel and go through it from the start.[4] But this novel was never completed, for the immediate outcome of his decision to go through his novel from the start was his first 'novel' as we understand it—*Rudin*.[5]

For more than four years—from 1851 to 1855—Turgenev wrestled with the problem of the novel as a genre before he finally decided upon writing what he called 'a large story' (*bol'shaya povest'*) which took the form of *Rudin*. Why was this? The most obvious reason is

[1] Letter to E. M. Feoktistov, 2 April (O.S.) 1851. Quoted from M. K. Kleman, *Letopis' zhizni i tvorchestva I. S. Turgeneva* (1934), 59.

[2] Letter to Louis and Pauline Viardot, 1/13 May 1852. *Sobr. soch.* (1958), xii. 110.

[3] Letter to P. V. Annenkov, 24 Feb. (O.S.) 1853. Ibid., 150.

[4] Letter to S. T. Aksakov, 2 June (O.S.) 1855. Quoted from *Soch.* (1930), v. 278.

[5] *Rudin* was begun on 5 June (O.S.) 1855. Annenkov, who possessed the first manuscript of the novel, wrote in his *Reminiscences*: 'The story was at first entitled *A Genial Nature* which was later crossed out and Turgenev inserted in his own hand—*Rudin*. It seems that the novel was conceived and written in 1855 in the country and in a very short space of time—seven weeks. A note on the manuscript states: "*Rudin*. Begun 5 June, 1855, on a Sunday, in Spasskoye; completed 24 July 1855 on a Sunday in the same place, in 7 weeks. Published with considerable additions in Jan. and Feb. numbers of *The Contemporary* for 1856."' *Lit. vosp.* (SPB., 1909), 493.

that Turgenev took a long time to recover from the unpleasant experience of his arrest and exile. In October 1852 he complained to
Konstantin Aksakov that he was unable to take up work on his novel
because 'I do not feel in myself either the inspiration or the strength,
without which one cannot write *firmly*'.[1] Another reason is that, at
thirty-four years of age, he was already being overtaken by a feeling
of premature senility. At the best of times Turgenev was prey to
hypochondria. This solitary residence in the country—far from
Pauline Viardot, far from friends and far from the stimulating atmosphere of Europe—served to accentuate his natural low spirits.
Nevertheless he succeeded in occupying himself with some literary
work. *Mumu*, probably the most famous of his many short stories
dealing with the problem of the serf-master—in this case, serf-mistress
—relationship, was written during the month that he was under arrest
in 1852, and while at Spasskoye later that year he wrote *The Inn*. Both
stories, incidentally, are based on Turgenev's recollection of the feudal
atmosphere which prevailed in his mother's household and which
he not only abhorred but regarded as manifestly evil. But close
acquaintanceship with the countryside seems to have turned Turgenev's
literary interest away from such rural problems as he had dealt with in
his *Sketches*, or the two stories of 1852, towards the problem of the
intellectual, with which he had begun his literary career. Such stories
as *The Backwater*, *The Correspondence* and *Jacob Pasynkov*, especially the
second, illustrate this renewed concern for the type of introspective
Hamlet, at the mercy of his weak will and his outraged sense of
inferiority, that he had examined in his *Hamlet of Shchigrovsky Province*
and his *The Diary of a Superfluous Man*. There is, however, a significant
difference. It is the same difference as was to be noted between the
earlier studies of the peasantry and the later studies in the *Sketches*—
an increasing compassion and understanding mark these studies of the
intellectual during the fifties. Moreover, as Granjard has noted, in all
his work between 1848 and 1858 Turgenev displays '*les accents élégiaques
la tonalité mineure*'[2] and it is this which comes to the fore very strongly
in *The Correspondence* and *Jacob Pasynkov*. Turgenev, after the shock of
1848 and the more personal experience of his arrest and exile in 1852,
had become contemplative and nostalgic. His gaze was turned back
to the achievements of the forties and his aim became one of

---

[1] Letter to K. S. Aksakov, 16 October (O.S.) 1852. *Sobr. soch.* (1958), xii. 120.

[2] Henri Granjard, *Ivan Tourguénev et les courants politiques et sociaux de son temps* (1954),
202.

reappraisal. *The Correspondence*, begun as early as 1844 and completed in 1854, illustrates the transition from censure of the intellectual who has wasted his life to an appreciation of the fact that this type of intellectual 'superfluous man' may not be entirely to blame.

In *The Correspondence*, the 'superfluous man', Aleksey, confesses to his correspondent, Mariya Aleksandrovna, that we, the intellectuals of his generation (i.e. of the forties)

are stupid, like children, but we are not as sincere as they are, we are cold as old men! But we haven't the wisdom of old men—that's why we're psychologists! Oh, yes, we're great psychologists! But our psychology borders on pathology, our psychology is a cunning study of the laws of a sick condition and a sick development, which is no concern of healthy people! But chiefly we are not young, not even young in our youth!

Yet, he asks himself, why do we indulge in this self-recrimination, why do we slander ourselves? The intellectuals of his generation had been young—'We also have been in Arcadia, have wandered through its shining fields!'—and had been touched by a love of high ideals, by a sense of purpose, by the purity of youth's enthusiasm. 'Surely then we deserved something better than life has brought us?' he asks. There is more in this cry than self-pity. It is a reproach to the social conditions of his age and the political oppression wielded by the autocracy. To which his correspondent, Mariya Aleksandrovna, answers:

You will probably agree with me that we women—at least those of us who are not satisfied by the ordinary worries of domestic life—receive our ultimate education from you, the men. You have a great and powerful influence over us. Now let's see what you do with us. We'll talk about the young girls, especially those who, like myself, live in the depths of the country—and there are many such in Russia. In addition, I know no others and so I cannot talk about them. Imagine to yourself such a girl. Her education is finished and she is beginning to live, to enjoy herself, but enjoyment alone is not enough for her. She demands much from life, she reads, she dreams . . . about love. Only about love and nothing else, you will say. Granted. But for her that word means a lot. Again I say that I'm not talking about a girl who finds it troublesome and boring to think for herself. . . . She looks about her and waits for the time when the man will appear for whom she has been yearning. At last he appears. She is carried away—she is like soft wax in his hands. Everything —happiness and love and ideas—has burst upon her on the instant of his appearance; all her fears are calmed, all her doubts are resolved by him. Truth itself, it seems, speaks through his lips—and she worships him, is ashamed of her happiness, learns from him, loves him. . . . Great is his power over her at this time. If only he were a hero, he would have inflamed her passion, he would have taught her to sacrifice herself—and all sacrifices would have been easy for her! But, alas, there are no heroes in our time. . . . Nevertheless he can direct her wherever he wishes and she dedicates herself to what interests him, his every word finds a place in her soul—and yet she still doesn't know how worthless and empty and false words can be, how little words cost him who speaks them, how little they deserve to be believed! And these first moments of bliss and hope are usually followed—due to circumstances (circumstances are always to blame)—by separation. . . .

Mariya Aleksandrovna's answer outlines the very substance of the relationships between hero and heroine which Turgenev is to examine in his novels. The important point, however, is that the heroes are not to be 'heroic', nor are the heroines to be totally self-sacrificing. Their relationship is to be at the mercy of 'circumstances'—the 'circum- stances' of Russian society, of the gulf that exists between the sexes or of 'Fate'—and separation, in one form or another, is to be inevitable. But the 'superfluous man' hero is no longer the man so hopelessly obsessed by his own egoism that others' feelings have to be sacrificed in order to salve his own vain self-pity. This 'superfluous man' is to be, like the Aleksey Petrovich of *The Correspondence* or the Jacob Pasynkov of the eponymous story, a man who has had ideals and has attempted to reintegrate his own personality, but whom society has spurned and whose life has been that of the unstable, uprooted wander- er (*skitalets*), dedicated to ideals that have faded and affairs of the heart that have ended in frustration.

If, then, one can give any direct answer to the question: why did Turgenev spend four years in wrestling with the problem of the novel? it must be that he had not, until 1855, sufficiently deepened his under- standing of human nature and human life, of human destiny and the world of nature to permit him to embark on what he called a 'large work'. He had also, of course, to realize that a 'large work' was not simply a work that was large in quantitative terms. In abandoning his work on his 500-page novel, *Two Generations*, he was tacitly acknowledging this.[1] For the 'largeness' of Turgenev's novels as we

[1] An extract (*Sobstvennaya gospodskaya kontora*) from the first part of this projected long novel appeared in the *Moscow Herald* (1859, No. 1). It is thought that the novel was based on a five-act comedy *The Lady Companion* which Turgenev had projected in 1849, but later abandoned. See I. S. Turgenev, *Soch.* (1930), v. 278; also, in the same edition, iv. 229. The content of *Two Generations* has been briefly described by N. M. Gut'yar; see N. M. Gut'yar, *Ivan Sergeyevich Turgenev* (Yur'yev, 1907), 157. The actual manuscript of *Two Generations*, however, remains unlocated.

now know them depends not upon their size but upon the depth of understanding of human nature which is revealed in them. It was this depth, it seems, which Turgenev was achieving during these interim years. He was re-exploring the problem of the intellectual, but he was also probing deeper into the significance of such 'superfluous men' as it was revealed by their lives.

In both *Hamlet of Shchigrovsky Province* and in *The Diary of a Superfluous Man* the aim was the portrayal of a particular type of intellectual and the result was a portrait limited to a particular occasion or episode in the hero's life. Even the underlying tragedy of the wretched *Hamlet* or the miserable Chulkaturin (of *The Diary of a Superfluous Man*) persecuted to death by his sense of failure were invested with a kind of sardonic humour. But neither Aleksey Petrovich of *The Correspondence* nor Jacob Pasynkov are portrayed sardonically. In both cases the study is more serious and 'elegiac'. Both are seen in the perspectives of their lives and the inferences of the portraits are consequently enlarged and deepened. Both are seen to die unfulfilled, but their lives remain as testaments of their refusal to conform and their respect for ideals that transcend the humdrum. The figure of Rudin is to represent a climax in Turgenev's examination of the problem of the 'superfluous man' intellectual, while the form of *Rudin*, the novel, is to combine the type of portrait based upon one episode from the hero's life which is to be found in *Hamlet of Shchigrovsky Province* and *The Diary of a Superfluous Man* with the type of extended portrait, after the pattern of a chronicle, which is to be found in *Jacob Pasynkov*. Similarly, the critically sardonic manner of the two earlier stories is to be discernible in the way Rudin is portrayed in his relationship with the heroine, Natal'ya, while the more elegiac tone, typical of the two later stories, is to mark the final stages of the novel.

But if Turgenev had thought his way through to an enlarged form of short story—what he called a *bol'shaya povest'*, as distinct from *roman*, a novel—which embraced an enlarged view of the type of 'superfluous man' whom he had examined earlier, then he had also enlarged and deepened his ideas about the nature of human destiny. It is his *Faust*, of 1856,—with its epigraph from Goethe, '*Entbehren sollst du, sollst entbehren*', and its final paragraph on the nature of life —which crystallizes Turgenev's ideas at this time. The work takes the form of a short story composed of nine letters (Turgenev frequently made use of such formal devices in composition: stories told by narrators gathered for an evening, extracts from diaries, exchanges of letters, etc.) and its content is semi-fantastic without any of the realistic, social-tendentious manner characteristic of his previous studies. But the first-person narration of this story is a pointer to the fact that Turgenev intended the moral at the end of the story to be in the nature of a personal statement on his view of life:

In conclusion I will say to you: I have derived one conviction from the experiences of these last years: life is not a joke or an entertainment; life is not even pleasure. . . . Life is a heavy labour. Denial, constant denial—that is its secret meaning, that is the clue to it; not the fulfilment of one's favourite ideas and dreams, no matter how lofty they might be, but fulfilment of one's duty must be the concern of man; if he has not fettered himself with the iron fetters of duty, he cannot reach, without stumbling, the end of his career; while in youth we think: the freer we are, the better, and the further we will go. Youth can think like that; but it is shameful to comfort oneself with an illusion when the stern face of truth has finally looked one in the eyes.

The undue pessimism of these words is not accidental. Its causes lie not only in Turgenev's temperament or in any accumulated bitterness deriving from his experiences during the fifties—the essence of this pessimism, after all, is distilled in his very earliest works—but also in the influence of German thought, possibly even of Schopenhauer, which became so popular during this decade. Yet in Turgenev's case the philosophical bases of this pessimism acquire a very personal meaning, particularly in reference to love and death. *The Correspondence, Jacob Pasynkov, Faust* are all studies in love and death. Turgenev outlines his attitude to this relationship between love and death in the most contemplative or 'philosophical' of his works during the fifties, *Journey into the Wood*, begun in 1853 and completed in 1857. Here man is regarded as 'a being of a single day, born yesterday and already today doomed to death,' like an insect. It is while watching such an insect that the narrator, at the end of the work, thinks to himself:

Looking at it, it suddenly seemed to me that I understood the life of nature, understood its undoubted and obvious—although still to many mysterious— meaning. A tranquil and slow animation, the leisureliness and restraint of its sensations and forces, a balance of health in each separate being—that is its very basis, its unalterable law, that is on what it rests. Whatever rises above or sinks below that level is discarded by it as worthless. Many insects die as soon as they experience the joys of love which upset the balance. . . .

For Turgenev love is an illness that upsets the balance of health in man's organism. In *The Correspondence* Aleksey, in his final letter, says:

Love is not a feeling at all—it is an illness, a specific condition of the soul and body; it does not develop gradually—one cannot doubt it, one cannot escape it, although it does not always make its appearance in the same way; usually it takes hold of a man without asking, suddenly, against his will—just like an epidemic or a fever. . . .

And in *Faust* Vera, the heroine, instantly falls sick and dies the moment that love is admitted between her and the narrator of the story.

But love and death, inextricably linked as they are in Turgenev's view of human destiny, cannot be fully understood without reference to Turgenev's view of nature as something that surrounds man and preys upon him. In a letter to Pauline Viardot of 1849 Turgenev described nature as 'indifferent'—

Yes, that's what she [i.e. nature] is: she's indifferent; the soul is only within us and, perhaps, a little around us . . . that weak glimmering which eternal night constantly strives to extinguish.[1]

and in his *Journey into the Wood* this 'indifference' of nature becomes horrific:

From the depths of the age-old forests, from the everlasting bosom of the waters the same voice is heard: 'You are no concern of mine,' says nature to man. 'I reign over my kingdom, but you must concern yourself with how not to die.'

Man, when he is brought face to face with nature, is filled with a sense of his individual doom and personal inadequacy:

. . . not just the bold hopes and dreams of youth are calmed and extinguished within him, seized by the icy breath of the elements; no—his whole soul droops and withers; he feels that the last of his brother human beings can vanish from the face of the earth and not one pine needle will shake on these branches; he feels his own isolation, his weakness, the accidental quality of his existence and with hurried inner terror he turns back to the petty cares and labours of life; he feels easier in this world that has been created by him—here he is at home, here he dares to believe in his own significance and his own strength.

[1] Letter to Pauline Viardot, 29, 30 May/10, 11 June 1849. *Sobr. soch.* (1958), xii. 82. Turgenev speaks of this 'indifference' of nature in connexion with a painful scene he witnessed in Russia, when a severe hailstorm suddenly destroyed a peasant family's harvest. The father of the family covered his head with his shirt after this catastrophe. 'It was the last gesture of the dying Socrates,' Turgenev remarks, 'the final and silent protest of man against the cruelty of his own kind and the callous indifference of nature.'

Man's insignificance in this cosmic view of human destiny embraced by Turgenev should not be underestimated. Man is at the mercy of natural forces and his aims and achievements are to be measured finally not in relation to his life, but in relation to the eternity of nature. Nature contains the unalterable, impassive laws whose existence man must admit to himself but which are external to him and incomprehensible to him, and even the merest intimation of them can cause man to feel an unearthly horror:

I sat down on a tree stump, leaned my elbows on my knees and, after a long silence, slowly raised my head and looked around me. Oh, how quiet and morosely melancholy was everything around me—no, not even melancholy, but dumb, cold and threatening at that moment! My heart shrank within me. At that instant, in that place, I sensed the spirit of death, I felt, I almost consciously knew its presence. If only there had been one audible sound, even a momentary fluttering of the leaves in the immobility of the wood which surrounded me! I again, almost with terror, lowered my head, as if I had looked somewhere where no man should ever look. . . .

Death, like nature and its laws, is external to man and nothing can mitigate the inevitability and the horror of it. Turgenev, of course, knew that nature had its beauty and an infinite variety of changing moods, but its relationship to man was impassive and unchangeable in the last resort: nature reigned supreme, while man had simply to concern himself with how not to die. Nature was eternal, while man was simply a creature of a single day. This view, though it may be pessimistic, has a decisiveness and ruthless unsentimentality which form the basis of Turgenev's philosophy of life. He had few variations to offer on these basic assumptions about human life and destiny. Steno is as circumscribed by these assumptions as is Nezhdanov, the hero of his last novel, *Virgin Soil*.

In any consideration of his novels, however, it is the political aspect of Turgenev's work which comes to the forefront. All his stories up to the middle of the fifties had been, broadly speaking, portraits of one or another type of individual depicted in one or another kind of situation or relationship. The social or political aspect of the portrait had been present by implication, but the society itself had not been presented in any detail. Turgenev's novels are to introduce us to particular societies as well as to particular individuals and the political implications of this broader view are at once to become apparent. Turgenev was to become the chronicler of his age in the sense that the cameos of his novels were to reflect the political and social issues of the larger picture, of Russian society itself, that extended out behind them. Indeed, contemporary critics were to judge his novels less from the point of view of artistic merit than from the point of view of their political and social message. His novels were to be regarded as fragmented reflections of, and personal comments upon, the development of Russian society and the ideological attitudes of the intelligentsia during the decades of the forties, fifties, and sixties. If he had few variations to offer on the basic philosophical assumptions of his art, then there are variations to be discerned in the political complexion of his novels. Similarly, although Turgenev's personal views remain consistently Westernist, in the way Turgenev traces the development of Russian society certain variations are apparent. They spring from his desire to be the dispassionate observer of the social scene, chronicling the development of social ideas with something of the historian's objectivity and allowing such changes as occurred to give a political colouring to his fiction that might run contrary to his own convictions.

Turgenev's approach to the novel, therefore, must be regarded as political and social, as well as literary. His interest in the novel, as early as 1851 in writing about Yevgeniya Tur's four-part novel, took the form of concern for Russia's social maturity. He was ready to ask himself whether 'the basic elements of our social life' were sufficiently obvious to permit the development of a new and larger literary genre that could reflect them. Ten years later, in 1861, there was to be no doubt about it: he had written four novels—*Rudin*, *A Nest of the Gentry*, *On the Eve* and *Fathers and Children*—all of which save *Fathers and Children* had been published, and that was to be published at the beginning of the following year. His doubts about the admissibility of the novel concerned with social problems had consequently been proved entirely groundless. But of more importance was the fact that he had made a remarkable and unique contribution to the development of the Russian realistic novel as a literary genre. These four novels, appearing between 1856 and 1862, constitute a moment of concentrated development in both form and content that is unparalleled in Russian literature. During these years Turgenev was to lay the basis for his own future fame as a novelist and was to provide an artistic example that could not be overlooked by the novelists who were to come to prominence during the sixties and seventies. It may be no exaggeration to claim that it was an artistic example which few novelists writing in any language have been able to overlook and, equally, which few have been able to improve on.

4

THE NOVELS OF TURGENEV
INTRODUCTION

In the 1880 edition of his *Works*, Turgenev assembled all his novels and introduced them to the reader with the following words:

Having decided . . . to include all the novels written by me (*Rudin, A Nest of the Gentry, On the Eve, Fathers and Children, Smoke* and *Virgin Soil*) in their right order, I consider it pertinent to explain, in a few words, why I have done this. I wanted to give those of my readers, who will take upon themselves the task of reading through these six novels one by one, an opportunity to convince themselves of the extent to which the critics have been just in reproaching me for changing my direction, for apostasy and so on. To me, on the contrary, it seems that I could be blamed rather for an excessive constancy and straightness of line, as it were. The author of *Rudin*, written in 1855, and the author of *Virgin Soil*, written in 1876, are one and the same person. Over this period I have aspired, to the extent that my powers and ability have permitted, conscientiously and impartially to depict and embody in suitable types both what Shakespeare calls: 'the body and pressure of time' and that rapidly changing physiognomy of Russians of the cultured stratum, which has been preeminently the object of my observations. It is not for me to judge the extent to which I have succeeded; but I dare to think that readers will no longer doubt the sincerity and single-mindedness of my aspirations. . . .[1]

It is only right, in studying Turgenev's novels, to bear in mind what he has to say about his 'constancy' and 'straightness of line' (*pryamolineynost'*). In terms of artistic form there is a monolithic quality about the development of Turgenev's novels. They all appear to be constructed of the same elements, the same literary properties, which are suitably rearranged and reassembled to suit the changed requirements of each novel but which are never noticeably altered. Perhaps, as Turgenev suggests, he can be 'blamed' for this undue orthodoxy. He was not eager for experiment, nor was he out to impress by employing sensational literary devices. The truth is that his was an age when craftsmanship was more essential to success than the gimmick,

[1] *Sobr. soch.* (1956), xi. 403-4.

and he was more aware of the need for tradition than the need to
break with it.

The two aims which Turgenev had always before him—that of
depicting 'the body and pressure of time' and the rapidly changing
face of cultured Russian society—unite in the primary artistic consideration of his novels: the fact that they are 'realistic'. Turgenev's
realism is to be defined, firstly, in common human terms. His novels
give us pictures of real life which are true to life and acceptable in
terms of a reality that every man can experience. Secondly, his novels
are realistic in the sense that they are 'social-psychological' representa-
tions of epochs in the development of Russian society. The two
definitions are complementary: the reality of the artistically trans-
formed experience must necessarily complement the reality of the
particular social-psychological problem which Turgenev sets out to
identify and depict. One is wary of pinning any label of 'realism' too
firmly to Turgenev's novels for the simple reason that it is a hackneyed,
blanket term, too often ill-used—as anyone who knows anything about
Socialist Realism will readily acknowledge—and open to multifarious
shades of meaning and doctrinaire interpretation. It is nevertheless
the quality of the real which is so unmistakable a characteristic of Turgenev's novels and which lends them the universality of inference that
must be a primary consideration, social significance apart, for it is here
that Turgenev's claim to fame resides.

It is instinctive to Turgenev to hide himself. His attitude towards
his fiction is one of sympathetic detachment, almost—though never
quite—indifference. His aim is to be dispassionate, leaving the axes to
grind themselves. There is here much artfulness as well as craftsmanship, but it is essentially his knowledge of his craft that is supreme.
For he knew that no writer could ever hope to divorce himself wholly
from his work and he did not labour the pretence of objectivity to the
point of denying himself, as author, any role in his fiction. He appears
in his novels as narrator, story-teller or observer of the human scene
and he is never a false narrator, story-teller or observer, parading in the
guise of some fictional 'I' or 'We' who may have opinions that run
contrary to those of the author himself. When Turgenev addresses
himself to the reader, it is Turgenev who is addressing us and we need
never have any doubts about his role. Percy Lubbock has observed
that 'Turgenev was never shy of appearing in his pages as the reflective-
story-teller, imparting the fruits of his observation to the reader',
though he adds that in an essentially pictorial form of novel, as are

Turgenev's novels, the intrusion of the author may weaken the general effect.[1] There are certainly instances when Turgenev's comments tend to violate the pictorial realism of his fiction, but it is equally remarkable how little this disturbs the balance of the composition. He is generally extremely frugal and apt in his personal comments, while his role as author of the fiction is always kept within strict bounds of artistic propriety.

In the greatest of his novels—*Rudin*, *A Nest of the Gentry*, *On the Eve*, and *Fathers and Children*—this objective detachment is to be seen at its best. Here Turgenev does not intrude into his fiction unnecessarily, either in the guise of narrator or as omniscient author. There are instances, admittedly, when Turgenev's personal sympathies and antipathies (more often the latter) colour the manner of description, but in no case can it be said that these novels acquire anything like the over-all bias which is, in a sense, the distinction and, more strictly, the weakness of his fifth novel, *Smoke*. In these first four novels the aim has been to allow the fiction to exist in its own right, to allow the story to tell itself, to let the reality of the portrait grow of its own accord. This is the essence of the realism in the Turgenevan novel. One is left with the impression that there is a reality in these novels not of Turgenev's making, which indeed surprises Turgenev as much as it may surprise and delight the reader, leaving one with a sense of having witnessed an incident in life that—as Turgenev puts it at the end of *A Nest of the Gentry*—'one can but point to—and pass on'. Here is the secret. Turgenev, in his artfulness, is the craftsman who likes to leave the impression that he has merely indicated with an elegant gesture of the hand the humour, pity, and tragedy of human life, whereas the elegant simplicity of the gesture only conceals an absorbing knowledge of his craft.

It is the objectivity of Turgenev's attitude that is the primary characteristic of his realism and it is for this purpose that he hides himself. But, accepting this, what are the constituent elements of Turgenev's realism? How does he succeed in giving the reader a picture of reality that is universally acceptable? There is obviously no one answer to such a question, but if we are to choose any primary constituent of Turgenev's realism that is both essential to his fiction, especially his novels, and universal in inference, then we must point to the importance of nature in his work. Nature in Turgenev's novels is both the natural scene that so often supplies the backcloth and human

[1] Percy Lubbock, *The Craft of Fiction* (1921), 121.

nature that occupies the foreground. The natural scene both reflects and contrasts with the human emotions of the heroes and heroines in the foreground: it reflects their moods and their hopes and their feelings and it sets in relief their tragedies. Correspondingly, the heroes and heroines only discover the full extent of their emotional attachment or incompatibility by acknowledging their human frailty in the face of nature's unchanging, ironic, Giaconda-like smile. The important thing is that nature is always the same, ever-present, ever demanding its rights, ever highlighting the ephemerality and accidental quality of human life and happiness. It is in Turgenev's poetic ability to understand and evoke the natural scene that his artistic mastery, which might be tempted so easily into the bathetic and meretricious, is astonishing for its delicacy of proportion and subtlety of feeling.

Compare, for instance, the way in which the scene is set in Chapter VII of *Rudin* for the first occasion when Rudin meets Natal'ya alone and the way in which the scene is set in Chapter IX on the occasion of their last meeting. On the first occasion the day is radiant, the grass after the brief rainfall begins to flow with emerald and gold, the sky has cleared and the garden where the hero and heroine are to meet is filled with freshness and quietness. On the second occasion, when Rudin is to fail to meet the challenge offered him by Natal'ya, the description emphasises the unnaturalness and barrenness of the environs of Avdyukhin pond, while its symbolic significance, with its associations of crime and mystery in peasant legend, is doubly emphasised by the fact that 'grey skeletons of massive trees towered here and there like mournful spectres over the low bushy undergrowth'—which is in striking contrast to the symbol of the apple-tree that has broken down under the weight of its own fruit (the true symbol of genius, in Rudin's opinion) or the strong oak-tree with its new leaves breaking through which Rudin had used previously (during his conversation with Natal'ya in Chapter VI) as a symbolic means of expressing his idea of love. Here the natural scene sets the mood for what is to follow or is symbolic of the feelings of one or another of the protagonists. Or in Chapter XX of *A Nest of the Gentry* when Lavretsky, on the day after his return to Vasil'yevskoye, plunges into recollections of his past life to the accompaniment of the slow movement of nature:

And once again he began to listen to the silence, awaiting nothing—and yet at the same time endlessly expectant: the silence engulfed him on every side; the sun ran its course across the tranquil blue of the sky, and the clouds floated silently upon it; it seemed as if they knew why and where they were going. At that very time, in other places on the earth, life was seething, hurrying, roaring on its way; here the same life flowed by inaudibly, like water through marshy grass; and until evening Lavretsky could not tear himself away from contemplation of this receding, outflowing life; anguish for the past was melting in his soul like spring snow and—strangest of all!—never before had he felt so deep and strong a feeling for his country.

Or a little later, in Chapter XXVII, the night scene captures his new mood of expectancy, of hopefulness, after the visit of the Kalitins to Vasil'yevskoye:

The charm of the summer night possessed him; everything around him seemed so unexpectedly strange and at the same time so long and so sweetly familiar to him; near and far—and one could see a long way, although the eye could not distinguish much of what it saw—everything was at peace; this very peace was redolent of youth bursting with life. Lavretsky's horse stepped out, rocking him evenly from side to side; its large black shadow moved along beside it; there was something secretly pleasing in the tramp of its hooves, something joyous and wonderful in the ringing cries of the quails. The stars disappeared in a bright haze; a crescent moon shone with a hard glow; its light flowed in a pale blue stream across the sky and fell in patches of smoky gold on the light clouds which passed close to it; the freshness of the air brought a slight moisture to the eyes, gently caressed the limbs and flowed freely into the lungs.

These descriptive passages are not introduced by Turgenev purely 'for effect'. They are all integral to the story or the demands of characterization, serving to evoke moods, to 'orchestrate' the feelings and thoughts of his protagonists, to introduce scenes and illustrate the psychological state of a person at a particular moment. Again, for instance, in *On the Eve* the scene in which Yelena and Insarov are to confess their love for each other (Chapter XVIII) is dramatically introduced by the description of the thunderstorm or, later in the novel, the concluding episode of their life together is foreshadowed by the incomparable description of Venice in the spring (Chapter XXXIII). Or in *Fathers and Children* when the brash nihilism of Bazarov so disturbs Nikolay Petrovich Kirsanov that he goes out into his garden in order to ask himself how anyone can fail to appreciate nature:

And he looked around, as if wishing to understand how anyone could fail to appreciate nature. Evening was already approaching; the sun was hidden behind a small aspen wood which lay half a verst from the garden: the shadow

from it stretched endlessly across the motionless fields. A peasant was riding at
a trot on a white horse along the dark narrow lane beside the wood: he could
be seen quite clearly, even to the patch on his shoulder, despite the fact that
he was in the shadow; the legs of his little horse flashed briskly and distinctly
by. The sun's rays shot through the wood from the far side and, penetrating
into its depths, suffused the trunks of the aspens with such a warm light that
they acquired the appearance of pines, while their foliage became almost pine-
blue, and above the wood there rose the coldly pale blue sky, slightly flushed
by the sunset. Swallows flew high above; the wind had quite died; late bees
buzzed lazily and sleepily in the lilac blossoms; midges swarmed in a column
above a solitary, outstretched branch.

The selectivity of the detail, the contrast of far and near, the immaculate water-colour sense which informs such descriptions—each
sentence a significant stroke in the composition of the picture—
naturally mirrors the balance and the careful assemblage of different
facets which compose his novels as a whole. But the brilliance of the
technical achievement still must not hide from us the fact that nature
in Turgenev's novels remains ironically beautiful and impassive; it
can reflect human emotions only when the emotions are projected into
it. As Shubin explains to Andrey Bersenev at the beginning of *On the
Eve*, when the latter has complained of nature being 'too satisfied with
itself' and awakening in him 'something disquieting, a feeling of
anxiety, of sadness':

'I only want to explain why nature, in your opinion, affects us in this way.
It is because it stirs in us the need for love, but is not capable of satisfying it.
It drives us quietly into others' living embraces, while we don't understand it
and expect something from nature itself. Oh, Andrey, Andrey, this sun and
this sky are beautiful, everything around us is beautiful, but you are sad; but
if at this moment you held in your hand the hand of some woman you loved,
if the hand and the woman were yours alone, if you saw with *her* eyes, if you
felt not your own isolated feelings but *her* feelings—then nature would not
awaken sadness and anxiety in you, and you wouldn't bother to note its beauty;
it would exult and sing, it would repeat your own song, because you would
have given it, dumb as it is, a tongue to sing with!'

At all other times nature is strikingly indifferent, though for Turgenev's purposes it has a formal function in his fiction as backcloth and
mirror of the human problems which occupy the foreground. It is
the staple element in that poetic atmosphere with which all Turgenev's
novels are invested. Perhaps, in the twentieth century, the idea that
nature can be the complement of human emotion smacks of sentimentality; it is a preciosity that 'good' writers might wish to avoid;

but it presumes a classical attitude to nature to which Turgenev avowedly adhered, which made sense to him and which was an integral component of his realism. It is to be emphasized that Turgenev's realism is not of the *tranche de vie* variety. His realism subsumes artistic tenets of form and manner which Zola-esque naturalism, stream-of-consciousness, the thraldom to Hemingway or—as in the Soviet Union—thraldom to extra-literary standards of value, have tended to force into the background, though such tenets have an importance in their own right which cannot be rejected out of hand. They are the rational disciplines of the writer-classicist as opposed to the anti-rational 'freedoms' of the writer-romantic. Both are expressions of attitudes of mind and artistic temperament that have an equal claim to be called realistic.

To this extent all Turgenev's novels have a distinct pattern to their internal construction. It is best explained on the analogy of the theatre, though it is achieved through a process of contrast which is only applicable in terms of the novel.

In the first place, there is a theatrical quality—not stagey or artificial but theatrical in the best sense—about the way in which Turgenev 'mounts' his novels. He gives each novel a location, a situation, in some cases only a house, as Dar'ya Lasunskaya's residence in *Rudin*, or a particular place, as Baden-Baden in *Smoke*, or a region with several different though mutually connected foci of interest, as in *Fathers and Children* and *Virgin Soil*, and such a location or situation serves to unify each novel, both physically and temporally. Indeed, the temporal unity is almost as important as the unity of place or location—so many of his novels are 'months in the country'—because it also serves to concentrate and limit the development of the fiction. This is the setting of the novel which circumscribes the action of the major participants as if they were performers upon a stage. Turgenev lets the reader know all the salient facts about those characters—in the shape of biographical excerpts and introductions—who are integral to each location or situation, to each 'place' in the novel, for they almost have the function of stage properties, characters of a particular place, conditioned by it and typical of it, who rarely if ever step out of the special place assigned to them.[1] In this way his novels give the appearance

---

[1] Henry James records Turgenev as saying of his characters: 'If I watch them long enough I see them come together, I see them *placed*, I see them engaged in this or that act and in this or that difficulty. How they look and move and speak and behave, always in the setting I have found for them, is my account of them. . . .' Henry James, *The Portrait of a Lady* (1921), i. p. viii.

ET

of being tableaux of a theatrical variety with just the required formal rigidity, the required attitudinizing; each episode in the action is like one scene upon a stage, neatly set and neatly accomplished; but such rigidity of form is purely an artistic tenet and does not offend against life. The impression created as a result of this method is not that life has been formalized to suit the tastes and designs of the author but that life itself seems simply to have imposed its own natural scheme upon the way in which the fiction is presented to us.

In the second place, again on the theatrical analogy, there is the arrival of the stranger, the unknown or only partly known quantity, whether hero or heroine, who steps into the fiction and at once provides the element of newness and contrast. All Turgenev's heroes are strangers to the situations of their respective novels: Rudin, Lavretsky, Insarov, Bazarov, Litvinov, Nezhdanov, while his heroines are integral parts of their novels' 'place', although they may still enter the fiction as unknown or only partly known quantities. It is in the relationship between the hero who enters from outside and the heroine who embodies the most characteristic or typical features of the 'place' of the novel that the contrast becomes apparent. It is always a contrast on two planes—that of the social or ideological, on the one hand, and that of the psychological or individual, on the other. Both planes of contrast are complementary and form unities, just as the natural scene of the background complements the human nature in the foreground and serves as a unifying principle in the novels. The contrast afforded by the presence of the stranger-hero in the 'place' of the fiction is usually, firstly, that between the new and the old, between the modern and the traditional, between the younger and the older generation, between experience and innocence, because the hero usually (the only real exception to this is *Virgin Soil*) personifies a new ideological attitude which is strange and alluring to the heroine of the 'place'. Rudin, for instance, is a fount of new ideas for Natal'ya; Lavretsky offers a new vision of the world to Liza; Insarov is an inspiration to Yelena; Bazarov is intriguing and strange to Odintsova; Litvinov offers hope of renewal to Irina—and in each case it is the ideas proffered by the hero that seem to have the major appeal to the heroine. For these ideas are the product of a different social experience, a different education, a different conditioning, and the heroine is attracted to the newness of these ideas as if they were guarantees of new and nobler psychological or individual characteristics in the hero. It is then, secondly, a disparity in psychological attitude which also affords the contrast. The love-stories in Turgenev are never between *similar types* of person; just as the heroes and heroines are typical of different types of social experience, education or conditioning, so they differ in psychological type. Yet to this extent they complement each other and reflect each other, set in relief their finer or their inferior qualities and become, perhaps even despite themselves, involved in that process of contrast which is the primary element in the love-relationship between hero and heroine in Turgenev's novels.

It is here that peripeteia has its part to play. The contrast of types afforded by the love-relationship follows a smooth course only once in Turgenev's novels (the Yelena-Insarov relationship in *On the Eve*) and even then it is doomed. In all other cases the process of contrast is brought to a head at one vital moment when the promise of mutual happiness, previously an underlying assumption of the relationship, is irrevocably destroyed. In no novel is the cause exactly similar, but in each case it is due to the revelation of some incompatibility between hero and heroine, whether of personality or circumstance, that clearly prevents any further development in their relationship. It is at this moment that the hero's or the heroine's true nature, delineated during the process of contrast in which both of them have been involved, is finally revealed in its weakness or its nobility. All the subsequent action of the fiction is influenced by this decisive moment of climax and takes the form of a protracted conclusion or epilogue.

A theatrical analogy, therefore, supplies the clue to the internal construction of the Turgenevan novel. It provides the skeletal design which is the basic form of Turgenev's realism in his novels in the sense that they are 'staged' in some realistic setting and have a common pattern discernible in their internal development. These are the formal properties of his novels that make them distinctive as realistic novels. But however important these aids to form, these constructional elements in the novel, may be, they are clearly not the sum total of Turgenev's art.

To argue that Turgenev understood the art that conceals art would be to understate the case. He understood supremely well that the novel had to have a 'story' and for it to have a story it had to be properly constructed. He chose as his metier the love story in its simplest form, a straightforward hero-heroine relationship, unencumbered by such niceties as the eternal triangle, the problem of divorce or inversion, but concentrating on the directness of the relationship itself and the extent to which it could serve as a means of revealing the individual characteristics of the two participants. It is the way Turgenev handles his love-stories that betrays his artistry, but it is here that he also conceals his art. For his love-story is never the *only* thing in his fiction, meaning that it is never the totality of his fiction to which all else is subordinated. The love-story is usually no more than the vehicle for supplying the contrast that is so essential for the characterization. Turgenev's novels are really elaborate portraits of one or another hero or heroine, whose features are shaded in with the gradations of contrast in the surrounding scene. All the subtle facets of his novels—the descriptive material, the subsidiary characters, the ideological problems, the psychological nuances, the contrasts of light and shade, the concise and pertinent dialogue, the persuasive and poetic style—are united in the single aim of painting a portrait and embellishing it with significant detail. The figures so portrayed dominate the novels, unify them, give them life, suffuse them with their own feelings. It is their lives and destinies that engage the reader's attention and make him feel the enchantment of involvement in new worlds and new ways of living. This is the enduring feature of Turgenev's art as a novelist. His heroes and heroines transcend the fictional matter of which they are composed and acquire living traits of personality to which the reader can immediately respond; and no matter how distant the epoch in which they lived, their lives still have reference to the present day.

In his first four novels Turgenev was to explore and elaborate his artistic technique, though the formal properties in each novel were to remain largely the same. For this reason I have chosen to examine these novels not as separate entities but as stages in the development of the Turgenevan novel, illustrating the development in terms of the structure, in terms of the ideas and ideals, and in terms of Turgenev's philosophy as it is revealed in the relationship between hero and heroine. The concentrated nature of the development is best examined, to my mind, in this way.

5

FOUR GREAT NOVELS
STRUCTURE

Rudin (1856) tells how a stranger, Rudin, arrives at the country residence of a wealthy widow, Dar'ya Lasunskaya, and is so successful in impressing the assembled company with his eloquence and charm of manner that he is invited to stay as a guest. As time passes, the widow's daughter, Natal'ya, falls in love with him, but the relationship is discovered, and Rudin is unceremoniously banished from the house. Years later, in 1848, he dies for his ideals on the Paris barricades during the Revolution. These bare bones serve only to indicate that the interest of the novel lies not in its story but in the way it is constructed, in the sociological problem it sets out to examine and in the subtleties of characterization which it embodies.

Turgenev begins the action of his novel with a short statement on the time and place. The first chapter of *Rudin* opens with the sentence: 'It was a calm summer morning.' The situation of the forthcoming action is then described. In the same way, as each of the minor characters is introduced, his or her significance for the fiction is neatly shaded in by some kind of biographical note. The first character is Aleksandra Lipina—'a widow', we are told, 'childless, who lived with her brother, a retired cavalry captain, Sergey Volyntsev'. This latter is only described as being unmarried and engaged in looking after her estate: this is significant, for Sergey Volyntsev is later to have an important role to play as the hero's rival. Pandalevsky is introduced in greater detail—for the reason that, though he is to play no major part in the development of the novel's action,[1] he is nevertheless to be the informant who brings about the hero's fall from favour. Each new character gives us a new idea of the kind of society to which we have

[1] It appears that Turgenev originally intended Pandalevsky to play a much more important role in the novel. He was to be Aleksandra Lipina's suitor and this relationship was to provide a parallel theme to that of the relationship between Rudin and Natal'ya. In abandoning this plan he made his novel less schematic and thus concentrated the interest of the fiction upon the figure of Rudin. See M. K. Kleman's commentary to *Rudin* in I. S. Turgenev, *Rudin. Dvoryanskoye gnezdo* (1933).

been introduced. This form of introduction to the central situation of the novel's action has led Edward Garnett to remark:

. . . the grouping of the characters is a lesson in harmonious arrangement. Note by what simple natural steps one passes from the outer circle of the neighbours of the wealthy patroness of art and letters, Darya Michailovna, to the inner circle of her household.[1]

This inner circle is introduced at the beginning of Chapter II. First, the house; then the hostess. By a natural progression the other members of her household are introduced: Pigasov, the children, Mlle. Boncourt. Although special attention is given to the hostess herself and to Pigasov, whose entire life story up to this time is retailed in a short biographical sketch, it is significant that no attempt is made at this point to establish either Lezhnyov, whom Aleksandra Lipina had met during her walk in Chapter I, or Natal'ya, who are both to play a more considerable part in the novel than Dar'ya Lasunskaya, Pandalevsky, and Pigasov. All this points to the assumption that the establishment of a scene, of a situation, is a first principle in Turgenev's method. With the establishment of a particular situation and the introduction of a number of characters, whose backgrounds are established by the biographical notes to which attention has been drawn, the only unknown quantities are those characters who are destined to have the largest part in the action of the fiction. In this way, the attention of the reader is focused upon the major characters and especially upon the hero who arrives, unheralded, at the very beginning of Chapter III.

The process of the hero's characterization begins immediately. It is developed, firstly, by means of that natural contrast which his presence in the 'place' of the fiction at once arouses, exemplified in the particular contrast between him and the intellectual misogynist, Pigasov, or in the way he wins the plaudits of Dar'ya Lasunskaya and the admiration of the young Basistov on the evening of his arrival. But the hero is still a stranger and the reader knows nothing of his background. How is this background to be explained without to some extent violating the pictorial immediacy of the realism which Turgenev has been at great pains to create? Must Turgenev retard the course of the action and introduce the relevant information about the hero's background in the kind of biographical note which he has used for his minor characters? Turgenev studiously avoids such an artifice in this case. The hero's characterization is developed, secondly, by one character

[1] Edward Garnett, *Turgenev: a Study* (1917), 62.

acting as a kind of *Icherzaehler* in relation to him. This, as it transpires
in the latter half of both Chapters V and VI, is to be the role of
Lezhnyov, the character who was only cursorily introduced previously
in Chapter I. He is to act both as commentator upon the hero, revealing
the necessary information about his background and personality
without which the reader would not be able to understand him fully,
and as a contrast, both in temperament and attitude, to his eloquence
and basically unpractical nature. In addition, Lezhnyov may be said
to act as a mouthpiece for Turgenev himself—a function that is
especially important in Chapter XII and the Epilogue. In this way he
appears as a chorus, an independent figure in the development of the
novel's action, yet essential for a proper understanding of the hero.
But Lezhnyov's role, despite the contrast he himself affords and the
contrast afforded by the successful outcome of his relationship with
Aleksandra Lipina, is chiefly that of commentator. It is in Rudin's
relations with Natal'ya that the process of characterization is finally
resolved.

Natal'ya is clearly impressed by Rudin's eloquence when he first
arrives, but they do not meet until the next morning (first part of
Chapter V) and on this occasion Rudin's fallibility is first intimated
by Natal'ya's remark to the effect that he should put his accomplish-
ments to some useful purpose. This intimation is at once followed by
the detailed biographical information which Lezhnyov has to offer
in the second part of Chapter V; and this information opens the way
for the reader's doubts about Rudin's 'genial nature'.[1] By the beginning of Chapter VI two months have passed since Rudin's arrival
and Natal'ya's feelings have undergone a marked change. It is, however, Rudin who speaks of love—very much, it seems, in the abstract
and apparently unaware of the effect this may have on Natal'ya
herself—and the genuineness of his feeling is at once called in question
by Lezhnyov's remarks in the latter part of the chapter. Proof of
Lezhnyov's remarks is to be found in Chapters VII, VIII, and IX—the
meeting in the garden on the Sunday morning when Rudin fails to
understand the nature of Natal'ya's feelings towards him, then his
sudden declaration of love in the summer-house, his visit to Volyntsev
and the final meeting with Natal'ya after Dar'ya Lasunskaya has
learned of their relationship from Pandalevsky. The 'unmasking' of
the hero who had been met with such approval and acclaim in
Chapter III is now complete, and it is his weakness in the face of

---

[1] The first title of the novel.

Natal'ya's demands that is the most telling moment in the process of characterization.

The central action of the novel is in two parts—the arrival of the hero (Chapters III-V) and, two months later, the hero's departure in disgrace from Dar'ya Lasunskaya's residence (Chapters VI-XI). Chapter XII and the Epilogue are by way of being a protracted conclusion. It may be seen, then, that this novel shows strong signs of being influenced by the short-story form. The two episodes of arrival and departure are almost separate stories. During the gap of two months separating the two episodes it must be assumed that Natal'ya falls in love, for she is in love by the beginning of the second episode. However, Turgenev has made no effort to illustrate this process. This is a weakness that shows the extent to which Turgenev had been unable, as yet, to achieve the special form demanded of the novel. In fact, this is a work, as the title indicates, which is designed as a vehicle for portraying the hero. The setting, Lezhnyov's commentary, the love-story all seem to be subservient to this end. Turgenev begins by introducing his hero into a strange milieu; on his first appearance he is accepted as being brilliant and new; then he is gradually stripped of his assumed brilliance; by the moment of his departure it seems that such lesser characters as Pigasov and Volyntsev have triumphed. It is only in Chapter XII and the Epilogue that the balance is gradually redressed and, largely through the agency of Lezhnyov as commentator, Rudin, the failure, acquires a measure of grandeur. His idealism finds its apotheosis in the final scene of his death on the Paris barricades.

Although in Turgenev's second novel, *A Nest of the Gentry* (1859), characterization is again all-important, as a novel this work is structurally more cohesive than *Rudin*. It tells the story of Lavretsky's return to his home in Russia after an unfortunate marriage. When he once again settles down in the circumstances that had been familiar to him as a child, he falls in love with Liza, a girl with strong religious feelings, and even hopes to marry her after learning of his wife's death from a report in a French newspaper. The report turns out to be incorrect and his wife's unexpected arrival brings the relationship with Liza to an end. Again the story is slight, and its very brevity reveals the extent to which this work depends for its effect upon revelation of character and evocation of atmosphere.

As in *Rudin*, the opening chapters of *A Nest of the Gentry* form an introduction to the society and environment in which the ensuing action is to occur. Here such characters of the 'place' of the fiction as are to have only an incidental part in what follows—Mar'ya Dmitriyevna Kalitina, Liza's mother, Marfa Timofeyevna Pestova, her aunt, Gedeonovsky, a friend and a great chatterbox, Vladimir Nikolaich Panshin, a young government official and Liza's erstwhile suitor, Lemm, an elderly German music teacher—are all introduced at some length (Chapters I-VII), whereas Liza, whose personality is to be such an important feature of the novel, is introduced with no more than a descriptive statement to the effect that she was 'a slender, tall, dark-haired girl of nineteen' (Chapter III). Lavretsky then makes his appearance and his significance for the fiction is explained in the lengthy digression of Chapters VIII-XVI which supply his genealogy. Chapters XVII-XXXIV constitute the central section of the novel and are concerned with the major episodes in the development of the novel's theme, the growing affection between Lavretsky and Liza and the gradual crystallization of Lavretsky's Slavophil views. Chapter XXV is an insertion which has the purpose of explaining Liza's background. The remaining chapters recount the return of Varvara Pavlovna, Lavretsky's wife, and the way in which both hero and heroine are obliged to forgo the mutual happiness which their relationship promised in favour of isolated devotion to their self-appointed tasks. The Epilogue is concerned chiefly with Lavretsky's return to the scene of the novel eight years after the events described in the previous chapters.

There is no division in this novel, as there was in *Rudin*, between the episode of the hero's arrival and the episode of the hero's departure. Interest is thus concentrated on the love-story itself and the way in which the relationship develops. This gives the novel a cohesion and completeness which *Rudin* lacked. Moreover, both hero and heroine seem to occupy the centre of the fiction in almost equal proportions, so that the novel is less exclusively a vehicle for the characterization of one figure and more a study in mutual contrasts.

Lavretsky's position in the fiction is explained (in the digression of Chapters VIII-XVI) before the central action of the novel begins. Liza, on the contrary, is in no sense a 'revealed' character before the action of the novel begins, and the method which Turgenev employs for her characterization is of some interest. Firstly, Liza is 'illuminated' by the two characters, Marfa Timofeyevna and Lemm. Their presence in the novel serves as a measure against which the character of Liza may be gauged. Marfa Timofeyevna, for instance, understands Liza because she is of the same blood and the same birthright, whereas

Lemm's understanding of and love for the young Russian girl is expressed in his love of music. Turgenev here succeeds in evoking the feeling of rapture which has arisen in Liza's heart not through any direct description of her love for Lavretsky, but by subtle intimations of her changing feelings, climaxed by the tumultuous music that Lemm plays late at night for the delight of Lavretsky at the end of Chapter XXXIV. It is only at this late stage in the novel that Turgenev chooses to reveal Liza's background (Chapter XXXV), which finally accomplishes her characterization in preparation for the final contrast which is afforded by the arrival of Varvara Pavlovna. But the revelation of Liza's character is also accomplished, secondly, by the use of a commentator. As a Russian critic has pointed out:

> If Marfa Timofeyevna and Lemm clarify for the thoughtful reader the figure of Liza simply by the fact of their presence in the novel, then the hero, Lavretsky, performs the same artistic function, but in a different way: throughout the novel he never ceases to be the faithful companion and the irreplaceable collaborator of the reader. The latter, without this co-operation from Lavretsky, would never be able to recreate the figure of Liza in his own mind.[1]

In fact, for formal purposes, the relationship of Lavretsky to Liza is approximately the same as the reader's relationship: she is an unknown quantity for both parties. One may quote as an instance of Lavretsky in his function of commentator the short interior monologue which occurs in Chapter XVIII, as Lavretsky is driving to Vasil'yevskoye. It is in this monologue that we obtain for the first time some concrete impression of Liza's outward appearance. Indeed, throughout the novel it is through Lavretsky's thoughts that we gain a fuller picture of her. Lavretsky is, as it were, the sensitive plate which reflects and interprets Liza to the reader. On the other hand, even though Lavretsky may be a commentator vis-à-vis Liza, his very function as commentator has the further, and concomitant, result of revealing his own personality. Lavretsky is not a kind of *deus ex machina* figure or chorus external to the main action of the fiction. He is more closely integrated into the fiction than was Lezhnyov. In this respect the structure of *A Nest of the Gentry* represents a marked advance upon the structure of *Rudin*. Lavretsky is not only the hero of the novel but also an intermediary between the heroine and the reader; as the novel progresses his own personality emerges more clearly, just as does Liza's, through

[1] D. N. Ovsyaniko-Kulikovsky, *Sobr. soch.* (SPB., 1913), ii. 243-4.

his agency. This balanced contrast endows the novel with a classical inner unity of form and an admirable shapeliness. The result is one of Turgenev's finest love-stories.

But the perfection of structure which Turgenev achieves in *A Nest of the Gentry* is still in many ways a perfection in terms of the short-story form, not in terms of the novel. The figures of the hero and heroine appear to dominate all other facets of the work, just as in *Rudin* all the elements in the fiction appeared to be made subservient to the task of portraying the hero. In *A Nest of the Gentry* all the minor characters—and it should be remarked in passing that Turgenev, who always excelled in portraying minor characters, produced here some of the most brilliantly drawn minor figures to be found in his novels —have specific roles allotted to them which contribute directly to the portrayal of either hero or heroine. These minor characters all stand on the periphery of the love-story which forms the central theme of the novel and they are, so far as the structure of the work is concerned, no more and no less important than the natural scene, the times of day or that pervasive atmosphere of summer with which Turgenev has invested his narrative. Indeed, the minor characters are simply parts of the atmosphere and their figures merge with it, dissolving into the background as soon as their formal roles are completed. But this atmosphere, poetic and elusive as it is, would not be present in the fiction at all were it not for the love-story, and neither love-story nor atmosphere would be successful were it not for the fact that Turgenev had chosen to limit the form of his work, circumscribing it in place and, more especially, in time (the duration of the action is approximately the same as in *Rudin*: about two months), so that in essence it is an elaborate *story* describing the brief and tragic relationship between hero and heroine.

The young critic, Dobrolyubov, writing of Turgenev's third novel, *On the Eve*, remarked:

Our author has never wanted and—so far as I can judge from his previous works—would not be capable of writing an heroic epic. His aim is quite different: from the entire Iliad and Odyssey he singles out only the story of Ulysses' sojourn on Calypso's isle and ranges no further afield.[1]

Dobrolyubov may have intended a rebuke in saying this, but the comment is very pertinent. Turgenev was not capable of writing epics

[1] N. A. Dobrolyubov, 'Kogda zhe pridyot nastoyashchy den'?', *Pervoye polnoye sobr. soch.* (SPB., 1911), iv. 63.

as such, yet his novels infer epic issues despite their structural resemblance to short stories. The love-stories in both *Rudin* and *A Nest of the Gentry* were carefully set in their proper perspectives by the biographical material provided for all the characters at different stages in the development of the fiction, and by the information offered in the Epilogues. The love-stories were thus made to appear as episodes from an epic, from the lives, that is to say, of the hero and heroine: it was their sojourn on Calypso's isle. That Turgenev originally intended *Rudin* to be simply an episode from the hero's life, with the tragedy residing purely in the unfortunate outcome of the love-story, is borne out by the fact that he did not add the final scene describing Rudin's death until the publication of the Osnovsky edition in 1860, four years after the novel first appeared. Similarly, *A Nest of the Gentry* simply recounts an episode in the lives of the hero and heroine and the tragedy that separates them is one of circumstance. Theirs was a brief idyll, but life went on afterwards. In his third novel Turgenev is clearly striving to enlarge both the matter and the manner of the kind of love-story form which he had chosen for his novels.

On the Eve (1860) tells the story of the heroine's, Yelena's, love for a young Bulgarian revolutionary, Insarov, who is studying at Moscow university. She falls in love with him because he represents for her a strength and purposefulness which she finds lacking in the young Russians of her own generation. Eventually she marries him, though against the wishes of her upper-class and rather stupid parents, and accompanies him on his return to Bulgaria to liberate that country from the Turks. However, he dies in Venice before reaching Bulgaria, and it is upon this note of tragedy that the novel ends.

The enlarged scope of this novel is to be seen, firstly, in the greater number of 'places' which form the setting of the fiction. In *Rudin*, for instance, the action was limited largely to the residence of Dar'ya Lasunskaya, while in *A Nest of the Gentry* it was largely restricted to the Kalitins' house in the town of O. . . . But in *On the Eve* the range is greater: the Stakhovs' summer *dacha*, Bersenev's lodgings, the Stakhovs' Moscow house, Insarov's Moscow lodgings, the concluding scenes in Venice; and the period of time occupied by the action of the fiction is correspondingly greater. Structurally, such enlargement of scope gives the work greater flexibility, the characterization is less constricted and in general the dimensions are those of a novel, not of a short story, although it must be admitted that it also gives rise to a certain looseness in the narrative thread that was not a feature of the two previous novels. The enlarged scope of the novel, however, is to be seen most clearly, secondly, in the resulting portraits of both hero and heroine. These portraits are not moments taken from a continuum, extending into both past and future, but last portraits: the action of the novel embraces not one episode in the lives of hero and heroine, however crucial that may be, but the *final* episode in their lives. Moreover, the looseness in the narrative structure is to some extent compensated for by the greater psychological depth in the portrayal of the central figure, the heroine. Also, the issues in the fiction unite the personal and the social, the individual and ideological in a more complex and pointed manner than in the two previous novels. This is 'a novel of ideas' and all the characters may be said to embody different ideas or ideological attitudes; they are thus more independent as elements in the fiction than were the minor characters in *Rudin* and *A Nest of the Gentry*, who gave the impression of being chiefly 'illuminators' of the hero and heroine.

The independence, for instance, of the two most important minor characters, Shubin and Bersenev, is illustrated in the opening scene of the novel by the banks of the Moscow river. Their conversation not only introduces the major issues that are to be raised during the course of the novel, and not only sketches in the importance of the hero and the heroine, but it also carefully indicates the differences of personality, temperament and ideas which distinguish them as independent characters in the fiction. These are the younger generation. Opposed to them, though more satirically drawn, are Yelena's mother and father, Anna Stakhova and Nikolay Stakhov, both introduced at length in Chapter III. Yelena herself is established in the fiction by the biographical material and the description of her personality provided in Chapter VI. As a consequence of this, it might be thought that the unknown quantity in the fiction—and hence its interest—would be the figure of the hero. Although it is certainly true that Insarov is an unknown quantity throughout the novel, this seems to be due less to the way in which his characterization is planned than to a failure on the part of Turgenev. Insarov, like Solomin of *Virgin Soil*, is a façade. He appears to have no inner world of his own, no existence beyond what he says and does. This is a serious flaw in his characterization, made doubly obvious by the fact that the real unknown quantity, and hence the interest of the novel as a vehicle for characterization, is the figure of the heroine. Yelena is portrayed with such depth and the process of her characterization is consequently so intriguing, that the figure of

Insarov, on whose characterization Turgenev has expended so little art, pales in comparison.

To quote Edward Garnett again:

... the reader may note how he is made to judge Yelena through six pairs of eyes—Stakhov's contempt for his daughter, her mother's affectionate bewilderment, Shubin's petulant criticism, Bersenev's half-hearted enthralment, Insarov's recognition, and Zoya's indifference, being the facets for converging light on Yelena's sincerity and depth of soul.[1]

This is broadly true, although the major instruments for effecting the characterization of Yelena are Shubin and Bersenev, especially the former, who uses his artist's eye to good purpose in illuminating facets of her personality which other characters fail to discern. Indeed, Yelena is subjected to close and continuous scrutiny by Shubin, and on several occasions during the novel he seems to acquire the role of commentator in revealing her personality and her significance to the reader (Chapters IX, for instance, XII, XX and latter part of XXX). But despite the fact that Shubin 'illuminates' Yelena in this way, this is no sense diminishes his importance as an independent 'spokesman of ideas', nor does it mean that he is given the role of commentator to the extent that Lezhnyov and Lavretsky were made to play this role in the previous novels. Though Yelena is presented to the reader partly through the contrasting views of her which are offered by the minor characters, her personality is given depth less by this objective 'illumination' of her than by a subjective manner of portraiture which demands the use of certain devices.

In the Preface to the 1880 edition of his novels Turgenev mentioned that he received the idea for *On the Eve* from the diary of his neighbour, Karateyev.[2] The only incident from the diary which appeared in the subsequent novel was the episode of the visit to Tsaritsyno described in Chapter XV. The fact that he took the idea for his novel from a

---

[1] Edward Garnett, op. cit. 95.

[2] Before leaving for the Crimean War, Karateyev left in Turgenev's hands a manuscript in which he described his relations with a young girl in Moscow. At first this girl had been fond of Karateyev, but later she had transferred her affections to a Bulgarian, Katranov, who did in fact return to Bulgaria to participate in the struggle of the Bulgarian people against the Turks, as does Insarov in the novel. Karateyev had hoped that Turgenev might find some way of having his manuscript published. Turgenev mentioned the matter to Nekrasov, editor of *The Contemporary*, but, owing to the diary-form of the manuscript, it was found unsuitable for publication and Turgenev subsequently made use of the story of the relationship between a young Russian girl and the Bulgarian patriot as the basis for his novel.

diary must have suggested to Turgenev that he could make use of the device of the diary extract in portraying the inner world of his heroine. This is borne out by the fact that the extracts from Yelena's diary are introduced in the chapter following the episode of the visit to Tsaritsyno. By making use of this device of the diary, Turgenev is able to show the gradual awakening of Yelena's feelings prior to the revelation of the fact in the following chapter (Chapter XVII) that Insarov is also in love with her. The love-story element in this novel is thus given depth largely through the way it is presented from Yelena's point of view. In addition, Turgenev also employs the device of the letter. In Chapter XXII Yelena's reactions to the suitor, Kurnatovsky,[1] whom her father has found for her, are given in the form of the letter that she writes to Insarov describing the occasion. All this illustrates the extent to which Turgenev has relied upon a subjective manner of portraiture in the characterization of Yelena. Indeed, the middle section of the novel's action seems to proceed by a succession of scenes, alternating between objectively described episodes, in which dialogue predominates, and passages of subjective psychological characterization: the episode of Tsaritsyno is followed by Yelena's diary, the episode in which Yelena and Insarov confess their love for each other (Chapter XVIII) is followed by a description of Yelena's inner state that evening (Chapter XIX), the episode in which Shubin shows his sculptures to Bersenev (Chapter XX) is followed by a further description of Yelena's feelings (Chapter XXI). Turgenev also makes use of such subjective material as dreams and delirium in depicting the inner state of his heroine and hero—something that he had avoided in the more objective manner of his previous novels.

The success of the novel, therefore, stands or falls by the figure of the heroine. What Yelena does, says, feels and thinks occupies the foreground of the fiction, while what Insarov feels is rarely made explicit. His function is almost equivalent to the function of Natal'ya in *Rudin*: the catalyst in the process of characterization. In this respect, *On the Eve* can obviously be compared with *Rudin*, as a novel that is designed

[1] As was apparently the case with Pandalevsky in *Rudin*, Kurnatovsky was originally intended to play a more important role in *On the Eve*. A list of the characters in the novel, with their ages and the initials of the living models, has survived, in addition to a preliminary sketch of the narrative, chapter by chapter. These documents reveal that Turgenev made changes during the composition of his novel—the most important of them being the change in Kurnatovsky's role—but in other respects he appears to have remained surprisingly faithful to his original plan. See André Mazon, 'L'Élaboration d'un roman de Turgenev: À la Veille, Premier Amour, Fumée', *Revue des Études Slaves*, v (1925), 244-68.

as a vehicle for portraying one central character, with the important difference that the minor characters are less like props to the central portrait. The work, in fact, represents a considerable step forward in the maturing of Turgenev's powers of characterization—despite the feebleness of Insarov's portrait—and in his understanding of the novel-form. He achieved in Yelena a much more elaborate portrait than any that he had achieved hitherto. Without, however, denying the un-doubted merit of this achievement, it is a portrait that has certain obvious blemishes. By any standards it is sentimental (largely due to the subjective manner, at which Turgenev was never very successful), yet the most significant blemish is that, by comparison with such major figures as Rudin and Lavretsky, Yelena is intellectually uninteresting. The intellectual interest seems to be distributed among such characters as Shubin, Bersenev and, to some extent, Insarov, or purely incidental characters such as Kurnatovsky and Lupoyarov. On the other hand, in contrast to Rudin and Lavretsky, she is portrayed as a decisive, resolute character, not compromised by the middle-aged failings of the 'superfluous man'. For Turgenev to perfect the type of character after which he had been striving—the Quixotic temperament rather than the Hamlet—he had only to combine the resolute characteristics discernible in his portrait of Yelena with the intellectual interest of such a figure as Rudin. This is what he succeeded in doing in painting the portrait of Bazarov in his fourth novel, *Fathers and Children* (1862).

Turgenev has said that he was first prompted to write about a hero of the type of Bazarov by the example of a young provincial doctor of his acquaintance who had died, presumably, about the year 1859. When he mentioned his intention to a friend whom he met on the Isle of Wight in August 1860, he was amazed to hear this gentleman reply: 'But surely you have already presented a similar type in— Rudin?' Turgenev adds: 'I was speechless: what was there to say? Rudin and Bazarov—one and the same type? . . . These words had such an effect on me that for several weeks I avoided all thought of the work on which I had embarked. . . .'[1] The gentleman's remark, however, is not so extraordinary as it may appear at first sight. It simply serves to underline the fact that Bazarov, like Rudin, was conceived as a hero designed to have more intellectual interest than Lavretsky, for instance, or Yelena. Like Rudin, he was intended to dominate the fiction, although—unlike the Rudin of the original version—he was

[1] *Sobr. soch.* (1956), x. 346–7.

conceived as a tragic figure whose tragedy would be climaxed by his death.[1]

Fathers and Children tells the story of Bazarov's return from the university in the company of his young friend, Arkady Kirsanov. They both stay for a while on the Kirsanovs' estate, where the contrast between the Fathers and the Children is initiated in the arguments between Pavel Petrovich Kirsanov and the hero, and later they visit the local town, where Bazarov meets the heroine, Odintsova. This meeting initiates the major love theme of the novel, but the action is by no means devoted exclusively to the development of it. Subsequently Bazarov visits his parents, spends a short while with them and then, to their understandable dismay, returns to the Kirsanovs' estate where the argument between Fathers and Children is concluded by the duel between him and Pavel Petrovich. Later Bazarov returns to his parents, where he decides to help his father, a retired army doctor, in his practice. Here he contracts typhus after performing an autopsy on a peasant killed by the disease and finally succumbs to it himself. As can be seen, there is more story content in *Fathers and Children* than in the previous novels, but this does not alter the fact that it is the characterization of the central figure which provides the interest of the fiction.

The objectivity of the work is remarkable on two counts. Firstly, in portraying Bazarov Turgenev has achieved a masterly portrait of a type—the type of the 'new man' of the sixties, the *raznochinets* intellectual or 'nihilist'—with whose political and social views he was manifestly out of sympathy. Secondly, the novel possesses an organic unity, in which there are no narrative devices that obtrude into the fiction to distort, however slightly, the final impression of naturalness. This is not to say that *Fathers and Children* is merely a factual document or chronicle, unenlivened by the author's technique as an artist. It simply means that the technique has been perfected to the point where such devices as the use of commentator (in *Rudin* and *A Nest of the Gentry*) or devices such as diary extracts and letters (as in *On the Eve*) are no longer necessary in the delineation of character. The emphasis

---

[1] Hjalmar Boyesen records Turgenev as saying (originally in 'A visit to Turgenev', *The Galaxy*, xvii (1874), 456–66: 'I was once out for a walk and thinking about death. . . . Immediately there rose before me the picture of a dying man. This was Bazarov. The scene produced a strong impression on me and as a consequence the other characters and the action itself began to take form in my mind.' Quoted from the Russian in 'K biografii I. S. Turgeneva', *Minuvshiye gody*, 1908, No. 8, p. 70. Turgenev writes to the same effect in his letter to Sluchevsky of April 1862.

now falls squarely on the scenic, pictorial objectivity of the narrative
and the artistic composition of the work, leaving the impression that
the novel is 'telling itself', as it were, almost without the author's
agency or participation.

In every respect this is more obviously 'a novel of ideas' than *On the
Eve*, although the ideological independence of each minor character is
linked, without being in any sense compromised or diminished, to the
development of the central figure, Bazarov, in a more compelling
manner than were Shubin and Bersenev to Yelena. This is due to the
fact that in *Fathers and Children* the minor characters are not only
spokesmen or embodiments of ideas or ideological attitudes, but they
are also representatives of a particular social class with specific class
attitudes; and Bazarov, opposed to them, is not only an opponent of
their ideas, but a spokesman for a new, emergent social class which
is to usurp the political and social authority of the older generation.
In his previous novels Turgenev had not delineated class distinctions
so clearly, but in *Fathers and Children* he carefully welds the social and
political issues, the ideological and class attitudes, into the structure of
his novel, creating a remarkable organic unity. The result is the most
artistically perfect, structurally unified and ideologically compelling
of Turgenev's novels.

Arkady Kirsanov and his father, Nikolay Petrovich Kirsanov, are
introduced in detail to the reader at the very beginning of the novel.
All the other characters—Pavel Petrovich Kirsanov, Odintsova,
Bazarov's parents and such lesser characters as Fenichka (the peasant
girl who has borne Nikolay Petrovich an illegitimate son), Kukshina
and Sitnikov, the talkative representatives of the younger generation
—are introduced into the fiction to the accompaniment of biographical
and other information sufficient to explain their significance. The
exception is again the unknown quantity, the hero, whose characterization is to provide the interest of the novel. Bazarov is not introduced
to the reader by means of any biographical excerpt which might set his
character in perspective; he is introduced, and his background lightly
sketched in, by the remarks made about him by the other characters
(particularly during the conversation between Arkady and Pavel
Petrovich in Chapter V). While these remarks serve to provide information about Bazarov without which the reader might not be
able to understand his significance for the fiction, they also serve to
illustrate the contrasting nature of Bazarov, arising from his different
social background. There are, of course, intimations in the fiction

that Bazarov is 'different' from the other characters, but Turgenev does not rely on his omniscient position as author of the fiction to emphasize this 'difference'. On the contrary, he allows it to be made clear by the natural contrast that arises initially from the fact that Bazarov enters the fiction unexplained and by the more definite contrast which is provided through Bazarov's contact with the other characters.

Bazarov is further highlighted in the fiction by the fact that the novel is so constructed as to isolate him from the other characters. This is achieved by giving the other characters not only biographical backgrounds or information sufficient to make their backgrounds comprehensible, but also specific 'places' in the fiction. Each character, with the exception of Bazarov, has his or her own 'place' or situation in the fiction: Nikolay, Arkady, Pavel—the poverty-stricken Mar'ino; Odintsova, Katya—the luxurious Nikol'skoye; the elderly Bazarovs —their humble estate; Sitnikov, Kukshina—the background of the town. With the exception of Bazarov and Arkady, all these characters remain in their own particular 'places' and are only comprehensible in relation to their 'places' (Odintsova and Sitnikov, admittedly, can be said to abandon their 'places' for short episodes—Odintsova to the town and to visit Bazarov on his death-bed, Sitnikov to Nikol'skoye (Chapter XIX)—but it is still true that they are only comprehensible in relation to their own 'places'). Moreover, each 'place' in the fiction and its occupants has the purpose of illuminating, by contrast, an aspect of the hero. Pavel Petrovich in Mar'ino illuminates the ideological aspect of Bazarov's significance for the fiction, the problem of the socio-political conflict between the generations; Sitnikov and Kukshina in the town illuminate the superiority of Bazarov by comparison with other members of the younger generation; Odintsova in Nikol'skoye illuminates the essential personality of the hero as a man, the duality in his nature; Bazarov's parents illuminate his egoism, the personal, as distinct from the ideological, barrier dividing the generations, and his individual insignificance as a human being, for their adoration of him is carefully offset by his own pessimistic musings on his destiny. Each 'place' in the fiction can therefore be seen as a stage in the process of the hero's characterization, and the stages are graded to elaborate and deepen the hero's portrait. Finally, Arkady ceases to play an active part in the fiction (after becoming involved in his love-story with Katya), and Bazarov is isolated as the central figure of the novel's action. In this way it can be seen that Turgenev emphasizes the tragedy of Bazarov's isolation, both as a social type and as a human being, by emphasizing his isolation within the fiction itself.

The process of characterization is also structurally integrated with the pattern of love-stories which, loosely speaking, supplies the plot of the novel and illustrates the ideological issues at stake. There are, in all, four different love-stories: (a) Nikolay-Fenichka; (b) Pavel-Fenichka, involving Bazarov; (c) Bazarov-Odintsova; (d) Arkady-Katya. All these love-stories express in one way or another an aspect of the conflict between the Fathers and the Children. The first love-story, between the land-owner and the peasant girl, implies at once the underlying social problem of the day: the relationship between land-owner and peasant on the eve of the Emancipation in 1861 (the action of the novel, it may be noted, occurs in 1859). The nature of this particular relationship between Nikolay and Fenichka also illustrates the moral failure of the older generation, of the Fathers, and it is a point at issue, in the early stages of the novel, between Nikolay and his son. The second love-story (it scarcely obtrudes as a love-story, but it must not be overlooked) is of considerably greater importance for the structure of the novel. So far as the external action of the novel is concerned, the fact that Pavel Petrovich sees Bazarov kissing Fenichka (Chapter XXIII) simply supplies him with grounds for challenging Bazarov to a duel. But the inner meaning of this episode must also be noted. The ideological conflict has already occurred (Chapters VI and X); the contrast with the members of the younger generation has been made (Chapters XII and XIII); the relationship with Odintsova has already been explored and has reached a climax (Chapters XV-XVIII), though it has not yet been abandoned; Bazarov's awareness of his own significance as a human being and his tragic destiny, despite the great future hoped for by his parents, has been made explicit in his conversation with Arkady on his parents' estate (Chapter XXI). Bazarov is now ready to reject the ideological and social precepts of the *dvoryanstvo*, the gentry; his desire to provoke a fight with Arkady in Chapter XXI foreshadows his readiness to accept the challenge that Pavel Petrovich offers him in Chapter XXIV. Yet the fact that they fight the duel ostensibly over Fenichka, the peasant girl, shows the way in which the ideological issues are welded into the structure of the novel. For Bazarov's readiness to fight the duel must be understood in the light of the fact that he is prepared not only to reject the *dvoryanstvo*, but also to devote his life to working for the peasants. His interest in Fenichka may be purely personal, but it is also given

ideological significance. Similarly, Pavel Petrovich's readiness to offer
the challenge must be understood in relation to the fact that for him
Fenichka bears a resemblance to a certain Princess R. . . . out of passion
for whom he had ruined his career and had been obliged to retire
to the splendid isolation of Mar'ino (the predicament of the 'superfluous man' *par excellence*), and in relation to the fact that the crux of
his earlier argument with Bazarov (Chapter X) had been the problem
of the peasantry, whom he had claimed to understand better than
Bazarov. His interest in Fenichka is also a mixture of the personal and
the ideological. The subsequent duel represents the climax in the
personal and ideological conflict between the two generations; and
the defeat of Pavel Petrovich is not simply the defeat of the older
generation by the younger, it is also the defeat of the gentry, the
dvoryanstvo, by the new class of the *raznochintsy*.

The third love-story, between Odintsova and Bazarov, is clearly
the most interesting, both because it concerns two people of widely
differing social status and because it serves, like all the major love-
stories in Turgenev's fiction, as a means of illustrating the differing
personalities of the two characters. It is, however, Bazarov who
emerges more successfully from this contrast. Odintsova is almost as
passive a participant in the relationship as was Insarov in *On the Eve*.
But, unlike the Yelena-Insarov relationship, the relationship between
Odintsova and Bazarov does not absorb the whole of the fiction.
There is no definite continuity to it and it is allowed to languish, in
contrast to the fourth love-story, between Arkady and Katya, which
is both the most conventional in the sense that it is between two
young people of similar social status and the most conventional in the
sense that it has a happy outcome.

It is in the different relationships involved in these love-stories that
an enlargement of both structure and content in *Fathers and Children* as
compared with the previous novels is to be discerned. In *Rudin*, for
instance, there had been a suggestion of triangular form about the
central love-story (Rudin-Natal'ya-Volyntsev), but the Rudin-
Natal'ya relationship had been the most important relationship in the
fiction, paralleled by the love-story between Lezhnyov and Aleksandra
Lipina. In the relationship between Rudin and Natal'ya, however,
there had been no explicit suggestion of social inequality, although
Rudin was banished from Dar'ya Lasunskaya's house because he was
not felt to be 'suitable' for her daughter; yet, despite his lack of rank,
he was of the same class. In *A Nest of the Gentry* the major love-story

between Lavretsky and Liza had been connected with the Liza-Panshin, Liza-Lemm relationships, but these latter had had little bearing on the central theme of the novel. Similarly, although Lavretsky's social standing was compromised by the fact that his mother was of peasant extraction, in other points of genealogy he was Liza's social equal. In *On the Eve* Shubin and Bersenev had been united by similar feelings for Yelena, but the love-story between Yelena and Insarov had been quite independent of them. In the social sense, the inequality between Yelena and Insarov was partly camouflaged by the fact that he was given Bulgarian nationality, although Kurnatovsky was thought to be socially more fitted for Yelena, and it can be seen that her parents' reaction to her marriage was one of shock not at the fact that Insarov was a Bulgarian but because he was of more modest social origins. In general, therefore, it can be said that in these three novels there had been a single love-story which was at the centre of the fiction and only in *On the Eve* did the relationship infer a marked social inequality. But in *Fathers and Children* there is a multiplication of love-stories in the structure of the novel, and all the love-stories, with the exception of the Arkady-Katya relationship, involve social inequalities. Inevitably this means that the novel embraces an enlarged view of Russian society, for all classes in Russian society are exemplified by this means: the gentry (*dvoryanstvo*), the new men (*raznochintsy*), and the peasantry. The single love-story in the earlier novels, standing at the centre of the fiction and absorbing the greater part of its interest, had not permitted such an enlarged view.

Yet, in structural terms, the main feature of *Fathers and Children* is the figure of Bazarov. The action of the novel hinges upon him almost exclusively. He is present in practically every scene of the novel, and it is his movement within the fiction that serves to link together the different 'places' or foci of interest which comprise the setting of the novel. Simultaneously, these 'places' and their occupants contribute, stage by stage, to the process of his characterization. A natural unity of form and content is thus achieved, which is the most striking development in Turgenev's exploration of the novel-form. The portrait of Bazarov that finally emerges from the novel is one that transcends all other issues in the fiction. Beginning on May 20th 1859, the action of the novel portrays Bazarov during approximately the last three or four months of his life. His portrait acquires finally a tragic grandeur, culminating in his death which is a moment unequalled in Turgenev's fiction.

The structural development that Turgenev achieved during the writing of these four novels is obvious. In a sense it may be thought that *Rudin*, *A Nest of the Gentry* and *On the Eve* were merely the preliminary sketches for that perfection of novel-form which Turgenev achieved in *Fathers and Children*, but each of the earlier novels had its own contribution to make and can be regarded as a separate stage in Turgenev's development as a novelist. During his own lifetime, however, this development in structural terms attracted less interest than the ideological or socio-political issues with which the novels were concerned. This is 'the body and pressure of time' and that 'rapidly changing physiognomy of Russians of the cultured stratum' which, as he mentioned in his Preface to the 1880 edition, had been preeminently the object of Turgenev's observations. Nowadays this aspect of his work may tend to detract from the popularity of his novels *qua* novels, for it dates them to an epoch which has little direct relevance to the present, but it is nevertheless their strength as a committed literature and this strength increased proportionately as Turgenev's command of structure became more marked.

IDEAS AND IDEALS

All Turgenev's heroes embody ideas and aspire to emulate ideals. The degree of success or failure which they experience in their lives is gauged by the extent to which they are able to put their ideas to the service of their chosen ideals. Rudin, Lavretsky, Insarov and Bazarov all aspire to put their ideas to the service of ideals that transcend the personal and all of them appear to fall short of their ideals while succeeding in justifying by their personal example the worth of their ideas.

When Rudin, already on the verge of middle-age, enters the house of Dar'ya Lasunskaya, he is confronted with a society in which ideas are either modish plagiarisms or the objects of cynical banter. This is not due to any marked discrepancy in age between Rudin and his hostess, herself middle-aged, or the Dorpat-educated Pigasov. It is simply that ideas are interesting frivolities which beguile the leisure hours of the wealthy *dame de salon* and supply grounds for Pigasov to trot out his misogynistic opinions. Pigasov has already, for the shocked amusement of Dar'ya Lasunskaya, cynically demolished music, contemporary literature and modern philosophy. No doubt, the dilettante approach to such matters current in the Russian society of the time was deserving of censure—and this lends a warped truth to Pigasov's criticisms—but his cynicism has demolished more than this pseudo-culture; it has demolished ideas as items of any value in social intercourse.

Rudin's only real triumph is his first, when, needled by the anti-idealist Pigasov, he demonstrates, rather crudely, the importance of believing in ideas:

'Generalities!' continued Pigasov. 'All these generalities, reviews and conclusions will be the death of me! It is all based on so-called convictions; everyone talks about his convictions, and goes around with them expecting them to be respected, what is more. . . . Bah!'
And Pigasov shook his fist in the air. Pandalevsky burst out laughing.
'Excellent!' said Rudin. 'Then according to you there are no convictions?'
'No, they don't exist.'
'That's your conviction?'
'Yes.'
'Then how can you say there aren't any? There's one you have for a start.'
Everyone in the room smiled and exchanged looks.

After this Rudin's superiority is unquestioned and his ideas are at once accorded the fullest attention. They are couched in an eloquent rhetoric that stirs the hearts of his listeners and subtly entrances them with its music. They flow out with such abundance that he finds it difficult to express himself as cogently as he might, but they are obviously the product of inspiration and have the appeal of poetry for those—particularly the younger ones—assembled at Dar'ya Lasunskaya's that evening. Their importance resides in the fact that they are not concerned with mundane issues. After the defeat of Pigasov over the question of believing in ideas, Rudin carries his argument a stage further by insisting that it is not facts in themselves that have paramount importance but the systems, the fundamental laws and general principles which can be discovered from the known facts. He exalts the intellect as fervently as Pigasov is prepared to deride it; and in this respect he acknowledges himself to be an idealist. But it is an idealism that bases itself upon the conviction that:

'all these attacks on systems, on generalities and so on are particularly distressing because, together with systems, people are denying knowledge in general, science and faith in science—and, at the same time, faith in themselves and their own powers. But people need this faith: they cannot live on impressions alone, and it is wrong for them to fear ideas and not trust them. Scepticism has always distinguished itself by barrenness and impotence. . . .'

which leads to the ideal transcending the purely personal:

'I repeat, if a man has no firm principle in which he believes, if he has no ground on which he stands firmly, how can he assess the needs, the significance and the future of his people? How can he know what he must do himself, if . . . ?'

This is quite sufficient to make Pigasov retreat from the argument, leaving the field of Rudin who—as may be noted—does not complete the sentence and will only complete it by throwing away his life on the barricades of 1848. But the rhetorical question initiates a theme that Turgenev is to examine in all his novels. Each hero is to pose himself the same question: 'How can I assess the needs, the significance and the future of my people? How can I know what I must do, if . . ?' and the answer is, in each case, made explicit by the example of the hero's life.

Rudin's triumph over Pigasov may be construed as that of a superior intelligence over a weaker, of the idealist over the cynic, of the *engagé* 'superfluous man' over the dispirited provincial intellectual of the Nicholaevan régime. In this contrast there is no conflict between generations, although Rudin is clearly a new social phenomenon in the salon of Dar'ya Lasunskaya where Pigasov has long been a habitual visitor. Yet the issue that really divides Rudin from Pigasov is the simple one of the opposition between altruism and egoism, between ego in the service of some higher cause and ego in pursuit of self-indulgence.

'Egoism,' Rudin concluded, 'is suicide. The egocentric man dries up like a solitary, barren tree; but egoism as an active aspiration to perfection is the source of all that is great. . . . Yes! A man must destroy the stubborn egoism in his own personality, in order to give it the right to express itself!'

It is the younger generation, Basistov and Natal'ya, who are most impressed by this evocation of higher principles; and it is indeed to youth that Rudin's message is addressed:

All Rudin's thoughts seemed to be directed towards the future; this lent them an air of impetuosity and youthfulness. . . . Standing by the window, looking at no one in particular, he spoke, and, inspired by the general sympathy and attention accorded him, by the proximity of the young women and the beauty of the night, carried away in the flow of his own feelings, he reached heights of eloquence and poetry. . . . The very sound of his voice, quiet and intense, heightened the enchantment; it seemed that some higher being spoke through his lips, which he had not expected. . . . Rudin spoke of what lends eternal significance to man's temporal existence.

'I remember a Scandinavian legend,' he said in conclusion. 'A king is sitting with his warriors in a long, dark hall, around a fire. It takes place at night, in winter. Suddenly a small bird flies in through one open door and out at another. The king remarks that the little bird is like man in this world: it flew out of the darkness and back into the darkness again, and did not stay long in the warmth and the light. . . . "Oh, king," the eldest warrior objects, "the little bird will not lose itself in the dark but will find its nest." It is just like our life on earth that is so fleeting and insignificant; but everything great on earth is accomplished only by men. For man the awareness of being the instrument of these higher powers must take the place of all other joys: in death itself man will find his life, his nest. . . .'

The essence of the message would seem to be religious—reminiscent of that idea of philosophy as service of the divinity which Turgenev had learned from Werder in Berlin (Rudin also spent a year in Berlin) —but it is a religion of service to humanity, to one's country and the liberation of one's people. Rudin speaks as the high-priest of this idea, with the inspiration not only of poetry but of some higher being who spoke through his lips: it is incantatory as well as edifying, sacred as well as poetic. Man, in the Christian spirit though not in the Christian manner, must be ready to sacrifice his life in the altruistic cause of serving his people. The idea is the corner-stone of that notion of the revolutionary as one dedicated to a sacred vocation which is to find its apotheosis—as for Rudin it was to be 1848—in the activities of Nechayev and his collaborators during the seventies.[1]

But Rudin's message is not overtly one of revolution, despite the fact that Turgenev took Bakunin as the model for Rudin's portrait. Rudin simply exemplifies the idealistic roots of the notion of revolution as a sacred vocation. In sociological terms, Rudin is supremely a product of the thirties, though he might be classified as 'a man of the forties' with all that man's Hegelianism, love of abstract general principles and vaguely defined but high-minded liberalism. He stands for culture

---

[1] I have mentioned Nechayev here, not because he was the most characteristic representative of the dedicated revolutionary, but because his sombre figure captured and horrified the popular imagination—and fired the creative imagination of Dostoyevsky and Turgenev—during the seventies. He is represented in Dostoyevsky's *The Possessed* (in the figure of Pyotr Stepanovich Verkhovensky) and he is a 'behind the scenes' figure throughout Turgenev's *Virgin Soil*. The best study in English of revolutionary activity in nineteenth-century Russia is Avrahm Yarmolinsky's *Road to Revolution* (1957).

and learning, for cultivation of the finer human emotions and a love of the beautiful in nature. *'Vous êtes un poète,'* is Dar'ya Lasunskaya's verdict, and one must agree with it, for it is the absence of the hum-drum, the mundane, the petty and conventional that distinguishes him from the provincial society to which he is introduced. His supreme asset is the music of his eloquence, which strikes the strings of his listeners' hearts and permits an immediate response to the flow of his ideas. He thus succeeds in enchanting everyone, though especially Natal'ya and the young Basistov.

The weakness of Rudin is the weakness of the poet *manqué*: he can utter poetry but he cannot make it. The subsequent episodes in the novel combine to illustrate the basic unpracticality of Rudin, the division between his heart and his mind, his words and his deeds. It is left to Lezhnyov to emphasize that his words will always remain words, and yet these very words 'are capable of upsetting, even of destroying, a young heart', referring to Rudin's relations with Natal'ya; for Rudin, to Lezhnyov, is clever but shallow, lazy and not very well-informed, and at heart cold as ice. He compares him with another friend, Pokorsky (modelled on Turgenev's friend, Stankevich), whom he had known at the university:

'Pokorsky and Rudin were quite unlike each other. In Rudin there was far more brilliance and thunder, more high-flown phrases and, perhaps, more enthusiasm. He gave the appearance of being much more gifted than Pokorsky, but in fact he was poverty-stricken by comparison. Rudin was excellent at developing any kind of idea and could argue masterfully; but his ideas were not born in his own head: he took them from others, particularly from Pokorsky. Pokorsky was soft and gentle in appearance, even puny—and he loved women to distraction, liked having a good time and would stick up for himself. Rudin seemed full of fire, courage and vitality, but spiritually he was cold and almost timid, unless his self-esteem was at stake when he would be up in arms at once. He strove in every way to win people over, but he won them over in the name of general principles and ideas, and in fact he had a strong influence on many people. But no one liked him. . . .'

Lezhnyov has to admit that he owed much to Rudin during his university years, particularly to that eloquence of his in which:

'Nothing remained senseless or accidental; in everything rational necessity and beauty received their expression, everything received a clear and, at the same time, mysterious meaning; each separate phenomenon of life rang harmoniously, and we ourselves, with a kind of scared, fearful reverence, with an ecstatic quivering of our hearts, felt that we were the living vessels of an eternal truth, its instruments, called to some great service. . . .'

The pity of it all was that Rudin could not live up to his eloquence. In his relations with others he showed a paradoxical pettiness and too great a willingness to interfere in other people's private problems which were no concern of his. This fault is exemplified not only in what Lezhnyov has to say about his relations with Rudin but—and much more scathingly—also by Rudin's behaviour towards Volyntsev over the question of their respective relations with Natal'ya. His intellectual superiority blinds him to the commonly accepted proprieties of social intercourse, and this weakness is exaggerated whenever he meddles in affairs of the heart.

But this weakness, although fully explored in the relationship between Rudin and Natal'ya, does not substantially alter the fact that he remains faithful to his principles. He remains a free agent, still ready to propagate his love of learning and his belief in the importance of ideas. As he tells Basistov when they journey away from Dar'ya Lasunskaya's house:

'Do you remember what Don Quixote said to Sancho when he left the Duchess's castle? "Liberty," he said, "my friend Sancho, is one of the most precious gifts Heaven has bestowed upon man, and happy is he to whom Heaven has given a crust of bread, without the obligation of offering thanks for it to anyone else!" What Don Quixote felt then, I feel now. . . . May God grant, my good Basistov, that you experience this feeling some day!'

Basistov is to remain the most outspoken champion of Rudin at all times. He defends Rudin against the cynical assaults of Pigasov and proclaims him to be a genius (Chapter XII). Rudin's eloquence has stirred him as it stirred Lezhnyov earlier. Even Lezhnyov is ready to admit his genius, but with important qualifications:

'Perhaps he has genius,' objected Lezhnyov, 'but character—it's his misfortune that he has no character. . . . Yet that isn't the point. I want to talk about what there is that is good and rare in him. He has enthusiasm; and that, believe me—for I speak as a phlegmatic man—is a most precious quality in our time. We have all become intolerably rational, indifferent and effete; we have gone to sleep, we have grown cold, and we should be grateful to anyone who rouses us and warms us, if only for a moment.'

Then he proceeds to offer a revised view of Rudin's worth:

'This coldness is in his blood—through no fault of his—but not in his head. He is not an actor, as I called him previously, not a swindler, not a scoundrel;

he lives at someone else's expense not like a sponger, but like a child. . . . Yes, he will certainly die somewhere in poverty and misery; but is that any reason for us to throw stones at him? He will not achieve anything himself precisely because he has no blood, no character; but who has the right to say that he will not contribute, has not already contributed, something useful? That his words have not sown many good seeds in young hearts, to whom nature has not denied, as it has to him, the strength to act, the ability to realize their own ideas? After all, I was the first to experience all this myself. . . .'

The vindication of Rudin offered by Lezhnyov is the vindication not of a genius, not of any romantic figure such as Lermontov's Pechorin, but of a man of talent who believed in ideas in a society to which ideas were either contemptible or matters of little consequence, who propagated these ideas and yet was not strong enough to implement them. Rudin is a type common, in a sense, to any society: the intellectual, absorbed in ideas, brilliant at currying interest in them, though incapable of putting them into effect. Edward Garnett remarks that 'an English Rudin would have gone into the Church, and as a Canon or Bishop would have attained celebrity by his gift of lofty and magnetic eloquence'.[1] The remark is ironically apt for nineteenth-century England; in the twentieth century he would probably have been a publicity agent. But in nineteenth-century Russia he was simply superfluous, a social phenomenon for which Russian society could offer no place. This was his fate, as Lezhnyov tells us:

'Rudin's misfortune is that he doesn't know Russia, and this is indeed a great misfortune. Russia can get on without any of us, but not one of us can get on without Russia. Woe to him who thinks so, and double woe to him who really does get along without her! Cosmopolitanism is rubbish, and the cosmopolitan is a nonentity, worse than a nonentity; outside nationality there is no art, no truth, no life, nothing. Without a physiognomy there is not even an ideal face; only a commonplace face is possible in such circumstances. But I will repeat that this is not Rudin's fault: it is his fate, a bitter, hard fate, for which we shall not blame him. We should have to go a long way to find out why such people as Rudin appear in our midst. We shall simply be thankful for the good that is in him. That is easier than being unjust to him. It's not our business to punish him, and there's no need to: he has punished himself far more severely than he ever deserved. . . .'

Russia, always prodigal in its waste of useful lives, simply rejected Rudin, the unconformist. The tragedy of the Russian intellectual of those years was the tragedy, as Lezhnyov remarks, of the rootless

[1] Edward Garnett, op. cit., 61.

cosmopolitan. Rudin's destiny is to become the homeless wanderer, travelling from failure to failure until the desperate reassertion of his death on the Paris barricades.

It is clear that the bias of Rudin's thoughts and aspirations is towards the West. His cosmopolitanism is that of the Westernist, like Turgenev himself but without Turgenev's gifts as a writer, while Turgenev's attitude to such cosmopolitan Westernism is as equivocal as Lezhnyov's —a blend of censure and sympathy. But the remarks that Lezhnyov passes on the inextricable link between nationality and art indicate the direction in which Turgenev's thoughts are moving. The intellectual of Rudin's type could not be the saviour of his country, but this was not to say that there were not other types of intellectual of a less cosmopolitan brand who might perform an equally, if not more, important service. Lezhnyov himself is one such type. Turgenev, always sensitive to new trends, could detect that the notion of service to one's country, with its religious connotation, would have special appeal to the religious instinct of the Russian. Slavophilism united the religious and patriotic instincts in a zealous brand of political conservatism which had little immediate appeal for Turgenev, the liberal, but Turgenev could appreciate that the Slavophils—and personal acquaintance with the outstanding Slavophils, Sergey Aksakov and his sons, Konstantin and Ivan, contributed much to fostering Turgenev's views on the matter—expressed more than the rather dogmatic views of a small minority group. They expressed a love of Russia with which educated Russians would feel a natural sympathy and which was often more genuine than the concern for Russia's future expressed by the dilettante liberals of Westernist persuasion. Lavretsky of *A Nest of the Gentry* is not a Slavophil in the dogmatic sense, but he represents the gradual transition from the modish cosmopolitan Westernism of the twenties and early thirties towards a more mature understanding of the significance of nationality which was a feature of the intellectual development during the forties. The Slavophils themselves, particularly Ivan Kireyevsky who may be regarded as the founder of what may be loosely described as the Slavophil movement, had begun as Westernists, under the influence of Schelling. But even Belinsky, the acknowledged leader of the Westernists, had been influenced by this intellectual movement away from superficial interest in Western, primarily German, philosophy towards an understanding of the need for Russia to follow her own path; and later Herzen was to identify his Westernism with a messianic view of Russia that was to approximate very closely to the Slavophil view. Indeed, Turgenev himself was to be practically the only Westernist of any standing who remained true to his Westernist ideals—during the sixties and seventies, that is to say. But in late 1856, when Turgenev first made plans for *A Nest of the Gentry* (though he was not to complete the novel until two years later), the issues between the Westernists and Slavophils had already crystallized and had even become a part of history. It was in that year that Ivan Kireyevsky died, while it was also in that year that the spokesmen of the 'new men', the radicals of the sixties, Chernyshevsky and Dobrolyubov, first came into prominence. The time had clearly come to offer an assessment of that movement towards a maturer understanding of nationality which had occurred during the forties, for the climate of opinion was already changing and the authority of Turgenev's generation was already being seriously challenged.

The genealogy of Lavretsky offers a case-history that reflects an epoch in Russia's intellectual development. He was of ancient noble lineage, and the brief outline of his ancestry mirrors that interest in the ancestral past which other writers, notably Pushkin in writing his addendum to *Eugene Onegin*, or Sergey Aksakov and Tolstoy during the fifties, had shown in their works. But Lavretsky's inheritance was not to be quite so blue-blooded as that of the Aksakov's Bagrovs or Tolstoy's Irtenevs. His father, Ivan, was not educated at home on the modest family estate but in the house of a rich aunt, on the understanding that he was to inherit her wealth. Here he was dressed up like a doll in the eighteenth-century manner and put in the charge of a French tutor, a certain M. Courtin de Vaucelles, a student of Jean-Jacques Rousseau, who taught him to read Diderot and Voltaire. He was scarcely twenty years old when the old aunt died, leaving her wealth not to him but to the French tutor whom she had made her husband at the end of her life and who had wisely made off to Paris with her money. Ivan, penniless, was obliged to return to the family estate. This 'nest of the gentry' appeared dirty and unkempt to the young man after his luxurious upbringing. His father was annoyed by his city ways—his frock coats, ruffles, his flute and his punctilious habits—and even more annoyed by all his talk of Diderot and Voltaire. But this eighteenth-century wisdom, of which his head was so full, had not entered his blood. His blood was roused by one of his mother's peasant maid-servants, Malan'ya, with whom he fell passionately in love.

This relationship between a young scion of the gentry and a peasant girl was sufficient to undermine the feudal ethic, especially as Ivan announced to his father that he intended to marry Malan'ya. His father, incensed by this unthinkable insubordination, drove his son from the house; but Ivan remained true to his word, married Malan'ya and set off for St. Petersburg to find a living. In doing this Ivan felt that he had justified his reading of Rousseau, Diderot and *la déclaration des droits de l'homme*. Meanwhile, he left his wife in the care of Marfa Timofeyevna. In St. Petersburg he was fortunate enough to obtain a post with the Russian mission in London, and shortly afterwards he was to learn that his wife had given birth to a son. This son was Fyodor Lavretsky, the hero of *A Nest of the Gentry*.

To begin with, then, the young Lavretsky's birthright was divided. But this was by no means so unfortunate a feature of his inheritance from his father as was the education that his father decided to give him when he returned to Russia after retiring from his post in London. He returned an Anglomaniac and he at once set about making a man— *un homme* was the expression he used—of his son by introducing the most idiotic of Spartan 'systems'. The result was only too clearly foreseeable:

The 'system' bemused the boy, sowed confusion in his head and cramped his mind; but, despite this, the new way of life had a beneficial effect on his health: at first he caught a fever, but soon recovered and became a sturdy lad. His father was proud of him and described him in his strange manner of speaking as 'a son of nature, all my own work'. When Fyodor was sixteen, Ivan Petrovich considered it his duty, in good time, to instil in him a contempt for the female sex—and the young Spartan, timid at heart, with the first down on his cheeks, full of sap, strength and new blood, made an attempt to appear indifferent, cold and rude.

However, the Anglomania of Ivan Petrovich, Lavretsky's father, was to receive a rude shock with the failure of the Decembrist revolt of 1825. He at once abandoned all his free-thinking, started going to church, taking steam baths and indulging his apathy in the manner of an Oblomov. His discomfiture was climaxed by sudden blindness, which necessitated that for the last three years of his life he should travel about Russia in search of a doctor who could cure it. He was now a petulant, complaining despot who rejected all the liberal theories and schemes on which he had prided himself earlier. But he could not reject so easily the curious and unbalanced education which he had bequeathed to his son. When his father eventually died,

Lavretsky was twenty-three, a man of mixed peasant-gentry extraction who was entirely without experience of the world.

Lavretsky's genealogy graphically illustrates the divided cultural inheritance, the incompatibility of the 'imitative' and 'indigenous' elements, which the post-1825 generation of Russian intellectuals had to accept from their fathers and attempt to assimilate. They naturally looked to the West for intellectual stimulus, because there was no comparable stimulus to be found in Russia; and Western ideas—so foreign, so enlightened, so intriguing—cast their spell over them. In Lavretsky's case, painfully aware of the inadequacy of his education and determined to improve it, he became a student at Moscow university. His age and the shyness inculcated into him by his father's 'system' were barriers dividing him from the other students, with the exception of one of them, Mikhalevich. But even friendship with Mikhalevich could not make up for his inexperience, and it is through his inexperience that he falls in love with the frivolous Varvara Pavlovna and makes her his wife. She is more enamoured of the Western life of the capital, St. Petersburg, than of her husband. Later, when they go abroad to Paris, Lavretsky discovers, to his under-standable amazement, that she has been unfaithful to him. His life is shattered by this revelation. He at once rejects his wife and takes to travelling, as his aunt, Glafira Petrovna, had threatened he would: 'You will find nowhere to make your nest, and all your life you'll be a wanderer.' For four years, in fact, Lavretsky hides himself in a small Italian town, watching in the papers for the increasingly scandalous reports which are circulated about his wife's conduct. Finally, when he has recovered sufficiently from the immediate impact of the shock—although a scepticism nurtured by his experiences and his early training has now taken a firm hold on him—he decides to return to the only 'nest' that he knows, his parental estate of Lavriky. It is to this 'nest' that he returns on a bright, spring day in 1842 when, like Rudin, he is approaching middle-age.

The whole of *A Nest of the Gentry* is symbolic of the painful readjust-ment to Russia, its meaning and its problems, which so many members of the post-1825 generation had to undergo. Their Western education had proved a wilderness which left them parched and hungry for roots which only Russia could offer, but Russia herself was as alien to them as any wilderness. What was there in Russia for them? Lavretsky's love for Liza epitomizes the answer. Russia offered a home, a dedica-tion, a purposeful fulfilment in the name of the ideals which their

Western education had taught them to reverence, but had made them incapable of implementing. Lavretsky's return to Russia and his decision to settle in Vasil'yevskoye underline the very human and personal nature of this dilemma. He has returned with an intolerable burden of scepticism and apathy, yet physically he is healthy and strong:

'Here I am as though I were at the bottom of a river,' Lavretsky thought again. 'And here always, at all times, life is quiet and unhurried,' he reflected: 'Whoever enters its charmed circle must submit to it; here there is nothing to worry about, nothing to disturb one; here success comes only to him who carves out his own unhurried path as the ploughman carves out the furrows with his plough. And what strength there is everywhere, what vigour in this wilderness! . . . My best years have passed in loving a woman,' Lavretsky continued to reflect: 'Now let this boredom bring me to my senses, let it calm me and prepare me to take up my task without hurry.'

The contrast between Lavretsky's willingness to accept and the inability to conform characteristic of a man like Rudin is made in the meeting between Lavretsky and Mikhalevich (Chapter XXV). Mikhalevich uses the phraseology of the thirties and in this respect he is no more than a man of words. The words recapitulate the vague idealism of Rudin—'Religion, progress, humanity!' he exclaims as he leaves—while his censure is directed at the same qualities that Rudin attacked in Pigasov: the absence of convictions, self-indulgent egoism, cynicism. But Mikhalevich also reiterates one of Lezhnyov's criticisms of his generation: that they are apathetic, and their apathy, possibly the result of disillusionment or an unbalanced education such as Lavretsky's, smacks of complacency. It is one of those criticisms which Turgenev is frequently to put into the mouths of his 'spokesmen', directed as much at a fundamental weakness in the Russian character as at the hostile prejudice of political opponents. Mikhalevich's criticism is concerned with the fallacious idea, common to many Russian intellectuals, more particularly the Slavophils, that, once they have discovered the Achilles heel of the Germans or what is wrong with the French and English, they can use this knowledge as a salve to their own self-esteem and as an excuse for their own indolence. This intellectual Oblomovism is more dangerous than any other kind. Yet, though Mikhalevich may be accomplished as a Demosthenes, he can offer no satisfactory answer to Lavretsky's question: what to do? His only answer is:

'And when exactly, where exactly have people decided to become apathetic?' he shouted at four o'clock in the morning, in a voice that was already a little hoarse. 'Here among us they have decided to! Now! In Russia! When each individual has a duty, a great responsibility before God, before the people, before himself! We sleep while time is passing; we sleep . . .'

It is a more forthright answer than any that Rudin could give. Perhaps this may be due to the fact that Mikhalevich—and the young Basistov in *Rudin*—are the first of the 'plebeians', the *raznochintsy*, to appear in Turgenev's novels. The presence of such figures in the predominantly upper-class world of Turgenev's fiction is a tacit admission on his part of their growing importance in Russian society. But Mikhalevich's answer is still no more than another version of the intellectual's sacred duty to serve his country and his people which Rudin had propounded on the evening of his arrival at Dar'ya Lasunskaya's. It is a call to action shouted in a void.

If Mikhalevich attacks the gentry Slavophilism which he detects in Lavretsky, this does not alter the fact that the real object of censure in the novel is the artificial Westernism of Panshin. Panshin, the aspiring government official and a distant relation of the local Governor, is personable, talented and ambitious. Unlike any other socially-significant figure so far encountered in Turgenev's novels, he, it is to be assumed, will shortly have the power and the authority to implement his ideas in the administration of the country. Russia, in his opinion, has fallen behind Europe and must catch up with her. Since Russia lacks the inventive faculty—she did not even invent the mouse-trap—she can only become fully European through borrowing from Europe:

'Among us,' he continued, 'the best minds—les meilleures têtes—have long been convinced of this; all nations are in substance the same; you have only to introduce good institutions, and that's the end of the matter. Certainly the institutions can be modified to suit the existing national customs; that is our business, the business of civil'— (he almost said: state)—'servants; but if the need arises, you needn't worry: the institutions will remake the national customs.'

This is the cosmopolitan Westernism of Rudin at its worst and it involves something akin to the policy of the Soviet government at some stages in its career: the indiscriminate introduction of institutions from above, without regard to national habits or customs. To Lavretsky the idea that 'all nations are in substance the same' is particularly offensive. He challenges Panshin by championing Russia's youth and independence, by asserting that though he might sacrifice himself and his own generation he would stand up for the younger generation, its convictions and its hopes. To which Panshin replies that intelligent people should change everything; and Lavretsky's answer to this, reflecting the political opinions of Turgenev himself, is to emphasize the impracticability of changing everything at once from above, regardless of Russia's particular character and without any genuine belief in an ideal, even a negative one. His own education can show the dangers inherent in this attitude. He demands a recognition of Russia's uniqueness, her own 'truth', and a willingness to reconcile oneself to it, to accept it as a protection against falsehood. It is a diluted Slavophilism which can appeal, as the success of *A Nest of the Gentry* was to show, to Slavophils and patriotic Westernists alike. Lavretsky's answer to Panshin is summed up in the simple words: 'To plough the land and to strive to plough it as well as possible'—to find his 'nest' in Russia, to acknowledge his duty to his country and to begin the work of preparing the way for social change.

The argument between Panshin and Lavretsky is the moment that resolves Liza's doubts and precipitates the climax in their relationship. The personal and ideological issues are now united: Lavretsky's personal happiness is achieved through recognizing the need to dedicate himself; and it is this self-dedication that unites hero and heroine. But *A Nest of the Gentry* is pervaded by an elegiac air, as though it were Turgenev's post-mortem on the destiny of his generation. Their Western inheritance and their disillusionment in the circumstances of Nicholas I's Russia were too crippling a burden, symbolized in the novel by the return of Varvara Pavlovna, to permit them to enjoy their new-found sense of purpose. Their destiny was, like Lavretsky's, to stand aside while the younger generation enjoyed themselves in 'the nest of the gentry'.

At this point in Turgenev's career as a novelist his studies in the intellectuals of his own generation appear to have obliged him to draw the painful conclusion that the future destiny of Russia did not lie in their hands. This, perhaps, may have induced him to draw certain more fundamental conclusions about human nature as a whole. In drawing such conclusions he was, firstly, admitting that his own contemporaries could no longer offer models for heroes of the future—that is to say, for the more radical, revolutionary aspirations that were discernible among the younger, post-Crimean generation—and, secondly, he was attempting to provide a universal yardstick of human types which could serve as a basis for his studies in the future. These conclusions were couched in the form of a lecture, which he delivered in 1860 but which had been composed at various times between early 1857 and late 1859, entitled *Hamlet and Don Quixote*.

Turgenev had been struck by a remarkable coincidence: the fact that the first edition of Shakespeare's *Hamlet* and the first part of Cervantes's *Don Quixote* appeared in the same year. His aim in examining these two heroes is to compare them and, in so doing, to rehabilitate the figure of Don Quixote, whose significance had been misunderstood by his contemporaries—even by such an important representative of his generation as Herzen—due to the absence of an adequate Russian translation of the Spanish classic.[1] But he opens his study with certain general remarks on the two contrasting poles in human nature:

All people live—consciously or unconsciously—on the strength of their own principle, their own ideal, that is to say on the strength of what they consider to be truth, beauty and moral good. Many receive their ideal ready-made, in already constituted, historically-defined forms; they live, making their lives conform to this ideal, occasionally falling away from it under the influence of passions or accidents—but they do not question it, they do not doubt it; others, on the other hand, subject it to the analysis of their own thoughts. However that may be, it seems that we shall not be far wrong if we say that for all people this ideal, this basis and aim of their existence is to be found outside them or within them: in other words, for each of us either our own *ego* has the precedent or something else, recognised as being higher than the ego.[2]

For Turgenev Don Quixote seems to epitomize the latter case. He stands for faith, faith in something eternal and unshakable, for truth that exists outside the individual, not easily attainable and demanding much self-less service and sacrifice, but attainable by virtue of the constancy with which such service and sacrifice are made. Don Quixote is dedicated to an ideal and is prepared to lay down his life in service of it; he values his own life only to the extent that it can serve as a means of realizing his ideal, to the extent that it can serve as a means of implementing truth and justice on earth. Don Quixote is entirely devoid of egoism. Hamlet appears to be the exact opposite. He stands primarily for analysis, for egoism and absence of conviction. He lives entirely for himself, yet, because he is an egoist, he cannot believe in himself; although his *ego*, in which he cannot believe, is very dear to him. It is the starting point to which he constantly returns,

[1] *Sobr. soch.* (1956), xi. 490-91.   [2] Ibid, 169-70.

because he can find nothing else in the world to which he can devote himself. Thus he is a sceptic, constantly preoccupied not with his obligations, but with his own condition; and, doubting everything, he also doubts himself and knows his own weakness—yet, ironically, this knowledge is also his strength. It is from this self-knowledge that there springs Hamlet's irony, which is opposed to Don Quixote's most important characteristic—his enthusiasm.

Turgenev admits that, in the final resort, Don Quixote, for all his belief in high ideals, is the prototype of comedy, whereas Hamlet, for all his self-analysis and self-knowledge, is the prototype of tragedy. But Turgenev is concerned less with this aspect of these two heroes than with their common human traits and the extent to which they offer a clue to an understanding of human nature:

We shall limit ourselves to noting that, in this division, this dualism which we have mentioned, we must recognize a basic law of human life; all human life is nothing more than the eternal reconciliation and the eternal struggle of two ceaselessly divided and ceaselessly interfused elements. If we were not frightened of confounding your ears with philosophical terms, we would be resolved to say that the Hamlets are an expression of the basic centripetal force of nature, by virtue of which every living thing regards itself as the centre of creation and views everything else as existing only for its sake. . . . Without this centripetal force (the force of egoism) nature could not exist, just as it could not exist without the other, centrifugal force, by whose law everything exists only for another (this force, this principle of dedication and sacrifice . . . is the principle represented by the Don Quixotes). These two forces of stagnation and movement, of conservatism and progress, are the basic forces of everything that exists. They explain to us the growth of a flower, and they offer us a clue to an understanding of the development of the most powerful of nations.[1]

For the purposes of Turgenev's fiction the opposition is best seen in the way he contrasts the head and the heart, the intellectual preoccupation of a Hamlet with the emotional dedication of a Don Quixote. Though he recognizes that humanity unites both elements, it is the type in which the heart, the centrifugal force, predominates over the head, the centripetal force, which is now to be of greater importance for him. On the Eve shows the way in which the Quixotic element now comes to take precedence over the Hamlet element in Turgenev's fiction, for this novel is concerned with the 'progressive' forces that began to emerge in Russian society during the fifties, as opposed to the more 'conservative' forces of the thirties and forties

1 Sobr. soch. (1956), xi. 180.

which Turgenev had illustrated in *Rudin* and *A Nest of the Gentry*. The opening conversation between Shubin and Bersenev reflects some of the issues that Turgenev had been considering, in a different form, in *Hamlet and Don Quixote*. Shubin, the aspiring artist, expresses the attitude of a Hamlet towards nature. The ants, beetles and other insects that he sees running about in the grass as he lies on the bank of the Moscow river seem to him to be astonishingly serious. They run about with such important expressions on their faces, as if they, re-presentatives of the centripetal force of nature, believed that life actually meant something to them and to them alone. For Shubin himself nature is only meaningful to the extent that it responds to his feelings or brings him happiness. But his companion, Bersenev, the aspiring professor, who has recently passed his university examinations, is less inclined to accept this egotistical view. Nature to him is as alien and threatening to man as it was to the narrator of *Journey into the Wood*: it contains both Life and Death. Love also contains Life and Death, in Shubin's opinion, but, so long as man is able to do so, he must search for happiness.

> Bersenev raised his eyes to him.
> 'Is there nothing higher than happiness?' he remarked quietly.
> 'What, for instance?' Shubin asked and stopped.
> 'Well, for instance, you and I, as you say, are young and let's say we're good people; each of us wishes for happiness.... But is this the kind of word: "happiness" that would unite us, inspire us both, make us extend our hands to each other? Isn't it egotistical, I mean, doesn't this word divide people?'
> 'And do you know any words which unite?'
> 'Yes; and there are quite a lot of them; and you know them as well.'
> 'Well, what words?'
> 'There's art—since you're an artist—fatherland, science, freedom, justice.'
> 'What about love?'
> 'Love is also a word that unites people; but not the kind of love that you want; not love-the pleasure, but love-the sacrifice.'
> Shubin frowned.
> 'That's all right for Germans; but I want love for myself; I want to be number one.'
> 'Number one,' Bersenev repeated. 'But it seems to me that to make oneself number two is the sole purpose of our lives.'

This passage from the opening conversation sums up the difference between Shubin and Bersenev and also foreshadows the new ideolo-gical bias that Turgenev is to give to the hero, Insarov, in his rela-tionship with Yelena, the heroine. Self-indulgent happiness, like self-indulgent egoism, is now to give way before the notion of love as wilful self-sacrifice in the name of such ideals as fatherland, science, freedom and justice—a new set of ideals, far more emphatic than the ideals of 'Religion, Progress, Humanity' which Mikhalevich shouted to Lavretsky upon leaving Vasil'yevskoye. And it is only the Quixotic type of man who can subjugate his egoism sufficiently in order to, as a number two in life, accomplish the realization of such ideals.

The theoretical and, in a sense, experimental nature of Turgenev's interest in the type of Don Quixote is revealed by the very shallow characterization of Insarov. Indeed, his Quixotic dedication to the ideal of liberating his fatherland, Bulgaria, is not far short of the comic—as Turgenev admitted that all Quixotic vocations might be. Both Insarov's parents—his father was a fairly prosperous merchant in Sofia —were put to death by the Turks when he was only seven years old. Subsequently he was educated in Russia. In 1848 he returned to Bulgaria to renew his acquaintanceship with his native country, but came back to Russia two years later to study at Moscow university. Here he occupied himself with Russian history, law and political economy, with translations and the preparation of a Russo-Bulgarian grammar. Beyond this and the fact that he is in two minds whether to study Feuerbach, nothing concrete or factual is offered to the reader as a basis for understanding his character. He is, and remains, as much a foreigner to the novel as he is to Russia. His appeal for Yelena resides simply in the fact that he has taken upon himself the sacred vocation of liberating his native Bulgaria from foreign domination. In the novel his activity in this respect takes the form of occasional sudden absences, which remain largely unexplained, and several visits to his lodgings by strange countrymen of his. That Turgenev made his hero a Bulgarian, and not a Russian, was due not only to the fact that Turgenev could see no Russian equivalents of the Insarov-type of revolutionary in the society of the time, nor to any marked degree to considerations of censorship, but more directly to the fact that the Quixotic type was a new venture for Turgenev, an excursion into a new form of characterization for which he was to provide theoretical justification in his *Hamlet and Don Quixote* but for which the only model was the figure of the Bulgarian patriot, Katranov, in the Karateyev diary. The weakness of Insarov, both as a fictional figure and as a personification of the Quixotic type, springs directly from Turgenev's inability to realize the theory in effective practice.

Other figures in *On the Eve* may lack the all-important appeal of

active revolutionary vocation which is Insarov's distinction, but they
are more real and sympathetic as characters. Bersenev, for instance, of
poor gentry extraction, was educated at first by his father—a man with
a Goettingen background, like Rudin, and just as dedicated and ineffectual as Rudin, for whom 1848 is a catastrophe—and later at
Moscow university, two decades after that university had had its
greatest fame with such figures as Herzen, Stankevich and Belinsky.
Bersenev represents the interim generation between Turgenev's and
the emergence of the 'new men', the Bazarovs. Bersenev had been
bequeathed the torch of enlightenment by his father and was inspired
with the ambition of becoming a professor, like the Granovsky whom
Turgenev had known in Berlin in the late thirties. But this is the limit
of Bersenev's ambition, and of his talent: he did not have the vocation
of revolutionary. Shubin, similarly, percipient and artistically gifted
as he may be, is a social gad-fly and no more. Yet Turgenev puts into
his mouth sentiments that are in the nature of a commentary upon the
important changes in the Russian social scene of which the events in
the novel are a distant reflection. They may sound odd from a character
such as Shubin, but they express the admiration and the envy that
Turgenev felt for what the younger generation, epitomized by
Yelena, was attempting to do. Shubin, speaking to Uvar Ivanych,
says:

'Yes, it's a matter of youth and glory and courage. Death, life, struggle,
defeat, triumph, love, freedom, fatherland. . . . It's good! It's good! God
grant it to everyone! It's not like sitting up to your neck in a swamp, trying
to make it appear that it's all the same to you when it is, in fact, all the same
to you! While with them it's a case of the whole world or bust!'

The Shubins and Bersenevs, like the entire Russian intelligentsia, are
up to their necks in a swamp. The image is to be compared with the
striking picture of the people abandoned in the swamp by their intellectual leaders, who have climbed the tree of knowledge and are
content to enjoy its fruits regardless of the cries for help from below,
which Dobrolyubov offers in his article of 1859, *What is Oblomovism?*
Where are the leaders, the exemplars? Shubin wonders:

'. . . We have no one as yet, no real people, no matter where you look.
It's all small fry, rodents, little Hamlets, carnivorous parasites, it's all sub-
terranean darkness and ignorance, it's all boasters, all windbags, all beating
their own drums! And then there are the others, who've studied themselves
in shameful detail, and constantly feel their pulses with each new sensation and

declare to themselves: "That's what I feel now, that's what I think." Now there's a useful, sensible occupation for you! No, if there'd been some real people among us, that girl, that sensitive spirit, wouldn't have left us, wouldn't have slipped out of our hands like a fish into water! What's it mean, Uvar Ivanych? When will our time come? When will real people arise among us?'

'Give it time,' Uvar Ivanych answered. 'They'll come.'

Uvar Ivanych's answer is the optimistic message of the novel—a message which is exemplified in the decision of Yelena to share Insarov's destiny. For the picture of intellectual society that Shubin paints resembles the 'dark kingdom' of the bourgeois or merchant milieu which Ostrovsky depicted in many of his plays, particularly in *The Storm*, first staged in 1860, the year that *On the Eve* appeared. Turgenev's novel and Ostrovsky's play both illustrate the attempt of the younger generation, exemplified in both cases by a young woman —Yelena in *On the Eve*, Katerina in *The Storm*—to escape from what Shubin calls 'a swamp' or what Dobrolyubov, writing of *The Storm*, called the 'dark kingdom' of Russian society, with its narrow and constricting conventions, its patriarchal structure, its intellectual stagnation and its spiritual poverty, best summed-up by the curious Russian word *poshlost'*. Again, in both cases, this attempt at escape was made instinctively, as a moral revolt against an immoral world. It was not inspired by close acquaintanceship with enlightened Western ideas, as was the case with Turgenev's generation. In fact, there is no member of the younger generation in *On the Eve* who had studied abroad, outside Russia, as had Turgenev himself, or Rudin, or, in a sense, Lavretsky. The younger generation had been driven to act out of impulse, out of instinctive conviction, in that Quixotic manner which Turgenev attempted to explain theoretically because it had never been a feature of the experience of his own generation. The major difference between Turgenev's Yelena and Ostrovsky's Katerina is one of purpose, largely to be explained by the social difference between them. Katerina of *The Storm* is driven to make her futile gesture of revolt and non-acceptance, because her social milieu appears to offer no other way of escape; but Yelena is at least given the opportunity of a purposeful choice in her love for Insarov, so that her purpose is united with his in active pursuance of a revolutionary vocation.

Yelena's choice, however, is not made on ideological grounds, so much as personal. She can admire Insarov's desire to liberate his country—'It is frightening even to speak these words,' she tells Bersenev, 'they are so great . . .'—but her devotion is instinctive. The social problem of her relationship with one of an inferior class is also veiled by the purely personal problem which it presents to her: she loves Insarov for his revolutionary ardour, class distinctions apart; and there is also the issue of the difference between the generations, which is presented in Yelena's case not as an ideological difference but simply as a difference between a daughter and her parents. The Stakhovs are represented as comic and ineffectual. This is especially true of Stakhov *père* who, like so many representatives of the older generation whom Turgenev depicts in his fiction, is morally compromised by an inability to conduct his love life with the right measure of social propriety. All the former 'superfluous men' in Turgenev's fiction, from the Hamlet of Shchigrovsky Province to a man such as Lavretsky, had been rendered ineffectual by emotional entanglements; in Nikolay Stakhov's case the emotional entanglement renders him both comic and unworthy—a significant distinction. Shubin remarks that it is scarcely credible that Yelena should be the daughter of such parents.[1] But it is this fact that emphasizes the difference between the generations. It is to be repeated again in *Fathers and Children* in the way that Nikolay Kirsanov is morally compromised—and, to this extent, his authority discredited—by his relationship with the peasant girl, Fenichka.

In fact, in *On the Eve* it is not difficult to detect that Turgenev is beginning to ascribe a moral superiority not so much to the younger generation as a whole but to a particular class—the class of the poorer gentry and the *raznochintsy*. Bersenev is of poor gentry extraction, while Insarov is, Bulgarian nationality apart, a *raznochinets*: both these characters are positive and purposeful figures in the fiction. Yelena, admittedly of gentry extraction, rejects not only her parents but her class as well in deciding to go off with Insarov. The bias against the gentry itself is further illustrated in the fiction by the treatment accorded to such younger representatives of that class as Kurnatovsky and Lupoyarov. Kurnatovsky, a slightly older version of the Panshin of *A Nest of the Gentry*, takes the same official view with his airy talk of the need to observe principles regardless of the consequences. But, as Yelena tells Insarov in her letter describing Kurnatovsky's visit, this young representative of officialdom is simply morally inferior to him. She quotes Shubin in justification:

[1] Henry James wittily remarks about Yelena's parents that they are 'loquacious domestic fowls who find themselves responsible for the hatching of an eagle'. Henry James, *French Poets and Novelists* (1878), 288.

'. . . Shubin approached me after dinner and said: Take this one [i.e. Kurna-tovsky] and the other one (he still cannot bring himself to pronounce your name)—they are both practical men, but look what a difference there is between them: in one case there's a real, vital ideal given by life itself and in the other there's not even a feeling of duty, but simply an official honesty and an ability without any content.—Shubin is intelligent, and that's why I've quoted his words to you: but in my opinion, what can there be in common between you? You *believe* in something, but that one doesn't, because *it's impossible to believe* only in oneself.'

Here is the Hamlet-Don Quixote dichotomy stated categorically by Yelena. Kurnatovsky is the Hamlet whose inability to believe in any supra-personal ideal is contrasted with the Don Quixote, Insarov, whose one claim to superiority lies in the fact that he does believe. Lupoyarov, who visits Yelena and Insarov just before the latter's death in Venice, is another brand of upper-class intellectual, the parody of a Don Quixote in his effusive enthusiasm and a rubbishy Hamlet with his dilettante pursuits. 'The younger generation are all for progress!' Lupoyarov exclaims during his breathless diatribe, but his chatter about progress is sufficient in itself to reveal that it is not his type or his class who will be the instruments of social progress. Insarov's verdict—'There's your younger generation for you!'—seems to emphasize both his own superiority and the contempt in which Tur-genev holds certain sections of the younger generation of the gentry.

On the Eve, whether referring to the eve of the Crimean War, since the action of the novel occurs in 1853 and early 1854, or to the eve of the emancipation of the serfs, since the novel was published in 1860, is certainly more concerned with anticipating the future than lamenting the past. The optimistic tone of the novel is to be seen both in the broaching of such new ideas as those to which Bersenev alludes in his opening conversation with Shubin—the words which unite people: art, fatherland, science, freedom, justice and the idea of love-the sacrifice—and in the new ideal of national liberation which is presented in the energetic Don Quixote-type revolutionary, the *raznochinets*, Insarov. These new ideas and this new ideal are given pertinence to the Russian scene primarily through the example of Yelena. However, as Dobrolyubov pointed out in his review of *On the Eve*, the presence of such a figure as Yelena in the novel merely foreshadowed the emergence of a Russian equivalent of Insarov as Yelena's male counter-part in Russian society. This Russian Insarov is to be dedicated not to the ideal of liberating his country from foreign domination, but to the ideal of cleansing Russian society of its 'inner enemy' which takes the form, as Dobrolyubov expresses it in his aesopian fashion, of 'the damp and foggy atmosphere of our lives'[1]—of Tsarism itself, that is to say, and the entire social, economic and political structure upon which the autocracy was based. The time is ripe for the emergence of such a new type in Russian society, in Dobrolyubov's opinion, and soon he will appear as a clearly defined figure in Russian literature.

Unquestionably, apart from Turgenev, there was no writer in Russia at this particular moment, on the eve of the emancipation of the serfs, capable of depicting such a figure. Dobrolyubov's words at the end of his review seem to be addressed directly to Turgenev. But the social changes which made the time ripe for the appearance of a Russian Insarov were the same changes as had brought to prominence Dobrolyubov himself. This young *enfant terrible* of the new radical publicism had joined the staff of *The Contemporary* in 1857, and was soon busily engaged in attacking all enemies of 'progress'. Tsarism was the main target, though naturally in an oblique manner for fear of the censorship, but the *dvoryanstvo* also came in for their due measure of censure. Chernyshevsky in his article on Turgenev's *Asya*[2] had launched this attack on the *dvoryanstvo*, or the liberal wing of it, in 1858 and it was to be followed in May of the following year by Dobrolyubov's article on Goncharov's *Oblomov*. This article carried the attack to the point of denying any moral or ideological leadership to the gentry as a class, since they were corrupted by the fact of serfdom on which their existence as a class was based. Social and political animosities, personal hatreds, the desire for radical change, the sincere wish to be rid of the past, the expectation of a brilliant reorganization of society on 'scientific' lines—all these currents of feeling and conviction had their part to play in the ensuing publicistic polemics of the years immediately preceding the Emancipation of 1861.

Of one thing we may be certain in speaking of these polemics: their consequences were tragic. In general, the Russian intelligentsia, from its inception as a discernible body of enlightened opinion in the Moscow university circles of the thirties, had been united in agreeing on the need for reform of such institutions as serfdom, the legal system and the autocracy. This does not mean that the Russian intelligentsia ever presented a monolithic front: it contained as many different shades of opinion as it had members, and none differed more than the

---

[1] N. A. Dobrolyubov, op. cit., 88.

[2] N. G. Chernyshevsky, 'Russky chelovek na rendez-vous', *Atseney*, 1858, No. 3.

Slavophils. But the attitude of the Slavophils was never as serious a threat to a certain unity of opinion among the intelligentsia as was the attitude of the radical wing, represented by *The Contemporary*, towards the more conservative or liberal wing, of which the most prominent representative was the exiled Herzen with his journal *The Bell*. The disagreement which split the intelligentsia into these two opposed and finally irreconcilable attitudes was rooted in the natural class antagonism that existed between the *raznochintsy*, on the one hand, and the gentry, on the other. For the *raznochintsy* the emancipation of the serfs was merely a step in the right direction, opening the way for socialism and a radical reconstruction of the economic, social and political bases of the Russian state; for the gentry the emancipation of the serfs, although recognized as essential by many enlightened serf-owners as a means of promoting a healthier social and economic climate in Russia, was a direct threat to their economic existence and their prestige as a class. In the circumstances, the *raznochintsy* were not frightened of revolution as a means of achieving political change, for as a class the *raznochintsy* had little to lose and much to gain by a revolution among the peasantry, while the gentry had everything to lose by a revolution of this nature and were quick to counsel political moderation when they realized the danger inherent in the militant attitude of their opponents. If the Russian intelligentsia had been able to maintain a united front at this mid-point in the nineteenth century, unified perhaps by those noble ideas which Turgenev had advanced in *On the Eve*, then internal dissensions would not have weakened their cause and the autocracy, already buffeted by the Crimean War, might have been obliged to grant wider reforms and even a modest degree of constitutional government. At this moment, however, a taking of sides occurred. Class interests made their inevitable contribution to the dissension between the parties; self-interest undermined the altruistic motives upon which the intelligentsia relied for its moral authority. And in 1859 the split between the two wings of the intelligentsia, between the older and the younger generation, became an open disagreement, readily discernible in the tone of Dobrolyubov's article on *Oblomov* or the tone of Herzen's article, *Very Dangerous*, which appeared in June 1859 in *The Bell*; while in that same month Chernyshevsky went to London to see Herzen in order, presumably, to discuss the split which now divided them. Turgenev was not an uncommitted party to these polemics, yet he was probably the only prominent figure of the time who had the gift of dispassionate observation.

For Turgenev the materialistic aesthetic views of Chernyshevsky and the hostility of Dobrolyubov, which was not far short of personal malice, constituted severe slights to his *amour propre* as 'a man of the forties' and were insulting to his liberal Westernism. Turgenev turned his back on *The Contemporary* and exhibited his dislike of *The Contemporary*'s new editorial policy by publishing *On the Eve* in Katkov's liberal journal *The Russian Messenger*. There is little doubt that Turgenev intended, in writing *Fathers and Children*, to attack the radicalism —or, as he expressed it, the nihilism—of the aggressively materialistic policies promoted by Chernyshevsky and Dobrolyubov. Much private rancour and personal conviction lay behind Turgenev's intention. But his anger was moderated by a spirit of integrity, compounded of common sense and his writer's sense of proportion, which diluted the hostility until it became an avowed though grudging admiration. His personal acquaintanceship with a living prototype of these 'new men'—the young doctor whom he mentions in his *Literary Reminiscences*—must have accelerated the process of reconciliation. In Turgenev's eyes these 'new men' remained primarily epitomes of a negative attitude, inimical personally to him because it denied any value to art save the materialistic or the functional, but also fascinating to him because its unsentimental boldness and toughness of mind both contrasted with the emotional fallibility of the gentry intelligentsia and appealed to the Quixotic streak in his own predominantly Hamlet-like nature. In a sense, the 'new men' were all that Turgenev wished to be and was not. Yet Turgenev was not willing to make his novel a propaganda work in their favour, nor was he willing to bias his fiction against them. His aim was simply to present as objectively as possible the ideological and class antagonisms existing between the Fathers and the Children in that crucial year of 1859 when the two wings of the intelligentsia were in open disagreement.

Practically all the controversy aroused by *Fathers and Children* centred on the figure of Bazarov. Turgenev's first official defence, as distinct from the defences he offered in his private correspondence, of his treatment of the figure of Bazarov appeared in his *Literary Reminiscences*, written at a remove of between six and seven years after the publication of the novel. The crux of his defence in this case is contained in the following sentences:

The entire cause of the misunderstandings, all—as one might say—the 'trouble' resided in the fact that the type of Bazarov as reproduced by me did not have the time to pass through the gradual phases through which literary types usually pass. It was not his lot, as it was Onegin's or Pechorin's lot, to undergo an epoch of idealization, of sympathy and acclaim. At the very moment when this *new* man, Bazarov, appeared, the author approached him critically . . . objectively.[1]

Certainly *Fathers and Children* is the most immediately topical, the least historical, of all Turgenev's novels. He had applied his talent for dispassionate observation in a spirit of objective, critical appraisal to the social phenomenon of the 'new man', and the resultant portrait could not be seen by his contemporaries in a sufficiently clear perspective for it not to appear either too hostile or too complimentary. But this was in no sense Turgenev's fault. The fault lay with his contemporaries, and evidence of the extent to which Turgenev's ultimate intention was misunderstood is reflected in his letter to Sluchevsky of April 1862.[2] It is here that he offers a detailed defence of his portrait of Bazarov and his attitude towards the younger generation. In the first place, Bazarov was to be thought of not so much as a nihilist—in the derogatory sense in which this title was used by the reactionary opposition—but as a revolutionary, as a 'pendant to Pugachov': here Turgenev was clearly acknowledging the revolutionary aspiration of the 'new men', the *Children*. In the second place, the novel was to be regarded as being directed entirely against the gentry as the leading class in Russian society: here he was acknowledging the moral superiority of the *raznochintsy* as a class. Finally, Bazarov was to be regarded as a tragic hero so far as the fiction was concerned. It is the first two points that are of the greatest importance for an understanding of the ideological problems examined in the novel.

Bazarov, when he arrives at Mar'ino on May 20th 1859, is the least poetic of Turgenev's heroes. He is self-assured, caustic, contemptuous of Nikolay Kirsanov with his admiration for Pushkin, adept at concise, even folksy, comments upon his hosts and his surroundings, indifferent to niceties of behaviour but percipient in his appraisal of character. There is no suggestion of caricature about the way he is presented, nor is there any suggestion of caricature about the representatives of the gentry. Hostility towards the 'younger generation' is expressed only in the portrait of the model servant, Pyotr. Arkady Kirsanov is presented, at this stage in the novel, as no less radical in his views than Bazarov, although he is a lesser personality and is not given, as is his

---

[1] *Sobr. soch.* (1956), x. 350.
[2] Letter to K. K. Sluchevsky, 26/14 April 1862. *Sobr. soch.* (1958), xii. 339-41.

friend, to a single-minded pursuit of the natural sciences. It may be remarked in passing that Bazarov's interest in the natural sciences is depicted in much the same sketchy fashion as was Insarov's revolutionary activity: Insarov disappeared from the centre of the fiction occasionally in order to attend to revolutionary matters, while Bazarov occasionally disappears from the scene to collect frogs for dissection or to pursue experiments with the aid of his microscope. In neither case is the practical dedication of the hero given more emphasis than the hero's beliefs. Bazarov's beliefs, such as they are, are first described by Arkady in the conversation with his father, Nikolay, and his uncle, Pavel Kirsanov, on the morning after his arrival:

'He is a nihilist.'

'A what?' asked Nikolay Petrovich, and Pavel Petrovich stopped at once in the act of raising his knife in the air with a piece of butter on the end of the blade.

'He is a nihilist,' Arkady repeated.

'A nihilist,' remarked Nikolay Petrovich. 'So far as I can judge that's from the Latin nihil, *nothing*; in that case the word must denote a man who . . . recognises nothing?'

'Better say: who respects nothing,' added Pavel Petrovich and once again busied himself with the butter.

'Who approaches everything from a critical point of view,' Arkady said.

'Isn't that the same thing?' asked Pavel Petrovich.

'No, it's not the same thing. A nihilist is a man who does not acknowledge any authorities, who does not accept a single principle on faith, no matter how much that principle may be respected.'

It is this last remark about principles which contains the crux of the argument between the Fathers and the Children. As Pavel Petrovich, 'the man of the forties', the spokesman of Turgenev's generation, is quick to point out, it had previously been thought that without such principles accepted on faith a man could neither progress nor live fully. Pavel Petrovich's championing of principles echoes, in a more sophisticated form, Rudin's words on the importance of convictions; and his remark that 'there used to be Hegelians, but now there are nihilists' supplies the socio-historical footnote to the emergence of this new phenomenon (as Dostoyevsky is to show just as graphically in *The Possessed* when he makes the revolutionary nihilist, Pyotr Verkhovensky, the son of 'the man of the forties', Stepan Verkhovensky). For Pavel Petrovich Kirsanov is practically the last of 'the men of the forties' to appear in Turgenev's major fiction, and in this sense he is—as Bazarov calls him—'an archaic survival', compromised by the emotional weakness so characteristic of his generation, yet also typical of his generation in his assertion of the need for principles and in his willingness to defend his own particular 'aristocratic' principles just as strongly as Rudin defended the principles of science and knowledge against the sneers of Pigasov. The difference between Rudin and Pavel Petrovich is that the one stood on the threshold of an epoch, offering new ideas and new ideals to a younger generation eager to accept and to practise them, while the other stands at the end of an epoch, his ideas and his ideals largely discredited or, when not discredited, pre-served by him in a tissue-paper of French phrases to protect them from corrosion by the outside world; and when they are finally exhibited, the younger generation, in the shape of Bazarov, either tramples on them or ignores them.

Bazarov tramples on two notions dear to Pavel Petrovich and his generation in their first short conversation (Chapter VI): the sanctity of art and the dilettante concern for 'science'. Bazarov's contention that 'a good chemist is twenty times more useful than any poet' carries the war right into the enemy's camp, for nothing could be more offen-sive to the 'superfluous man' intellectual, with his carefully nurtured sense of the beautiful. When Pavel Petrovich, in his aristocratic con-tempt for such materialism, suggests that Bazarov believes only in science, the latter retorts that he believes in nothing, least of all in 'science' as a general concept, since there are only sciences, in his opinion, as there might be different trades or vocations. This utilitarian, hard-headed attitude is the primary characteristic of Bazarov. It demands an acknowledgement of the need to begin at the beginning, to learn the alphabet before proceeding to discuss general conclusions; it rejects out of hand all sentimentalism, whether in treating facts or human beings. To Bazarov Pavel Petrovich's emotional weakness is a matter for contempt. A man must be his own master through his knowledge of himself and of the facts of life. Moreover, Bazarov practises these precepts. He is no sentimentalist about the Russians ('The only good point about a Russian is that he has the lowest opinion of himself'), nor about nature, which stirred the heart of Rudin and continues to stir the heart of Nikolay Petrovich ('Nature's not a temple, but a workshop, and man's the worker in it').

Of course, there is much in Bazarov's uncompromising attitude that is to be deplored as adolescent and thoughtless. His hard-headedness in exalting facts at the expense of aesthetic sensibility is as narrowly doctrinaire as any blind conviction, however pragmatic. But his single-mindedness, his incontrovertible sense of purpose, redeem the follies of his impetuosity and contribute to his triumph over Pavel Petrovich in their second conversation (Chapter X). If the first conversation had simply delineated the essential elements of difference between the two representative types, then the second conversation elaborates these differences by setting forth the issues which were the talking-points in the dispute between the two wings of the intelligentsia during 1859. Thus, Pavel Petrovich upholds the aristocracy, quoting the English example, and defends his own idleness in respect of the *bien public* by asserting the principle of individuality, though he gives it a socio-political tinge—which Rudin, for instance, had never given it—in equating it with the principle of aristocratism. 'Aristocratism, liberalism, progress, principles'—Bazarov rejects these words, the highsounding ideals of the liberal wing of the intelligentsia, because they are alien and un-Russian. To Bazarov it is only necessary to act, for all logic, whether of history or otherwise, is a meaningless abstraction when it is a question of man's economic subsistence; and so he will act in a spirit of denial with the aim of sweeping away the ideals and principles of the past in order to prepare the way for the elementary practical tasks of the future.

Bazarov's denial of the value of principles extends to that principle of altruistic service which had been so prominently mooted in *On the Eve*. It is an unnecessary piece of romanticism, in his opinion, especially as the object of such service, the Russian peasantry, is deserving not of the sympathetic romanticism which Pavel Petrovich is willing to accord to its patriarchal institutions and its love of tradition, but only of censure and contempt for its superstitious ignorance. The attitude to the peasantry is the fundamental point of difference between the Fathers and the Children. To Pavel Petrovich Bazarov is no Russian if he does not believe in the Russian peasantry, yet Bazarov has no wish to turn the peasantry into another principle to be accepted on faith; Bazarov protests that his peasant heritage gives him more right to call himself a Russian than does the profession of faith in the peasantry which Pavel Petrovich extols as a mark of his patriotism. The absence of sentimentality or romanticism in this attitude leads Pavel Petrovich to accuse Bazarov of propagating materialism—and this is, strictly speaking, true, although it is no eighteenth-century materialism but a materialism based upon the economic facts of the situation; and such a situation can no longer be treated simply as a matter for condemnation or be passed over with reference to the corruption in the bureaucracy or be explained away by talk of parliamentary institutions and a new legal system. Such publicism alone is quite insufficient to mend this situation, although it seems that the nihilists have no other way of dealing with the problem than by employing denial and abuse—at least, that is Pavel Petrovich's contemptuous conclusion.

It rests with Arkady, the representative of Pavel Petrovich's own class, to suggest the political means at the disposal of the nihilists: the use of force, of revolution. This incenses Pavel Petrovich, for it strikes at the roots of all the civilized ideals which his class and his generation held dear: it is the weapon of the Kalmuk and the Mongol, not of civilized man. It naturally presupposes the denial and rejection of all that civilization has achieved so far, and Pavel Petrovich can see signs of this in the rejection by the younger generation of all classical art, even of Raphael, which is seconded by Bazarov in his assertion that Raphael is not worth a brass farthing—a deliberate piece of gratuitous iconoclasm similar to his rejection of Pushkin in favour of *Stoff und Kraft*. But it would be wrong to assume that Bazarov is any less aware than Pavel Petrovich of the value of civilization. Bazarov is neither a Kalmuk nor a Mongol: the difference between the generations is the more tragic because it is in essence no more than a difference of background and attitude. For Pavel Petrovich civilization is an aristocratic principle, a priceless artistic and cultural heritage far removed from the mundanities of economics, but for Bazarov civilization, no less priceless in the last resort, is to be sought primarily in economic terms and an initial premise of any civilization must be the well-being of the majority in a rationally ordered society. It is this which makes Pavel Petrovich as blind to economic problems as it makes Bazarov blind to the values of art. The final disagreement between them—a difference now as much between personalities as between attitudes—is occasioned by the ignorance of Pavel Petrovich about conditions prevailing among the peasantry. Bazarov cannot see one peasant institution which does not merit complete and ruthless denunciation. Even such an institution as the peasant *obshchina*, or commune, so revered as a sentimental link with the past by the Slavophils or as a nucleus of agrarian socialism by Herzen or as a basis for social reform in the countryside by Chernyshevsky, and such an institution as the peasant family are fit, in Bazarov's eyes, rather for censure and denunciation than for acclaim and approval. In dismissing these institutions he tears away from under Pavel Petrovich's feet the romantic groundwork of illusions and hopes about the peasantry entertained by the gentry intelligentsia. The ideological alternative which he has to offer is not in the least grandiose: the recognition of the importance of the natural sciences and the effective study of them, for this will be the new groundwork once the past has been swept away. And he abruptly ends the argument with his decision to go off and dissect frogs.

Bazarov's superiority, if only in point of strength of will and unsentimental reasoning, is exemplified in this argument with Pavel Petrovich; his superiority as a representative of his generation is exemplified in the contrast afforded by his meeting with Sitnikov and Kukshina. The satirical tone which Turgenev adopts in describing the habits and mannerisms of officialdom in the town is unmistakable (Chapter XII). This satirical tone is to be discerned equally clearly in his treatment of the sycophantic Sitnikov, with his Slavophil costume and his offensively garrulous manner, which Bazarov can so quickly deflate by a reference to his capitalist father, and the 'emancipated' Kukshina, anxious to adopt the right 'progressive' pose and even touchingly idiotic with her professed discovery of a new mastic from which she can make unbreakable dolls' heads. Their dilettante chatter, peppered with references to such fashionable figures as Liebig, George Sand, Fenimore Cooper, Bunsen, Proudhon, Macaulay and Michelet, sets in relief the taciturn indifference of Bazarov. Personalities as such are of no interest to him. The 'newness' of Bazarov is illustrated here by the fact that he takes no part in Sitnikov's and Kukshina's discussion about individuality which, although debased by them into matter for frivolous comment, shows the extent to which they are still pre-occupied with the ideas of the forties. To Bazarov Odintsova is at first simply 'a luxurious body', interesting purely from the anatomical point of view. This attitude of the hero towards the heroine is a new departure in Turgenev's fiction, but it is quite in character for Bazarov to behave in this way. Whatever Turgenev's intention in deliberately emphasizing the uncouthness of Bazarov—and one may justifiably suspect that Turgenev did not have the best of intentions at this stage in the portrayal of his hero—the result is to underline the fact that Bazarov does not adhere to the exalted view of individuality held by Belinsky (to whose memory the novel is dedicated), although in its final form the portrait of Bazarov as a practical reformer would probably have appealed to Belinsky more than any other hero in Turgenev's fiction.

Bazarov states his own position on the question of individuality when speaking to Odintsova (Chapter XVI):

'All people are alike, both in body and soul: each one of us has a brain, a spleen, a heart and lungs similarly arranged; and the so-called moral qualities are the same in all of us: the slight variations mean nothing. One human example is sufficient to judge all the rest. Human beings are like trees in a forest: no botanist is going to occupy himself with each individual birch-tree.'

Here the brash scientism of Bazarov is carried to its logical extreme. All intellectual or moral differences are explicable on physiological grounds, and it only remains for the same scientific principles to be applied in the sphere of sociology for all maladjustments to be overcome:

'The lungs of a consumptive are not in the same condition as yours or mine, although they are arranged in the same way. We know approximately what causes physical ailments; and moral diseases merely spring from bad education, from all the rubbish with which people's heads are filled from childhood; in a word, from the chaotic state of society. Change society, and there will be no diseases. . . . At least, in a correctly ordered society it will be entirely immaterial whether a man is stupid or wise, good or bad.'

There is no need to dwell on the false premises of this simplist view: it is the miracle of the God that failed. Odintsova humorously sums it up by remarking that 'we shall all have the same kind of spleen'—and that comment is sufficient. But for Bazarov, in his capacity as a doctor, this view is a matter of principle. During the course of his relationship with Odintsova experience is to teach him that individuals are more important than ciphers, yet it is this view that exemplifies the ideological 'newness' of Bazarov and sets him apart from all previous Turgenevan heroes.

This ideological 'newness' is further accentuated by Turgenev in two ways: in Bazarov's rejection of the gentry, the *dvoryanstvo*, and in his eventual decision to put his knowledge to effective use by assisting his father in his medical practice. In the first case, Bazarov's 'newness' as a social phenomenon is revealed in the fact that his hatred, unlike Insarov's, is directed not at a national enemy but at a class enemy. During their conversation in the hay-stack (Chapter XXI), Bazarov reveals the instinctive gulf that exists between himself and Arkady, and it is not a gulf so much between generations as between classes, the *raznochintsy* and the gentry. Later, after Bazarov's triumph over Pavel Petrovich in the duel, Bazarov is to be much more explicit in his condemnation of the gentry. When he describes the duel to Arkady, he refers directly to the 'feudal' company that he had been keeping; and he tells Odintsova when he leaves her that he had been mixing for too long in spheres alien to his nature, comparing himself to a flying fish that can stay in the air for a short while but must eventually flop back into the water. Saying goodbye to Arkady, his condemnation is blunt:

'. . . We are saying goodbye for ever, and you can feel that yourself. . . . You have behaved wisely; you're not made for our bitter, harsh, solitary existence. You haven't the audacity or the anger, only a youthful boldness and a young man's ardour; and that's no good for what we have to do. Your kind, the gentry, can never go beyond a noble passivity or a noble indignation, and that's all nonsense. You don't fight, for instance—though you imagine yourselves to be a lot of fine fellows—but we want to fight! Yes, indeed! Our dust'll eat out your eyes, our dirt'll soil you, and you haven't even grown up as much as we have, you're still in love with yourself, you still like to reproach yourself; but still you're a soft, liberal gentleman—et voilà tout, as my parent expresses himself.'

Although Bazarov might be tempted to classify it as yet another brand of romanticism, he does have an ideal. When he speaks of 'our bitter, harsh, solitary existence' it is no bravado but conscious recognition of the fact that his task can only be accomplished in isolation; and his task is to work among the peasantry, whom he despises as much as he despises the gentry. In the final estimate, there is little to choose between Bazarov and other 'superfluous men' in Turgenev's fiction, for Bazarov is also represented as a superfluous figure in society. The difference is that Bazarov is not one for heroics: he does not throw away his life on the Paris barricades like a Rudin, but sacrifices himself reluctantly in the cause of improving his medical knowledge and, equally reluctantly, in the cause of helping the peasantry. The death of Bazarov is a curiously ironic prophecy, for 'the men of the sixties', of which Bazarov is the first fictional representative, were to show the way to that mass movement of the Russian intelligentsia 'into the people' (*khozhdeniye v narod*) which was to be, figuratively speaking, the death of the Russian intelligentsia in the sense that it was to be the downfall of the intelligentsia's apolitical aim of spreading enlightenment. Admittedly, Turgenev intended—if we are to accept his letter to Sluchevsky—that certain political motives could be imputed to Bazarov, but these are neither elaborated nor made explicit in the novel. He may be accepted as a type of revolutionary, as a nihilist, as a *raznochinets*, but as the embodiment of an idea he stands for no more than practical reform, solitary endeavour, purposefully un-romantic and wilfully unsentimental, in the name of social improve-ment. Turgenev seems to have achieved Bazarov's portrait despite himself, and yet it is a portrait that summarizes all the positive virtues towards which all Turgenev's previous studies had been directed. It is the ideological climax of his first four novels, though ironically Bazarov is the least idea-conscious of all his heroes.

HERO AND HEROINE

Ideas and ideals have their particular place in Turgenev's novels, as a prelude to the love-story that is to follow. They are the distinction of his fiction, its strength as a committed literature, but they are not its magic. The magic of Turgenev's novels and their appeal as works that transcend the problems of their age lie in the fact that they are love-stories full of poetic echoes, permeated with the nostalgia of the fairy-tale and the freshness of life, tinged with the bright colours of immediate human experience but blurred at the edges by a saddening awareness of hopes faded. Turgenev's heroes may have their ideas and may seek to emulate their ideals, but it is the heroines who reveal their true natures, embodying moral standards which are the subtlest test of the hero's moral worth. It is in the relationship between hero and heroine that the profounder issue of human happiness is raised. It is here that the heart speaks and not the head, and the resulting in-compatibility contains the seeds of tragedy.

Natal'ya in *Rudin* is scarcely more than a girl. She is of a serious cast of mind, with a youthful eagerness for self-dedication first hinted at in her statement that she has been reading a history of the crusades; she is formidably innocent and by all accounts attractive. To Rudin she is at first no more than a young girl, whom he can envy or pity for her youthfulness. But it is certainly her youthfulness that initially attracts him—'The entire aim of science', he says, 'is to attain by conscious effort what youth has freely given it'—and the note of nostalgia for youth departed is a significant part of Rudin's romantic armoury. When Herzen criticized Turgenev for offering a self-portrait in his depiction of Rudin,[1] he may have had this feature of

1 Quoted from Soch. (1930), v. 284.

Rudin in mind, since this nostalgia for youth departed exactly reflects
Turgenev's constant preoccupation with the problem. Youth, ever-
green and romantic, was always Turgenev's favourite theme, perpetually re-explored and recreated in the colours of high summer with
an almost pathological minuteness. In this sense, Rudin is a replica of
previous 'superfluous men' in Turgenev's fiction, wistfully deriving
enjoyment from the thought that for him the passions of youth are
gone forever.

Enamoured of this brand of self-indulgent melancholy, which can
serve equally well as an excuse for his complacency, Rudin can speak
airily of the poetry in nature and in life, of the need to put his talents
to some useful purpose, without any sense of guilt at the futility of such
talk. His personality is complex, but to Natal'ya the absence of purpose
is immediately apparent. He reads to her *Faust*, the works of Hoffmann
and Novalis, expounds German philosophy, but there is always the
excuse of the apple tree broken down under the weight of its own
fruit which appears to absolve him from completing his projected
oeuvre on the tragic element in life and in art. The stumbling block, as
he admits, is his inability so far to clarify for himself the tragic significance of love. 'Who,' he asks, 'can dare to love in our time?' He will
analyse love's symptoms and its secrets and yet he will not admit that
the tragic aspect of love is unhappiness—that to him is more like the
comic side of love because he, preciously harbouring his emotional
pretence, has the words for love but not the instinct. It is Sergey
Volyntsev who has the instinct.

Lezhnyov can illustrate from his own experience the danger of
Rudin's emotional pose, his intellectual and not his instinctive preoccupation with problems of the heart. The vacuity of Rudin's
utterances about love—which reflects in a more sophisticated form the
Byronic 'coldness' of Onegin—is illustrated by his remarks to Natal'ya
after Lezhnyov has already depicted him as an emotional philanderer.
The past of which he dare not speak, his heart that has already grown
cold in the experience of living—these are facets of the pose; but he
has another motive to offer:

'. . . I expect much, but not for myself. . . . I shall never abandon active work,
the bliss of activity, but I have already rejected personal enjoyment. My hopes
and my dreams, on the one hand—and my personal happiness, on the other—
have nothing in common. Love (at this he shrugged his shoulders) . . . love is
not for me; I . . . do not deserve it; a woman has the right to demand everything
of a man, but I am no longer capable of surrendering myself entirely.'

This, as it transpires, is to be taken as a singularly truthful admission, although Natal'ya can do no more than regard it as a call for altruistic self-sacrifice, adding more fuel to the romantic fervour which Rudin's words have already kindled in her. It is just this that Rudin fails to perceive. He can go on to talk glibly about the vocation of women, about Natal'ya's feelings and the happiness which she can anticipate from Sergey Volyntsev, insensible to the real nature of her emotions. Then, when Natal'ya rounds on him with the reproachful: 'You understand everything, then you ought to understand me!', it is almost as if he had talked himself into a sudden realization of the fact that he can no longer 'deceive' her and that—possibly for the first time in his life—he has to acknowledge the profundity of emotions that words alone cannot express.

Pigasov obliquely emphasizes this basic weakness in Rudin's nature when he speaks of the difference between the bob-tailed and the long-tailed: a contrast in types which foreshadows Turgenev's study of the contrast between Hamlet and Don Quixote. Rudin must be taken as belonging to the bob-tailed variety, whose weakness is a lack of self-assurance. Indeed, the outcome of Rudin's sudden, ill-considered decision to declare his love to Natal'ya is clearly suggested by Pigasov's remarks, as it had been suggested earlier in Lezhnyov's condemnation of him. Moreover, once his love is declared, he has to bolster his feeling of inadequacy by at once informing his rival, Sergey Volyntsev, of the fact, though the latter can scarcely be expected to understand the exalted sense of propriety which prompted Rudin to make such a confession. The result is to pillory Rudin, to strip him of all his previously assumed grandeur; and it is just this that Turgenev does in the way he describes Rudin before the last meeting with Natal'ya at the Avdyukhin pond:

Rudin, intelligent, perspicacious Rudin, was not in any condition to say truthfully whether he loved Natal'ya, whether he was suffering or would suffer when he parted from her. Why then, without pretending to be a Lovelace—we must do him that much justice—did he deliberately turn the poor girl's head? Why did he wait for her with secret anxiety? There is only one answer: no one is as easily carried away by his emotions as a dispassionate man.

It is not surprising, therefore, that Rudin cannot meet the test which Natal'ya has to offer him. Yet the test is a supremely personal one and it lays bare the central thesis of Turgenev's philosophy of life: whether man has any right to personal happiness in defiance of the impersonal destiny which makes him no more than a creature of a single day, born yesterday and already dead tomorrow. Such happiness is what Rudin had unwisely anticipated in declaring his love to Natal'ya, but he is quick to realize that the hope was futile, that circumstances—whether his own weakness of will, his poverty, Dar'ya Lasunskaya's displeasure, the fact of fate itself—must oblige him to submit to a destiny that precludes him from enjoying such happiness. In this respect, Rudin may be taken as expressing a specifically Turgenevan attitude that is largely divorced from the other issues with which he is connected, so that when Natal'ya attacks him for failing to offer any advice except: 'Submit' she is mistaking the personal or Turgenevan aspect of Rudin for the Rudin who had previously extolled the virtue of freedom and self-sacrifice in the name of an ideal. Rudin certainly remains true to these principles of his, as his words to Basistov on leaving Dar'ya Lasunskaya's house, the conversation between Rudin and Lezhnyov in the Epilogue and his death on the Paris barricades reveal. It is personal happiness which is foredoomed; other happiness, achieved in altruistic endeavour, may be conceivable, although such happiness can never be as complete and secure as the happiness of a requited love.

Natal'ya is not compromised by the *malaise* of will, the essential futility, which foredooms Rudin to the act of submission at this final meeting. She had come to him eager for self-sacrifice, ready to leave her home and anxious to believe in him, but his only reaction had been to give in at once as soon as he learned that their relationship was known to her mother. Natal'ya has every right to pronounce judgement on Rudin for his faint-heartedness at such a moment, but it is in this very respect that the hero and heroine are presented as basically incompatible, as head and heart divided by different motives and intentions. It is Rudin's lack, not of understanding as such, but of emotional understanding, emotional response and emotional instinct —of heart, in other words—which divides him from Natal'ya. There is no denying that the possibility of happiness was there, as Rudin remarks in his letter to Natal'ya: 'Our lives could have been joined—and now they will never be united.' It is his 'strange, almost comic fate' which prevents him from facing up to the right decision at the right time. But, like all Hamlets in Turgenev's fiction, Rudin knows his own weakness, his emotional fallibility, and his advice to Natal'ya is always to follow the instincts of her heart, though he admits that it is advice which refers more to him than to her. The real tragedy of their relationship is summarized in a sentence towards the end of the letter: 'If only I had at least offered my love as a sacrifice to my future task, my vocation; but I was simply frightened of the responsibility laid upon me and so I proved myself unworthy of you.' If, in other words, he had said 'yes', then personal happiness could have been united with the altruistic notion of service to his country of which he had spoken so eloquently earlier and which had appealed so strongly to the zeal for self-dedication in Natal'ya's nature.

The irony, and the tragedy, of this situation is underlined by Turgenev through the overlapping of the time-sequence of the novel at this point. It must be assumed that Rudin writes his letter of re-nunciation and farewell at the same time at Lezhnyov makes his proposal of marriage to Aleksandra Lipina (end of Chapter X and Chapter XI). This device emphasizes the contrasting destinies, the contrasting resolutions of the problem of personal happiness, which are exemplified by these two figures: Lezhnyov in marital happiness, Rudin in becoming 'an eternal wanderer'. It is a contrast that Turgenev is to use again (particularly in *Fathers and Children*), with the bias always in favour of the marital happiness, although it is always the renunciation of such happiness which is the more inevitable of the two choices for the hero.

The youth of the heroine and the maturity of the hero may make it seem that in both *Rudin* and *A Nest of the Gentry* the incompatibility is one between different generations. However, the relationship is more subtly grounded than this in both cases. A difference in age there most certainly is, but the essence of the relationship lies in the mutual need which the one has for the other, the lack of which makes both of them incomplete. Natal'ya's innocence needs the experience of Rudin, whereas Rudin's intellect needs the emotional enthusiasm of Natal'ya. Without this Rudin will remain 'unmade', as he puts it, incomplete, his potentialities and talents unrealized to the full, and Natal'ya will remain similarly incomplete as a person whose zeal for service is left untapped. An equivalent need, despite the marked difference in age, is felt between Lavretsky and Liza. To both heroines the heroes may be in the nature of father-figures, loved as much out of a desire to find father-substitutes as for any intrinsic attraction they may possess: it is not difficult to recognize in this a Freudian off-shoot of Turgenev's unhappy, complex and neurotic nature. But to explain it in Freudian terms—or any other non-literary terms, for that matter—is to shed light on the author's attitude to his fiction though not on the significance of the fiction itself. The mutual need of hero and heroine must be understood as one of self-fulfilment, self-completion, supposedly to be attained in the happiness of a requited love, though in fact—as all Turgenev's studies ultimately reveal—such fulfilment is an impossibility, the love is always guilty and, in part, illicit. To express this Turgenev has resorted to the idea of 'fate'. Man, in Turgenev's view of things, is 'fated' never to complete himself, never to attain full realization of himself and his potentialities; and this applies equally to hero and heroine.

The guilty nature of personal happiness is illustrated in Liza in *A Nest of the Gentry*, whereas the more affirmative view is offered by the hero. Liza's is a unique and remarkable portrait in Turgenev's gallery of heroines. Her mixture of candour and deep feeling, of lucidity and superstition, of lyrical youthfulness and earnest religious devotion is the novel's poetry, so carefully blended that her image calls to mind not a face or a voice but the nostalgic residue of a love song or the compact and exactly phrased lines of an immaculate sonnet. The elusive quality of this portrait is due chiefly to Turgenev's supremely light but precise touch, which sketches the outline but never shades in the portrait unduly, and to the fact that her character is illuminated from different points of view—by Lavretsky himself, whose view of her alters as his feeling for her increases, subtly enriching and enhancing the lustre which her image sheds through the pages of the novel; by Marfa Timofeyevna who sees her with the sensitive yet scrupulous eye of an older generation, bound to her by a blood relationship; and by Lemm, whose love of music evokes the mysterious and lyrical enchantment of her nature. For all these characters Liza represents a kind of personal fulfilment, a precious salvation—for Marfa Timofeyevna because she seems to regard her almost as her own daughter; for Lemm because his love for her is equated with, and expressed by, his love of music; for Lavretsky because she is for him, despite the distant kinship, a symbol of the Russia to which he has returned for succour and re-dedication after the wilderness of his earlier years. Yet Liza herself is impervious to these emotional needs, unmoved, almost impersonal, wrapped with a dedicated absorption in her nun-like calm. Her devotion was to God alone, we are told, under the influence of the devout peasant woman, Agaf'ya, and there is a streak of the mystical in her nature which prevents her from accepting any but a divinely-given happiness. Resignation or submission to fate is not for her a matter of the moment, but a deeply ingrained conviction which pervades her view of life.

When she questions Lavretsky about his wife, it is on his guilt that she insists at first, as one who has violated a divine law in breaking the bonds of his marriage (Chapter XXIV). He must ask forgiveness of his wife, in her opinion, and Lavretsky is justifiably annoyed at such a suggestion, but to Liza he has no option: 'One must submit to fate ...' 'If we do not submit to fate ...' she goes on and the sentence remains unfinished, to be completed only when her relationship with Lavretsky ends in the return of Varvara Pavlovna. For her religious view is deeply pessimistic, as she explains to Lavretsky when they discuss the topic on the next occasion (Chapter XXVI): 'One must be a Christian not in order to perceive the divine or the earthly, but because every man must die.' Lavretsky resolutely opposes the fatalism of this view. He reiterates Rudin's advice to follow the dictates of the heart (Chapter XXIX):

> 'Be obedient to your heart; it alone will tell you the truth,' Lavretsky interrupted her. 'Experience, reason—all that is dust and vanity. Do not deprive yourself of the best, the only happiness on earth.'

But this is where Liza cannot agree, since in her view 'happiness on earth does not depend on us'. Lavretsky, speaking from experience, insists that such happiness can only depend on oneself, on the instinctive appeal of the heart and not on any feeling of duty or sense of renunciation. But the bold affirmation of these words is soon to be disproved. Even when Lavretsky has finally confessed his love to her, Liza can only remark that 'it is all in God's hands'—and this is a God not of charity, but the God of an avenging fate, a wrathful Jehovah, who will inevitably strike down those who have dared to seize a chance of the happiness that he jealously withholds from them until death.

The tone of Lavretsky's soliloquy after the return of his wife (Chapter XLI) shows the extent to which he has now come to accept Liza's view. His earlier affirmation now presents itself to him as an illusion, as a self-indulgent yearning for a happiness which no man, not even the peasant who has no choice but to be contented with his fate, can ever hope to attain. Everything depends on the luck of the roulette wheel. But though he may accept Liza's view, he still does not realize the stern morality in which her view is grounded. To her their happiness was guilty and punishment must come sooner or later. In fact, it has come sooner, as she tells him when they meet in Marfa

Timofeyevna's room, and she is able to prove her dictum that 'happiness does not depend on us, but on God'—or, in other words, that man is never 'fated' to enjoy temporal happiness and that the mutual self-fulfilment which the relationship offered is impossible. The final poignant irony, of course, is that Liza does not realize the extent to which she loves Lavretsky until the return of Varvara Pavlovna, and personal acquaintanceship with her, has exhibited to her the justice of Lavretsky's censure and his own moral superiority. When she speaks to Marfa Timofeyevna for the last time, she admits that she had had hopes of happiness, but she is still unable to overcome the sense of guilt, of her own personal sin, which had accompanied her feelings for Lavretsky; though it is no longer a feeling of guilt exclusively for herself, but for her father and the way he made his money, for the whole social milieu to which she belongs, and in this it reflects that rejection of the gentry and its 'nest' which is to be increasingly Turgenev's concern in his two subsequent novels.

The poetical blandishments of Turgenev's fiction, the finely wrought love-stories and the prevalent note of youth are the slenderest of outer coverings for a philosophy of life which denies life itself and has much in common with a death-wish. None of his novels expresses more powerfully and more uncompromisingly the pessimistic futility of his vision of the world than *On the Eve*. Yet this is a novel which in its outward proclamation of national freedom and a revolutionary ideal is certainly more optimistic than either *Rudin* or *A Nest of the Gentry*. The key to this paradox is to be found in the way that Turgenev intentionally divorces the personal from the social, the individual from the ideological in his novels, balancing the one against the other in opposing poles of optimism and pessimism. The more optimistic the ideological tone of his work, the more pessimistic is the individual view of destiny: it is this, above all else, which is illustrated by *On the Eve*. Moreover, it is in his examination of the problem of human happiness that a continuity of thought is apparent which is not so readily discernible in his examination of the ideological problems of his time. Thus the musings of Lavretsky in the Epilogue of *A Nest of the Gentry* show the way directly to Bersenev's opinions on the nature of happiness as they are expressed by him in his conversation with Shubin at the beginning of *On the Eve*, despite the fact that these are two different generations speaking. Still more striking as an example of this continuity of thought is the similarity between the sense of guilt at her personal happiness experienced by Liza and the sense of guilt which

Yelena experiences at the end of *On the Eve*, although more than a decade (1842-1854) and new historical circumstances and new ideas must be assumed to separate them.

Yelena, like Liza, brings with her into the novel a heritage of early religious experience. Her childhood friend, Katya, first inspired in her the idea of living in 'the freedom of God'. Yelena's instinctive sense of dissatisfaction and rebellion stems from this vision of escape suggested to her by Katya. Here, despite the unduly sentimental quality of Yelena's portrait, is an expectant optimism, a youthful zest and a craving for love which are more affirmative and purposeful than were the equivalent aspects of Liza's character. But 'the freedom of God' is an illusory ideal. Increasingly, as the novel progresses, the ideal of freedom is shown to be compromised by a God who is far from merciful, a God who finally avenges the sin of happiness as devastatingly as did Liza's God in *A Nest of the Gentry*. When Shubin is speaking about himself as an artist to Yelena (Chapter IX), he mentions the idea that people like him are God-forsaken or 'crushed by God' and so have no choice but to submit. Yelena appears to him to be quite a different sort of person and it is for this reason that he is ready to admire her and is prepared to admit that he had previously misjudged her character. But the God who seemingly oppresses him is the same God who oppresses Yelena and finally reduces even the noblest of human aspirations to dust and ashes.

Shubin may discern this fact—the contrasting statues of Insarov, the 'national liberator', on the one hand, and the butting ram, on the other, reveal the extent to which Shubin can maliciously describe the nobility of Insarov as a social ideal while at the same time representing his all-too-human insignificance—but this fact has not the personal meaning for him that it has for Yelena. In the same sense, Shubin may represent the idea of mutual self-fulfilment in his statue depicting his own emaciated face beside the concupiscent features of Annushka, but he has done no more than represent the idea. He has not had the living experience of it, just as he has not been able to understand Yelena fully. Like a commentator, Shubin is able only to underline the idea that Turgenev is attempting to examine in the relationship between Yelena and Insarov—the idea, that is to say, of mutual self-fulfilment. For behind all Turgenev's thought on the contrasting natures of Hamlet and Don Quixote there lies the idea that man can only fulfil himself by uniting in himself these twin poles of human nature, just as the core of the ideological problem in *On the Eve* is the need to discover the unifying words which will unite men in altruistic self-sacrifice. On the personal plane, for Yelena, as for Insarov, their relationship is represented as a process of unification, of the one fulfilling the other, although it is only for Yelena, as the central character in the fiction, that this idea is given particular meaning. And in Yelena's case her love for Insarov is always compromised by a feeling of guilt at the idea that it might be a self-indulgence.

The extracts from Yelena's diary reveal the personal nature of her dilemma. Because she does not feel the affection for her parents that she thinks she ought to feel, she regards herself as being

. . . a great sinner; perhaps this is why I'm so sad, why I have no peace. Some hand rests on me and oppresses me. Just as if I were in prison and the walls were about to fall in on me. Why is it that other people don't feel this?

The sense of personal guilt is already there, then, before she meets Insarov. It may be interpreted as a feeling of guilt at the social milieu in which she has been brought up, as was Liza's, but it is also closely associated with her feelings for Insarov. Contentment and peace of mind come to her after she has known him for a while; yet as soon as she realizes that she loves him, she at once invokes God's pity on herself for daring to write such a 'fateful' word as 'love' in the last entry in her diary. A similar fear of such self-indulgent emotion is expressed by Insarov, as Bersenev informs her on the same day that she makes this last entry in her diary: he did not want 'for the satisfaction of his personal feelings to betray his cause and his duty'. So he has gone away. The inevitable accompaniment of the disharmony wrought in her nature by her love for Insarov is fever and panic. Turgenev dwells uncompromisingly on the hours of torment she spends before she goes out into the thundery rain to meet Insarov and he embellishes the meeting with an unnecessarily pretentious symbolism, both in the portentous remarks of the old beggar-woman and in the fact that their love is consecrated in the wayside shrine, so that Yelena may indeed now be, as Insarov expresses it, 'my wife before men and before God'. Yet this is a God who proposes and disposes at will, more often the latter. Their love and their hope of mutual self-fulfilment in their happiness are at the mercy of this God—'Let God punish me if I'm doing wrong!' Insarov exclaims at the same moment that he proclaims that they are now 'united for ever' (Chapter XXIII). And it would seem that their happiness is to be particularly short-lived, for within a day or so Insarov is already in the grip of an illness

IT

that is, in fact, to undermine his health and is to contribute to his
death at the end of the novel. Although he recovers on this occasion,
the way their relationship has been imperilled emphasises the close
identity of love and death in Turgenev's view of the world (reflecting,
incidentally, what Shubin and Bersenev have to say of this problem in
Chapter I) and also illustrates the extent to which their happiness is
guilty. When they meet for the first time after his illness, Insarov says:

'Tell me, has it occurred to you that this illness was sent as a punishment
to us?'
Yelena looked at him seriously.
'That thought had occurred to me, Dmitry. But I had thought: what can I
be punished for? What duty have I violated, what have I sinned against?
Perhaps I have a conscience different from other people's, but it was silent;
or perhaps I'm guilty before you?—I'll be getting in your way, I'll be stopping
you. . . .'
'You won't stop me, Yelena, we'll go together.'
'Yes, Dmitry, we'll go together, I'll go with you. . . . That's my duty. I
love you. . . . I have no other duty.'
'Oh, Yelena!' Insarov said: 'What unbreakable chains every word you say
puts on me!'
'Why talk about chains?' she exclaimed. 'You and I are free people.'

But essentially they are not free people although they may appear to
have taken their destiny into their own hands. At this moment it may
seem to Yelena that their happiness, their identity, their mutual self-
fulfilment as human beings has been achieved, but the bond which
unites them is extremely slender. Despite the fact that Yelena in her
love for Insarov regards the emotion not as a self-indulgence but as a
duty which involves the sacrifice of her home and her country, the
projected happiness of their relationship is compromised at the outset
by the enfeebled state of Insarov after his illness and is finally doomed
irrevocably.

The pessimism of Turgenev may be too unremitting for contemporary tastes, too 'Slav' possibly (whatever that all-too-fashionable
cliché-term may mean), but it is not sentimental. It is an outcry
against the apparent irrationality and injustice of human existence.
When Yelena is ultimately driven to reproach God for failing to make
happiness more than an accident of human existence, it is Turgenev
who is speaking:

'Oh, God!' Yelena thought, 'why is there death? Why partings and sickness
and tears? Or why is there this beauty, this sweet feeling of hope, why the

comforting sense of a sure refuge, of some safe defence, of immortal protection? What is the meaning of this smiling, beneficent sky, this happy, peaceful earth? Can it be that everything is only inside us, while outside us there is an eternal cold, an eternal silence? Is it that we are all alone, isolated —while everywhere out there, in all those unplumbed abysses and deeps, it is all strange to us? Then why this thirst for prayer and its joy? ("*Morir si giovane*" resounded in her soul). . . . Can it be possible to pray for the past, to retrieve it, to save it. . . . Oh, God! Is it impossible to believe in miracles?' She rested her head on her clenched fists. 'Is it all finished?' she whispered. 'Can it all be finished already? I have been happy not only for minutes, or hours, or whole days, but for weeks at a time. And by what right?' She began to be frightened of her happiness. 'And what if happiness is impossible?' she thought. 'What if happiness is not given freely? Then happiness was heaven, but we were only mortals, poor, sinning mortals . . . *Morir si giovane*. . . . Oh, away, dark death! It is not only for my sake that he must live!'

'But what if this is a punishment,' she thought again: 'What if we must pay in full for our guilt? My conscience was quiet, it is quiet now, but is that proof of my innocence? Oh, God, can we be such criminals! Can you, who created this night and this sky, want to punish us because we loved each other? And if so, if he is guilty and I am guilty,' she added in a sudden fury, 'then, O God, grant that he, that both of us, should at least die an honourable, glorious death— out there, in the fields of his native country, and not here in this dead room.'

But the destiny of Yelena and Insarov is not heroic; it is tragic. In Turgenev's philosophy just as the harmony of nature is upset by such an emotion as love, so happiness is only to be attained at the expense of another's unhappiness—an idea which Dostoyevsky is to repeat in substantially the same form in his Pushkin speech. Yet this is not the essence of the tragedy, nor is it the essence of the guilt which Yelena feels. The tragedy is not the outcome of any incompatibility between Yelena and Insarov, but the result of Turgenev's tragic view of human life. After Insarov's death, Yelena feels that:

There were no reproaches in her heart; she did not dare to ask of God why he had not had mercy, why he had not had pity on them, why he had not protected them, why he had punished them more than their guilt deserved, if indeed there had been any guilt? Each one of us is guilty by virtue of the very fact that we are alive, and there is not a single great thinker or a single benefactor of humanity who, on the strength of the good he has done, can ever hope that he has the right to live. . . .

This idea points at once to the tragic aspect of Bazarov's portrait in *Fathers and Children*. It reveals the continuity of Turgenev's thought on the nature of human life, just as the final words in Yelena's letter to her mother express the idea of the death-wish:

> Fate did not unite us in vain: who knows, perhaps I killed him; now it is his turn to draw me after him. I have looked for happiness—and I will probably find death. It seems that's as it should be; it seems that there was guilt. . . . But death covers everything over and reconciles everything, isn't that so?

As Yelena realized in her delirious dream, as she travels with her girlhood friend, Katya, and falls into the abyss, only to hear Insarov's voice cry out to her, the notion of 'the freedom of God' is an illusion in the face of death. This is the meaning of the dream to her. Afterwards she cannot pray; it remains for her only to acknowledge the force of the death-wish and to accept the notion, here so clearly expressed in Turgenev's own terms, that:

> Death is like a fisherman who has caught a fish in his net and leaves it for a time in the water: the fish still swims about, but the net surrounds it, and the fisherman will take it when he wishes.

Although the tone is remotely biblical, there is no suggestion of a Christian ethic here. It is not Christ who fishes for men in Turgenev's world, but death. Death as a reconciliation of the problem of self-fulfilment is the last message of On the Eve, as it is to be an underlying assumption throughout the portrayal of Bazarov in Fathers and Children (once, that is to say, he has met Odintsova). In other words, life can offer a possibility of mutual self-fulfilment through love in the relationship between a man and a woman, but the happiness of such fulfilment comes too close to the divine for it to be countenanced in earthly terms. It is not a feature of human destiny to experience such happiness except as fire accidentally stolen from the gods or as a particle of divine bliss that is naturally accompanied by a feeling of guilt at having usurped more than humanity is permitted to experience. Death alone offers the true possibility of reconciliation; and it is here that the death-wish has its part to play. In effect, Turgenev's thought at this point comes very close to—precedes, in fact—Dostoyevsky's thought on the question of the man-God (it is significant that, with the exception of Botkin, only Dostoyevsky should have understood what Turgenev was trying to say in Fathers and Children[1]), despite the fact that Turgenev's thought is both more limited and more pessimistic.

[1] See Turgenev's letter to Dostoyevsky, 30/18 March 1862. Sobr. soch. (1958), xii. 334-5. Also letter to K. K. Sluchevsky, 26/14 April 1862.

Turgenev had perceived just as clearly as Dostoyevsky was to perceive later that man's aspiration to attain a heroic self-sufficiency involves the usurpation of a right which is not a part of human destiny. It is the usurpation of a divine right, a manifestation of diabolical arrogance, a symptom of the nihilism of the age. In *Fathers and Children* Turgenev alters the emphasis in his study of human nature by concentrating less on the problem of mutual self-fulfilment in the relationship of hero and heroine and more on the idea of man, the usurper of a divine right, whose arrogant self-will proclaims for itself a self-sufficiency in life which contravenes the limits of human experience and gives rise to a dilemma that is only to be resolved in death.

The process of self-realization begins in Bazarov's case after his meeting with Odintsova. Previously his dislike of romanticism and sentimentality had led him to dismiss any suggestion that there could be anything 'mysterious' about the relationship between a man and a woman (his condemnation, for instance, of Pavel Petrovich in Chapter VII), or that any special importance should be attached to differences between individuals. Yet he is soon to realize that his relationship with Odintsova has revealed to him the romantic in his own nature. In fact, it is this aspect of the relationship which is most important: it is not mutual self-fulfilment, but self-realization that his relationship with Odintsova has to offer him. Odintsova herself admits as much in one of their final conversations (Chapter XXVI), when she says: 'We did not need each other, that's the main point; in us there was too much that . . . how can I put it? . . . that was too much the same.' At the beginning of the relationship they did not realize this, but Turgenev makes it clear that Odintsova did not really desire any more than she had already, although she may have thought she did, and that it was only curiosity which prompted her to take an interest in her outspoken and opinionated guest. For Bazarov's part, he is drawn to her because her aristocratic beauty and coldness are a source of fascination to him, although in social origin and in temperament she has much in common with him. The common factors between them, therefore, preclude the 'need' of self-fulfilment in their relationship, but provide a basis for expanding upon the superior individual qualities of Bazarov.

To the extent that he had been indifferent to the importance of individuality, Bazarov had never really imputed an importance to himself as an individual, despite the fact that he had clearly felt himself superior to other representatives of the younger generation, such as

Sitnikov and Kukshina. In the first extended conversation that he has with Odintsova (Chapter XVII), the contrast between them is made clear: he knows the extent to which his feeling for her has changed and he knows equally well, as he tells her, that she is incapable of reciprocating his feelings—'You want to fall in love, but you can't: that's your misfortune.' Here it is as if the roles of Rudin and Natal'ya had been reversed, except that Bazarov is far more percipient than ever Rudin was. But the climax of the conversation is concerned with the perennial question of the difference between altruism and egoism. Odintsova asks:

'Then you think it's easy to surrender oneself to something completely?'

'It's not easy if you start thinking about it, start prevaricating, start reckoning your own worth, start thinking much of yourself, that is; but if you don't think about it it's easy to surrender oneself.'

'How can one fail to think a lot of oneself? If I haven't any worth, who'd want my devotion?'

'That's not my business; it's for the other person to decide how much I'm worth. The chief thing is to know how to surrender oneself.'

Here Bazarov repeats an adage more suited to the lips of a Bersenev —as he admits a sentence later, this sort of thing is not 'in his line'— but, however uncharacteristic the remark may be, it reveals that he has not yet 'thought about' the importance of his own personality. When Odintsova immediately asks him whether he thinks he can surrender himself, he replies noncommitally: 'I don't know, I don't want to boast.' It is an answer, however, which suggests that he is not entirely unaware of his own superiority.

Odintsova has already paraded many of her Hamlet-like qualities before him, and Bazarov has reciprocated with staunchly Quixotic singleness of mind. In their second conversation, when the relationship is much closer (Chapter XVIII) and is to be climaxed by Bazarov's profession of his love, Odintsova begins by offering the Hamlet-like view of happiness:

'Tell me, why is it that when we are enjoying music, for instance, a fine evening, conversation with sympathetic people, it all seems to be more an intimation of some measureless happiness existing somewhere else and not real happiness—that is, the happiness we possess ourselves? Why is this?'

—and Bazarov's reply, in characteristically Quixotic manner, is to deny that such thoughts ever enter his head. Immediately following this, in just the same way as Shubin noticed the superiority of Yelena,

Odintsova begins to suggest to Bazarov that he is a superior individual. How then, she asks, can he be content with becoming a provincial doctor? Bazarov's simple answer at this point is that the future, for the most part, does not depend on us but that, should an opportunity present itself, he will do something useful. He is simply not interested in what is 'going on' inside him. Again, therefore, Bazarov rejects the idea that his own personality has any special importance. In fact, what is 'going on' inside him drives him finally, with unequivocal directness, to blurt out his profession of love in a mixture of passion and anger—and it is this moment which not only conclusively reveals the predominantly Quixotic element in his nature but also constitutes an admission of the fact that he has had to acknowledge the importance of his own feelings. From this moment Bazarov is compromised, as are all previous Turgenevan heroes, by a realization of the self-importance which results from being made aware of his own feelings; from this moment traits of Hamlet, illustrated by his increasing in reflection and speculation about himself, become discernible beneath the Quixotic façade.

The most important outcome of the relationship, however, is the fact that it reveals the superiority of Bazarov as an individual. Odintsova has failed him, as Rudin failed Natal'ya. The difference is that there was no 'need' of mutual self-fulfilment between them: Bazarov's superiority was an assumption of the relationship from the beginning. But now that the superiority is proved, Bazarov cannot help but attach greater importance to his own personality; and this is at once made apparent with the sudden arrival of Sitnikov. If Bazarov had previously been indifferent to his own superiority vis-à-vis other representatives of the younger generation, Sitnikov's arrival now leaves him in no doubt about his superior position. Speaking to Arkady, he says:

'You, my boy, are as stupid as ever, I see. Sitnikovs are essential to us. I need, don't you see?—I need such oafs. It's not for the gods to bake the pots!'
'Well!' Arkady thought to himself, and then for the first time the bottomless abyss of Bazarov's self-importance was revealed to him in an instant. 'You and I, it seems, are the gods? That is, you're the god, while I suppose I'm the oaf?'

Arkady's thought simply underlines the new importance of Bazarov. Bazarov is not only exceptional in Turgenevan terms, as a hero who can wilfully reject feminine society—he says as much a little later to Arkady, after they have left Odintsova's estate—but exceptional also in human terms. A man must be untamed, he claims, quoting a

Spanish proverb. The notion of self-will has its seeds here. But a man who believes in nothing except the natural sciences, who accepts no authority, must go one stage further; he must proclaim himself as God. Bazarov, the nihilist, has no belief beyond himself, no will greater than his own, and in this self-sufficiency he exhibits that 'bottomless abyss' of arrogance and self-will which is characteristic of the man-God.

In the eyes of his elderly parents—among Turgenev's most perfect creations—Bazarov is unquestionably a superior being. Their adulation of him subtly sets in perspective his own human insignificance. Chapter XXI, the most interesting chapter in the novel, illustrates—as Shubin's two statues illustrated the dual aspect of Insarov—the difference between the great future which can be expected for a man of Bazarov's calibre and the unimportance of the man himself in relation to nature and eternity. Arkady extols Bazarov's greatness, to his father's unconcealed pleasure and delight, but in the midday sun Bazarov's own view of himself pales into insignificance. He is now fatally tainted with the weakness of all Hamlets: a preoccupation with self. It is now that he sees himself, regardless of his own superiority, as man, the creature of a single day:

'The little spot I occupy is so tiny in comparison with the rest of space, where I am not and where no one is concerned with me; and the amount of time which I shall succeed in living is so insignificant in comparison with eternity, where I haven't been and I won't be.... But in this atom, this mathematical point, the blood circulates, the brain functions and desires something...'

Of course, it is nonsense for him to think such thoughts, and he realizes this, but unlike his parents he has reached the point where he is aware of his personal insignificance. His is the dilemma of the man who, though he may know his human insignificance, can still feel his own self-importance. The difference between 'knowing' and 'feeling', between head and heart, is clearly emphasized. Bazarov *feels* himself to be a superior man—a 'real man', as he calls himself—and this feeling of superiority makes him despise the peasants, the Philips and Sidors, for whom he will have to sacrifice himself. On the other hand, he *knows* the inevitability of his own death—'the weeds will grow out of me', he says, while the peasants will live in their white-washed huts. To Arkady this is an unprincipled statement, but for Bazarov there are no principles in life, only feelings; while man's only certain knowledge is the fact of his insignificance. This conversation with Arkady reveals all the complexity of Bazarov, the mixture of Don Quixote and Hamlet, the man of feeling compromised by the knowledge of the inevitable flaw in his humanity.

Bazarov can now set out to fulfil the social task of breaking with the gentry and working among the peasants, but his personal task is the more isolated and the more painful. He deliberately turns his back on the possibility of happiness by forfeiting his relationship with Odintsova, although he is still in love with her. The contrast between his future role in life and the role of Arkady is underlined in Chapter XXVI by the simple device of juxtaposing the two relationships (Bazarov—Odintsova, Arkady—Katya). During their stroll in the garden Bazarov and Odintsova hold a post-mortem on their relationship, admitting that the passions of youth are gone forever, while Arkady, an instant after their departure, proposes to Katya. Marital bliss, the Tolstoyan ideal, offering self-realization and self-fulfilment, is what Arkady achieves, whereas for Bazarov it is a question of filling the suitcase of his life with something, no matter what, provided there is no empty space. In fact, Bazarov is now represented as a man whose individual purpose in life is already superfluous: the only 'nest' for him is death—which points the moral at the end of Rudin's Scandinavian legend. In Turgenev's philosophy there are only these two alternatives. Man can love and find fulfilment in love, as Arkady, or he can die. Bazarov, as he tells Odintsova in the last moments of his life, had 'fallen beneath the wheel'. There is no further point in thinking about the future—not even about love, the true form in life, because his own material form in life is already disintegrating. He had thought:

'I'll do a lot yet, I'll not die! There's a task to be done and I'm a giant! But now the task of the giant is—to die decently, though no one cares about that. . . .'

This is the personal task, common to all men in the frailty of their humanity, which Bazarov has to face. Here the social significance of Bazarov is finally superseded by the more universal issue of his tragic destiny as a man who has no choice in life except to die. He knows that he is no longer 'needed' in life:

'I am needed by Russia. . . . No, obviously I'm not needed. And who is needed? The shoemaker's needed, the tailor's needed, the butcher . . . he sells meat . . . butcher . . . stop, I'm losing my way . . . there's a forest here . . .'

He is man, the single creature, born yesterday and dead tomorrow, menaced at all times by impassive nature and the surrounding darkness.

His last word is 'darkness', reflecting the idea of man as the sole re-
ceptacle of spiritual life which 'eternal night constantly strives to
extinguish'.[1] He will find reconciliation only in his death and life
in the promise of eternity.

Can love, sacred, devoted love not be all-powerful? Oh, no! No matter
how passionate, sinning, rebellious is the heart hidden in the grave, the flowers
growing on it look at us serenely with their innocent faces; they speak to us
not only of that eternal peace, of that great peace of 'impassive' nature; they
speak to us also of eternal reconciliation and of life everlasting . . .

These words at the close of the novel may be taken as an epitaph
on Bazarov, the tragic hero of Turgenev's most tragic novel, but the
three dots which suggest the unspoken moral of the ending also reveal
the tragic paradox in Turgenev's thinking. Turgenev did not believe
in the possibility of 'eternal reconciliation' and 'life everlasting'. Those
who wish to believe may do so, is the silent admission of the three
dots; but for Turgenev, in his lack of religious faith, death was
corruption and annihilation, while life was to become no more than a
'tragic comedy', increasingly circumscribed by the demonic and the
supernatural, in which the human will was powerless to overcome the
forces ranged against it. Bazarov's death illustrates the inability of man
to attain that heroic self-sufficiency, the unification of Hamlet and
Don Quixote, which is his only hope of reconciliation in life. No other
Turgenevan hero is to be so convincingly real, so utterly of this
world, as Bazarov; and nothing shows more convincingly than his
death the extent to which Turgenev had plumbed the secret of life
only to discover its—to him—essential meaninglessness.

THE ACHIEVEMENT

Turgenev's achievement in these first four novels is to be measured
in literary terms by the fact that before their appearance during the
six-year period 1856-1862 there was no tradition of the novel in
Russian literature; while after their appearance there could be no other
tradition except that of the novel. Turgenev raised the art of the novel
to an eminence surpassing all other genres; it was in the nature of
things that the novel should have pride of place in the future.

Before Turgenev wrote these four novels, Russian literature had

[1] See the quotation on page 44.

seen the appearance of several isolated works which could, both in formal terms and in point of literary merit, be described as novels— *Eugene Onegin*, *A Hero of Our Time*, *Dead Souls*, *Who is Guilty?*, *An Ordinary Story*,[1] to name the only outstanding examples—but these could not be taken as representing a tradition. They were the first stages, necessarily hesitant and experimental, in the forging of what was later to be the tradition of the Russian realistic novel, though in essence these novels were amalgams of other traditions, such as the poetic narrative, the *conte* and *Novelle*, which had been developed to a significant degree of technical perfection in Russian literature before the middle of the century. Turgenev's contribution to the establishment of a tradition of the novel was twofold: firstly, in enlarging the short-story form into the form of the novel, and, secondly, in elaborating his own form of novel into a distinctive work of literary art. The only other writer to achieve anything like a similar mastery of the new genre was Goncharov with his *Oblomov* (1859), yet Goncharov's work has none of the formal perfection and technical accomplishment of Turgenev's novels. Similarly, although Tolstoy had written his semi-autobiographical trilogy, *Childhood*, *Boyhood* and *Youth* in the fifties and Dostoyevsky published his first novel, *The Insulted and Injured*, after his return from exile in 1861, these two works are either not, strictly speaking, novels—as in the case of Tolstoy's work—or, if novels, are artistically clumsy by any standards. It is only Goncharov who challenges Turgenev in the novel at this time, and he did not possess the gift of composition or the ability to assimilate and condense the properties of his fiction into a compact and artistically harmonious form, which is the special mark of Turgenev's genius.[2] One may criticize Goncharov for a certain clumsiness or formlessness, but one could never level such a criticism at Turgenev. In the technical sense, therefore, Turgenev's novels can be said to show the way to future developments, and the success of his endeavour lay in the extent to which he was able to promote a tradition in the novel that did not hamstring those who came after him.

[1] These works are by Pushkin, Lermontov, Gogol, Herzen, and Goncharov respectively.

[2] Mention may be made of two lesser-known writers, Pisemsky and Pomyalovsky, who were prominent at the time. In 1858 A. F. Pisemsky (1820-1881) published his novel *A Thousand Souls*, a vivid, documentary account of country life, reminiscent of Gogol's *Dead Souls*, while in 1861 N. G. Pomyalovsky (1835-1863) published two shorter works, *Bourgeois Happiness* and *Molotov*, which deal with the emergence of the new social type, the *raznochinets*. Although both writers are of interest for students of Russian literature, their novels are markedly inferior to Turgenev's.

The relatively small scale of his novels was a guarantee, in effect, that his total achievement in these first four novels would not desiccate the literary field for subsequent developments in the genre. This becomes all the more apparent when one realizes that his concern was not grandeur of scheme but delicacy of proportion. By being aware of his own limitations as a writer and of the limitations which artistic propriety demanded in the kind of novel which he had chosen, he was able to infuse the novel as a genre with a special freshness and original appeal that were very far from exhausting its potentialities. He was conscious throughout of the lack of a tradition and the need for it. This is one of the reasons why his novels have a formal conservatism about them, being composed so often of the same literary properties which undergo variations but which are not noticeably altered from one work to another. But in the final estimate such orthodoxy and restraint were less a conservatism than a means of reinvigorating and giving enduring shape to that hydra-headed, chameleon-like creature, the realistic novel.

Turgenev took his example from Pushkin and specifically from Pushkin's *Eugene Onegin*. Pushkin's 'novel in verse' is composed of narrative and commentary. The narrative has the form of a love-story, universal in its tragic implications but of specific social significance in its relation to the Russian scene, while the commentary is realistic and topical. Turgenev adopted the same method. His novels are constructed of these same elements, though more closely fused together, so that the commentary is not presented as a separate component of the fiction but as an integral part of the composition, related by one means or another to the love-story and to the characterization of the central figure. Structurally Turgenev elaborated and perfected the formal scheme which he adopted from Pushkin, enriching it with his own poetic manner and transforming it into a much more forceful and pertinent medium of social expression. But the debt to Pushkin is discernible in each of his first four novels. It is this which sets Turgenev squarely in the tradition of nineteenth-century Russian literature, which in so many respects sprang from, and was in so many ways indebted to, the genius of Pushkin. In Turgenev's case the debt took the form, apart from such specific structural borrowings, of an admiration, above all, for a sense of proportion, of harmonious balance in the unifying of the different fictional elements. This sense of unity is essentially classical. Pushkin possessed it innately. But to suggest that it is necessarily an innate gift, inaccessible to others less gifted, is only partially true. Pushkin's possession of this gift enabled him both to be a continuer of the eighteenth-century classical tradition and, when romanticism had given way to more realistic trends, to apply classical forms to his realistic work. As a result, in Russian literature the classical tradition was perpetuated even into the age of realistic prose fiction, providing a formal blueprint and a sense of 'belonging' to old traditions which was clearly not the case in nineteenth-century European literatures where a sense of classical form, seriously undermined by the 'freedoms' of the romantics, had to yield increasingly before the demands of naturalism in the novel. A fact often overlooked in discussing the development of Russian literature is that classicism, in whatever form, did not exist before the middle of the eighteenth century, and when it appeared it was strange and alien to Russian thinking, to be aped in its European dress as any other European fashion. It was left to Pushkin's unique genius to assimilate it into Russian literature. The fact remains, however, that this classical tradition was always in some measure a stranger to Russian literature, in the sense that it was of Western origin and therefore only accessible to those who had been educated according to Western standards. It may be called an upper-class or gentry tradition, since it was only the upper classes who had access to the classical spirit through their knowledge of Latin and Greek and their close acquaintanceship with Western culture. It is this which identifies Turgenev so closely with Pushkin. Other prominent writers—Gogol, Lermontov, Grigorovich, Goncharov and Dostoyevsky, for instance—were either totally unaffected by it or were never steeped in it, through being more 'Russian' in background, to the extent that Pushkin and Turgenev were. The great exception is Tolstoy, whose novels have the same quality of classical objectivity, coupled with a particularly classical view of man's destiny. Tolstoy's Olympian manner owes much to Pushkin's example. And in terms of the development of the realistic novel, Turgenev stands midway between Pushkin as the progenitor of the genre and Tolstoy who took the classical inheritance a stage further by identifying it with the epic (*War and Peace*) and the tragedy (*Anna Karenina*). But Tolstoy might not have achieved his own enormous enlargement of the form of the realistic novel had Turgenev not made his contribution to the establishment of a tradition. His achievement may seem small by the side of Tolstoy's, but it was of inestimable value as a catalytic agent in precipitating the growth of the more elaborate genre.

Though Turgenev took his formula from Pushkin, his problem as a writer was how to enlarge the short-story form into what he called 'a large story' (*bol'shaya povest'*) and what we would nowadays call 'a novel'. It was a problem of a very personal nature, since Turgenev was aware both of his own limitations and, as his halting approach to the problem of the novel during the early fifties indicates, of no firm guiding tradition. The result was that he took the form of the short story, of which he was such a master, and, in order to achieve the larger form, multiplied it until it became a novel. *Rudin* graphically illustrates this process. It is a novel composed of two main events, the arrival and departure of the hero, which almost have the form of two separate stories. They are united only by the unity of place and the process of characterization. But the process of characterization involves two story elements: the love-story between Rudin and Natal'ya and the parallel story element contained in what Lezhnyov has to tell Aleksandra Lipina about Rudin's background. These elements are welded together to achieve an elaborate portrait, but it is not difficult to perceive the different elements themselves and thus to assess the extent to which this novel is a composite of lesser forms multiplied into the form of a novel. *Fathers and Children*, however, illustrates the extent to which Turgenev had succeeded in overcoming the problem of assimilating the short-story form to the form of the novel. There is one unifying element in this novel, that of the hero, and all other aspects of the fiction are unified in the process of the hero's characterization. *Fathers and Children* is an organic whole as a novel. One cannot separate it into different formal elements. By gradual stages—through *A Nest of the Gentry* and *On the Eve*—Turgenev achieved this perfection of form and as a result not only effected a transition from the short story to the novel but also established a tradition of the novel in Russian literature. It is no exaggeration to claim this. It was out of his sense of classical unity, of classical balance and harmony, that he was able to attain such perfection and there was no one among his contemporaries who could afford to overlook the achievement.

A remarkable feature of the achievement, however, is its concentrated nature. In the space of six years Turgenev was able to effect the transition and in such a way that, as the formal problems were resolved, so the artistic mastery increased. Yet the concentrated nature of Turgenev's achievement merely mirrors the concentrated nature of Russian literary development as a whole during Turgenev's lifetime, between the fifty years 1830–1880. At the beginning of the period, so far as the novel was concerned, the only extant completed work of any importance was Pushkin's *Eugene Onegin*. By the end of the period, the tradition of the Russian realistic novel had been fully established and there were to be no further significant developments in the genre during the remaining twenty years of the century. Within this period of fifty years, however, two phases are discernible: from 1830 to 1848 and from 1855 to the end of the period. The first phase is marked by the appearance of the novels by Pushkin, Lermontov, Gogol, Herzen and Goncharov which have already been mentioned. This first phase was then followed by a period of seven years—1848-1855—when no novels worthy of the name appeared. The place of Turgenev's four novels may therefore be seen as being at the beginning of the second phase, as a continuation of the development so abruptly curtailed in 1848, as an assimilation and bringing to perfection of the forms prevalent in the first phase, though at the same time as a maturing of the genre in preparation for the more elaborate developments that were to occur in the latter part of the sixties and in the seventies.

In his first four novels Turgenev showed an admirable historical sense. The distinction of these novels as realistic works lies in their historical authenticity. They are portraits not only of particular heroes, or heroines, but of particular epochs. Increasingly, however, the historical sense can be seen to give way to the political sense, the documentary manner to the polemical, observation of the past to censure of the present. This is accompanied by a gradual broadening of the bases of the novels, a diminution of the importance of the single love-story (*Rudin*), a distribution of the ideological interest (*On the Eve*), a multiplication of the love-stories and a consequent enlargement of the ideological and sociological issues (*Fathers and Children*). Yet the unity remains. It remains because the central figure remains at the centre of the novel, unifying all the different issues. Moreover, it is in the unity given to the fiction by the central figure that a balance is maintained between the ideological matter, on the one hand, and the human problem, on the other, between the ideological significance of the hero and the personal problem of his relationship with the heroine, between the rational failings of the head and the intuitive strength of the heart. The central figure thus unifies the two views of human destiny which are to be found in Turgenev's fiction, of man as the rational being who aspires to put his ideas to the service of realizable ideals and of man as the insignificant creature of a single day, at the mercy of nature and eternity. It is in this duality that the real 'realism' of Turgenev's four great novels resides. It is here that Turgenev reveals himself as the realist thinker as well as the realist novelist. Man is here represented as the only gauge of reality, its centre and its essence, whose existence is the only guarantee of truth, whose aspirations are ennobled by the very fact that they are only mortal aspirations and whose hope for the future is made tragic by the fact that there can be no hope for man beyond the reality of his own being. It is here that Turgenev's historical sense acquired philosophical depth, making his novels not only great works of art that combine the ideological and personal in a delicate harmony but revelations about the human condition which tells us truths about man that have an enduring meaning. This is the true measure of Turgenev's achievement.

A paradox exists, however, at the very centre of it. It is the paradox of the unheroic hero. None of the heroes in these first four novels is, in the true sense of the word, heroic. They are too real or too human to be heroic in the traditional sense. This is at once their incontrovertible merit and their weakness. They succeed as heroes because their merits and their shortcomings are neatly balanced so as to provide the central interest of the novels. Only in *On the Eve* does the hero fail to achieve this and his failure is counterbalanced by the emphasis placed upon the heroine. But the success of the novels as unities, as portraits, depends upon the extent to which the hero or the central figure, however paradoxically unheroic in human terms, is capable of being the heroic centre of the fiction and of maintaining the interest of the fiction from start to finish. This is the principle upon which Turgenev's novelistic method is based. During the course of the first four novels more and more emphasis came to be laid on the unifying function of the central figure as less emphasis was laid on the unifying function of the single love-story. The love-story still remained important as a means of characterizing the central figure but, as in the case of the relationship between Bazarov and Odintsova, it was no longer related so closely to the ideological matter of the novel. This centrifugal movement away from the single love-story meant that, were it not for the unifying role of the central figure, the novel was in danger of disintegrating into a number of separate themes. Moreover, if the central figure failed, the novel would suffer not only structurally but aesthetically as well. These were dangers inherent in Turgenev's method. He avoided them in his first four novels very largely because he was constantly improving his technique, constantly moving forwards, assimilating the short-story form into the form of the novel and bringing it to maturity by a process of accretion and elaboration.

But the danger remained. The years 1860-62 are a climacteric in Turgenev's career. In these years he brought the forms of both the short story and the novel to perfection. Alongside *Fathers and Children* one must place that most enchanting and brilliant of his stories, *First Love*. In both these works the inspiration is at its greatest. The vitality is there, in form and in manner, in the evocation of mood and in the depth of human understanding, in the pervasive summer warmth which can give man the illusion that happiness is possible and in a view of life that recognizes the tragic implications in it but does not overwhelm it with pessimism. During the remaining years of the sixties, however, a moody pessimism was to inform Turgenev's work which upset the balance of his former view. The disturbance of the finely balanced equilibrium was to contribute to the breakdown of the formal unity in his own kind of novel, as a study of *Smoke* will show.

6

THE NOVEL AS POLITICAL PAMPHLET

SMOKE

THE critical reception accorded to *Fathers and Children* was in itself
sufficient to bring Turgenev to the verge of despair. It was the novel,
as he wrote with laconic sarcasm in his *Literary Reminiscences*, 'by
virtue of which the favourable disposition towards me of Russia's
younger generation was ended—and ended for good, it seems'.[1]
Partly Turgenev was reaping the whirlwind. Having established
himself as a social novelist of advanced views, the champion of the
younger generation (particularly in *On the Eve*), he had—largely un-
wittingly and with the best of intentions—come to occupy a false
position on the intellectual scene, posturing as the friend of youth
while continuing to believe in his own ideals which the younger
generation of the time did not share. The whirlwind took a material
form in the political disturbances in St. Petersburg of May 1862, of
which Turgenev was a witness. He had little realized how dangerous,
politically, his Bazarov might be or the extent to which he might be
politically compromised by the critical storm which his novel aroused.
The fires and looting were simply a manifestation of the animosities
hinted at in the novel. The intellectual polemics of 1859, during the
summer of which Bazarov argues with Pavel Petrovich, were already
to have assumed a much more violent form three years later, after the
Emancipation edict of 1861. They were a prelude to an ever increasing
number of political disturbances and acts of terrorism, notably such
events at the Karakozov affair of 1866, the activities of the *Nechayevtsy*,
the breakdown of the populist movement of the seventies into the
terrorism of the *Narodnaya Volya* and the Vera Zasulich affair of 1878,
all of which found reflection in the literature of the period and all of
which were early landmarks on the long journey to the revolution of
1917.[2] But Turgenev was a genuinely peace-loving man, more so even

---

[1] *Sobr. soch.* (1956), x. 346.

[2] In 1866 a young man of radical views, Karakozov, attempted to assassinate the Tsar,
Alexander II. His attempt was a failure. The subsequent outcry led to the banning of

than his great contemporaries, Tolstoy and Dostoyevsky. No matter that this was a love of peace due in large part to the epicurean slothfulness of his nature; it was also a love of peace which, in its abhorrence of violence, exalted the peaceful, civilizing virtues of European culture and enlightenment above all the fanaticism, political terrorism and police repression which had overtaken Russia.

Apart from being attacked by Antonovich in *The Contemporary* as a traducer of the younger generation,[1] Turgenev was also attacked by the conservatives for offering too sympathetic an interpretation of the radicals in his Bazarov. Such criticism—though in a less malevolent form—could have been expected. The most unexpected attack came from an entirely different quarter and, though it was less aggressive and overtly scurrilous, it was all the more hurtful because it seemed to Turgenev to be in the nature of a betrayal. It came from Herzen, who had been Turgenev's personal friend for almost twenty years and was the acknowledged political spokesman of Turgenev's generation. To describe the attack as unexpected is not to suggest that Herzen was making a new departure, but Turgenev could reasonably have supposed that he would not have had to suffer the treachery of a Brutus in addition to the other wounding assaults.

Herzen, immediately after the failure of the 1848 revolution, had changed his mind about the West. During the whole of the fifties his publicistic work had betrayed increasing signs of a vaguely romantic delusion, based on the assumption that the West was no longer the cradle of revolution, that the ideals of 1789 had become lost in the bourgeois materialism of Western Europe and that Russia, despite its backwardness, represented the only hope of moral regeneration in the future. It was this attitude of mind which formed the starting-point of his polemic with Turgenev. Between July 1862 and January 1863 he published in his emigré journal, *The Bell*, a series of eight letters addressed to an anonymous correspondent (though it was scarcely necessary to affect this rather ingenuous disguise, for it became obvious during the course of his letters that they were addressed to Turgenev)

The Contemporary. Narodnaya Volya or 'People's Will' was a terrorist organization which gave its name to a journal published between 1879 and 1885. In its terroristic activity in the name of 'the people's welfare and the people's will' it epitomized that notion of revolution as a sacred vocation which was implied by Rudin. In 1878 Vera Zasulich attempted to assassinate General Trepov. She was tried by jury and acquitted, much to her own surprise and the surprise of officialdom. Dostoyevsky attended her trial and is supposed to have based the trial scene in *The Brothers Karamazov* on it.

[1] M. A. Antonovich, 'Asmodey nashego vremeni', *Sovremennik*, 1862, No. 3.

under the general title of *Ends and Beginnings*. In these letters Herzen restated his view that Europe was on the royal road to a state of bourgeois philistinism (*meshchanstvo*) in which, not the Don Quixotes, not the dedicated revolutionaries such as Mazzini, but the merchant, the shop-keeper, the petty bourgeois element would be the leaders of the people. In Herzen's view, there was no longer any real God, no true ideal for which Christ could suffer in the West. Russia, on the other hand, only distantly related to Europe, may have to pass through the bourgeois forms already established in Europe, but it will ultimately discover its own social forms because the Russian people themselves, the peasantry, are uncontaminated by Europe's evils. Couched in the brilliant, oddly cosmopolitan, needlessly elliptical style so characteristic of Herzen, with a disorganized manner of exposition which is not far short of being deliberately perverse, *Ends and Beginnings* contain flashes of insight that are arresting, interspersed with many wrong-headed notions on the opposition between the general categories of Russia, on the one hand, and Europe, on the other.[1]

Herzen's thought always tended to be analytical; Turgenev, both as an artist and as a thinker, always tended to be syncretic. Opposition between two general categories of the kind which Herzen emphasized in his *Ends and Beginnings* was offensive to the Turgenev who, as all his literary work had shown, was always striving to achieve a unity of form and content, of man's propensities as a Hamlet with his inclinations as a Don Quixote. But this particular opposition, so clearly and unwisely biased in favour of the Russian peasant at the expense of European civilization, was more than offensive—it appeared to be a libellous act both against Turgenev himself and against the spirit of Russian Westernism. Turgenev had perceived the danger in this romantic view of Russia's potentialities which had gained so much ground among his contemporaries since the Crimean War and had censured it, in his own way, by providing a last glimpse of Pavel Petrovich Kirsanov, at the end of *Fathers and Children*, adorning the terraces of Dresden and professing Slavophil views, since such views were now considered socially *très distingué*. It was the same kind of modish, woolly-minded Slavophilism which Turgenev detected in Herzen's open letters to him, and he was angered by it. He had originally wanted to make a public reply. However, after being warned that such a course would be unwise in the changed circumstances which prevailed

1 See A. I. Herzen, 'Kontsy i nachala', *Polnoye sobraniye sochineniy* (P-grad, 1920), xv. 239-306.

in Russia after the May riots, he decided to answer Herzen privately. The result of this and other acts, such as his rejection of the Ogaryov address[1] and his behaviour during the 'affair of the thirty-two' (about which later), was to make it appear that he was currying favour with the Russian authorities. In fact, Turgenev had no desire to curry public favour with one political faction or another. He wanted to be on peaceful terms with as many factions as possible, but this desire for the best of all worlds was not to prevent him from vigorously defending his Westernist ideals against Herzen's attacks. He gave direct and incisive answers—in illuminating contrast to Herzen's discursive obloquies—to all the points raised against him. However, his defence rested on two main arguments: that it was not the Russian peasantry but the educated classes of Russia who understood the need for, and the meaning of, revolution, and that it was not a question of Russia being superior to Europe but precisely the reverse, because Russia belonged to Europe and needed Europe. These opinions Turgenev stated in a number of private letters, to others as well as to Herzen, during the latter part of 1862.[2] One cannot fail to see that, as was the case with Turgenev's attitude to the polemics in the immediate pre-Emancipation years, in this post-Emancipation epoch he still retained his common sense and his writer's sense of proportion. His assessment of Russia's internal situation and of Russia's relationship to Europe was both more sober and more far-sighted than Herzen's or Ogaryov's or Bakunin's. Revolution among the peasantry was nonsense; the Russian peasants were innately conservative. Disgust at the educated classes was misplaced; they were the only guarantee of civilization in Russia. To imagine that Russia could rejuvenate Europe was romantic Slavophilism; Russia's only chance of development was through accepting the superiority of European civilization and through adherence to Westernist ideals. In retrospect, it is astonishing that such commonsense views should have been disputed at all. But they were open to dispute because they were 'old-fashioned', products of the intellectual life of the forties which had grown stale after the failure of the European ideal in 1848 and the patriotic emotions which had

[1] N. P. Ogaryov (1813-1877), the life-long friend of Herzen, collaborated with him on The Bell and proposed in 1862 that an address should be sent to the Tsar, calling for the summoning of a Zemsky sobor or assembly of the people (i.e. peasantry) so that they could air their grievances after the Emancipation. The address was sent to Turgenev for his signature but he rejected it. For details of this and the other disagreements between Turgenev and the London exiles, see Chapter IX in Granjard, op. cit.

[2] See A. I. Herzen, Poln. sobr. soch. (P-grad, 1920), xv. 306 et seq., 485 et seq.

been aroused in Russia by the Crimean War. In upholding these views Turgenev was being reasonable and consistent, but such virtues could not overcome the overwhelming desire for something new, for radical political and social change, for new economic forms and new intellectual idols, which had seized hold on all wings of the Russian intelligentsia, except the most conservative, after the Emancipation. No one was ready to pay any attention to an ageing novelist whose last work had been so roundly condemned and who had, by all appearances, opted out of the political struggle.

Yet Turgenev had not planned to opt out. His first plans for *Smoke*, which was to offer a public defence of his position, were made in 1862 and the action of the novel, when it finally appeared five years later, was set in the summer of that year. Turgenev's dilemma is to be seen in his first literary work after *Fathers and Children*, the pseudo-realistic prose poem, *Phantoms*, of 1863. In this brief sketch he represents himself as being transported by a phantom lady—who is given the rather incongruous name of Ellis—in a series of nocturnal travels across Russia and Europe to witness scenes from both past and present, such as the wild waves off the Isle of Wight, the Rome of Julius Caesar, the tranquillity of the Isola Bella, the Volga at the time of Stepan Razin, the night-life of Paris, the Black Forest and the white nights of St. Petersburg. It is a highly artificial work, extremely personal and rather vain. In the reactions of this nocturnal Icarus to the scenes which Ellis has to show him one may easily discern the political antipathies and the neurotic fears of the author. His dislike of Caesaropapism and the imperialism of Napoleon III in France is matched by his abhorrence of the Razin-type *jacquerie* in Russia, just as his disgust at the degeneracy and greed of Paris is matched by his revulsion against the coldness and banal pretentiousness of St. Petersburg. Where, then, is this night bird to find his nest? The work concludes with an evocation of the futility of human existence and the stark meaninglessness of dissolution and death. This note of Schopenhauerian pessimism is repeated and elaborated in *Enough!*, subtitled *An Extract from the Memoirs of a Deceased Artist*, which Turgenev wrote between 1862 and 1864. The infinite pettiness of life, the infinite repetition and monotony of human history, the infinite *ennui* of having known all that there was to be known and having experienced all that there was to be experienced in life— in these circumstances man's only wisdom lies in the knowledge of his personal insignificance and the fact that, as Turgenev quotes from Shakespeare:

> Life's but a walking shadow; a poor player,
> That struts and frets his hour upon the stage,
> And then is heard no more: it is a tale
> Told by an idiot, full of sound and fury,
> Signifying nothing.
>
> (*Macbeth* V, v)

Even Shakespeare himself, if he were to live again, would not discern anything new in humanity. The miscellaneous and essentially simple picture of human life would reveal itself before him in all its alarming sameness.

The same gullibility and cruelty, the same urge for blood, for gold, for filth, the same trumpery enjoyments, the same senseless sufferings in the name of . . . in the name of just the same rubbish that Aristophanes laughed to scorn two thousand years ago, the same crude baits for which that oft-trapped animal—the human crowd—will fall just as easily, the same seizures of power, the same habits of servitude, the same kind of lies—in a word, the same busy jumping of the squirrel in the same old wheel. . . .

Even the power of art and beauty is insufficient to alter the fact that man is a child of nature, at nature's mercy, brought low by nature, his glorious works destroyed by it. Death is the only reality; human achievement is a dream that evaporates in the sunlight. So Turgenev pronounces his verdict of 'Enough!' on human life and for the rest will retire into silence.

Turgenev's thought in these works can be seen to be a continuation of the philosophic pessimism which emerged so clearly in the final stages of both *On the Eve* and *Fathers and Children*. However near the truth these reflections on life may be, their pessimistic tone is so unrelieved that it borders on the ridiculous; and there is probably some justice in the scathing satire which *Phantoms* and *Enough!* received at Dostoyevsky's hands in *The Possessed*. One cannot, however, discount the pathological element in them, for it is evidence of the breakdown of the rational 'objectivity' which had previously marked Turgenev's attitude. It is only logical to suppose that where there is no faith to protect the reason against the irrationality or 'impassivity' of the external world, evil is made all the more potent and can even assume the proportions of an obsession which has a reality of its own. This seems to have been the case with Turgenev. Love itself, it seems, will come to be identified with an obsession that possesses and paralyzes man's will (as will be shown later, in discussing *Smoke*); it is this idea, accentuated by the fear of the unknown, bound up with his neurotic horror of death as it is expressed in *Phantoms*, which is to admit something demonic into Turgenev's fiction, and in his lack of faith he is unable to exorcise it. But, these considerations apart, *Phantoms* and *Enough!* can be regarded, in determining his political position at this time, as neither more nor less than an expression of the sense of total isolation which he experienced after the personal calumnies visited on him in 1862.

After having already been discountenanced by the younger generation, his political isolation was accomplished by his break with the London emigrés after Herzen's attacks. This rupture was finalized by an event of some public importance: the inauguration of a Senate commission in St. Petersburg to look into the activities of the London emigrés—Herzen, Bakunin and Ogaryov—some of whose letters had been intercepted after the capture of two of their couriers on the Austro-Italian border in July 1862. Among the incriminating documents handed over to the Russian authorities were several which referred directly to Turgenev. As a consequence, he was implicated in this 'affair of the thirty-two', as it came to be known, and was summoned to appear before the commission. At first—since he was residing abroad—he refused, excusing himself on the grounds of illness and old age (though he was only forty-five), but later he took the advice of the Russian Ambassador in Paris and sent a petition to the Tsar in which he outlined his case and begged for clemency. His case was fairly simple. He could now disown his connections with the London emigrés without resort to mendacity because, despite his former close relations with Herzen and Bakunin in particular, he no longer shared their opinions and there was no need to pretend that he did. By the time Turgenev finally returned to St. Petersburg and appeared before the commission (in January 1864) official disapproval had lessened. On June 1st (O.S.) 1864 it was officially admitted that he had had no connections with the London emigré circle and he was consequently exonerated of all blame attaching to those implicated in the 'affair of the thirty-two'. Naturally this act of clemency on the part of the authorities had the effect of alienating Herzen in no uncertain manner. Although, before Herzen's death in 1870, their relationship was to be resumed, it was never as friendly as it had been formerly. Irrespective of the verbal truth of Turgenev's remarks about his connections with Herzen and his associates, his attitude towards the authorities over the 'affair of the thirty-two' was in fact sycophantic and graceless, and it was scarcely likely to endear him either to the young radicals, whose leader, Chernyshevsky, was exiled to Siberia in 1864 (less than a fortnight before Turgenev was exonerated by the commission) or to the progressives of an older generation. But if he had broken with former friends in the political sense, he had also broken with Russia in the literary sense. He no longer felt at home in a Russia that refused to listen to him and wilfully misinterpreted his work. Critical now of his friends, he also became critical of Russia. In this isolation, partly forced upon him and partly self-imposed, he preferred for the time being to remain silent and to make his nest in the peaceful circumstances of Baden-Baden among friends of a different kind.

From 1863 to 1871 Baden-Baden was the centre of his life. He was drawn to it because Pauline Viardot and her family had taken up residence there after her retirement from an active career as a concert singer. She gave singing lessons and occasional recitals, held musical gatherings at her house and composed, with the aid of Turgenev, home-made operettas with such titles as *Le dernier sorcier, L'ogre, Trop de femmes* which contained plenty of female roles and suitable minor roles for Turgenev himself. He was now more than her admirer, her lover from afar. He was her personal friend and counsellor, always in attendance, as solicitous and devoted as any loving husband; and he was equally devoted to her family, the family triumphs and tribulations. In order to perpetuate this close relationship, which has been described as, and probably took the form of, 'an unofficial marriage', he decided to build a house in Thiergartenstrasse on a plot of land adjoining the Viardots' villa. The work made slow progress, money was not forthcoming in sufficient quantity from his Spasskoye estate, but eventually his house, in the style of Louis XIII, with spacious, elegant rooms to show off his collection of paintings, and a miniature theatre for Pauline Viardot's concerts, was completed in 1868 and Turgenev settled into it to enjoy a contented middle-age. These Baden-Baden years were years of idyll. He enjoyed a personal happiness in the fruition of his relations with Pauline Viardot that he could only have dreamt of earlier and only occasionally was his peaceful life interrupted by rude incursions from the outside world to upset his aristocratic temper, such as the visit of Dostoyevsky to implore him for money for his gambling or to insult his Germanophile sympathies after the publication of *Smoke*. Throughout these years, however, Turgenev maintained his contact with Russia either through letters and journals, or through occasional visits to St. Petersburg and contacts with Russians, of all shades of political opinion, who visited Baden-Baden. But he continued to harbour a grudge against the Russia that had rejected him. His anger smouldered for four years, from 1863 to 1867, when it finally crystallized in the most bitterly outspoken of all his novels, *Smoke*, which was to gain him still more enemies, though it was also to clarify his own thoughts on the problem of Russia and Europe.

Smoke tells how the hero, Litvinov, returning to Russia after spending four years in Europe to acquire a technical education, stops for about a fortnight in Baden-Baden to await the arrival of his fiancée. Here he accidentally meets the heroine, Irina, whom he had known earlier during his student days in Moscow, falls in love with her and proposes that she should leave her husband to go away with him. This unexpected and overwhelming passion which he feels for Irina means that he has to break with his fiancée. When Irina reluctantly refuses him, he is obliged to return to Russia heart-broken and despairing, and only several years later does he recover sufficiently from the shock of his Baden experience to beg forgiveness of the fiancée whom he had wronged. Upon this slight, almost anecdotal, narrative framework is hung a series of satirical scenes and interludes depicting the left wing of the Russian intelligentsia and the members of the right-wing official set who have gathered in Baden-Baden during the August of 1862.

The novel is unified by the presence of Litvinov in practically every scene and the unifying function of the hero is enhanced by the unity of place, since all the events occur in or around Baden-Baden, and by a remarkable unity of time in the novelistic form, since all the events occur between approximately August 10th and August 22nd. But it is upon the unifying function of the hero that structural unity of the novel as a whole depends. It is also in this respect that *Smoke* is structurally weaker than Turgenev's previous four novels. The hero's obligatory presence in each episode of the fiction, often as a kind of observer-narrator, means that the natural process of contrast and revelation which had been such an important feature of Turgenev's method of characterization hitherto is now largely abandoned. Litvinov is in no sense an unknown quantity in the fiction. In this novel it is an essential principle of Turgenev's method, both of characterization and narration, that the reader should accept Litvinov not only as the hero but also as an intermediary between the reader and the fiction. In the role of intermediary Litvinov's personality must necessarily be effaced. He will observe the emigré intellectuals of left-wing persuasion, for instance, such as Bambayev, Voroshilov, Gubaryov and Madame Sukhanchikova, or the members of the official set, such as Irina's husband, Ratmirov, and the generals and their ladies, without obtruding into the fiction unduly. Technically this allows Turgenev to present the fiction from Litvinov's point of view and to pass comments on the significance of the events and personalities witnessed by Litvinov in a manner consistent with the demands of realism. But the efface-ment of Litvinov's personality in this function of observer-narrator is damaging to his role as the hero of the novel. His personality is represented as being strikingly ordinary, unheroic almost to the point of dullness. Turgenev in this case has carried the paradox of the unheroic hero too far. Previously he had been more cunning, allowing both the personality and the ideological interest of the hero or heroine to remain partly concealed so that the hero or heroine consequently became a matter for speculation both for the other characters and for the reader. Litvinov is too ordinary, too 'revealed' a hero to be matter for speculation.

But this weakness was clearly intentional, if not actually intentional as a weakness in his characterization. Litvinov's 'ordinariness', his average qualities, the absence of too much of the Hamlet or the Don Quixote in him, relate him at once to such average figures as Lezhnyov, Lavretsky, Bersenev or Arkady Kirsanov who, like him, were re-presentatives of the middle or lower stratum of the *dvoryanstvo*, cultured but not too cultured to be practical, sensible but not too sensible to become prey to the heart's desires. By making such a figure the intermediary between the reader and the fiction, and by revealing so much about him, Turgenev was obviously making a strong bid to gain the reader's sympathy for his Litvinov not only as a man but also as an ideological figure. Litvinov is a representative of his, Tur-genev's, class, a good example—or so one may be permitted to take it —of the class of educated Russians whom Turgenev had defended so vigorously in his polemic with Herzen. Moreover, Litvinov is an antidote to the type of Bazarov, a practical type from the *dvoryanstvo* as Bazarov was a practical type from among the *raznochintsy*. By such ideological standards, therefore, Litvinov can be represented as a thoroughly acceptable hero. He becomes at once part of the polemical or pamphlet element in this novel, the yardstick of common sense against which the degree of absurdity or the degree of reasonableness of the other polemical figures can be gauged. However, to the extent that there is no process of contrast and revelation in the way he is presented, he cannot be said to represent the main ideological interest of the novel. This novel is not an elaborate portrait of either a single hero or a heroine whose problem unites both the ideological and the personal issues in the fiction, even though it may have been intended as such a novel. This is the measure of Turgenev's failure in *Smoke* by comparison with his previous work. For *Smoke* is not the portrait of a hero or a heroine, but the portrait of a society, complemented by the history of the relationship between Litvinov and Irina during the ten days or so that they are together in Baden-Baden.

The weakness in the characterization of Litvinov is a weakness at the very centre of the novel, disrupting its unity and upsetting the balance between its various parts. As a result, the novel separates into four different themes, four different component elements, which are unified only by the most tenuous of strands: the presence of the hero. Of these four different themes three absorb the ideological interest of the fiction. They are the satirical depiction of the society of the left-wing intelligentsia, on the one hand, and the equally satirical depiction of the society of the official set, on the other—accompanied by the third theme of Potugin's commentary. The fourth theme is the history of the relationship between Litvinov and Irina. The element of political pamphlet in this novel is very considerable. The whole novel is biased in its favour, as a condemnation of the left wing and the right wing and as a proclamation of Turgenev's personal views through the mouth of Potugin. The relationship between hero and heroine, though it reflects some of the ideological issues at stake in the novel, does not entirely redress the balance. It is largely separate from the other elements in the fiction, with its own form of introduction and its own conclusion. The integrated, unified novel-form, towards which Turgenev had been progressing in his first four novels and which he brought to a pitch of perfection in *Fathers and Children*, seems to have broken down under the weight of polemical matter in *Smoke*. This is the major reason why one cannot number it among his great novels.

Although in formal terms the novel may lack unity, in its evocation of the Baden-Baden scene, in its percipient and exquisitely cruel character sketches of the minor figures, in its barbed and masterfully exact dialogue, *Smoke* is in the direct tradition of Turgenev's realism. He knew the world of Baden-Baden intimately and he has captured the atmosphere of the place with an arresting truthfulness. The season, the surrounding countryside, the noise of the casinos and the restaurants, the constantly provocative, ingenuous, nervously excited squabbling and arguments of the Russian intellectuals, forever conscious of being strangers in these cosmopolitan surroundings, the air of transience about the life of Baden-Baden itself, the slightly dowdy elegance—it is all there, exactly felt and exactly depicted. It is a curiously modern novel. This may be due to the fact that the circumstances of the novel —the bourgeois world of nineteenth-century Germany as distinct from the feudal world of nineteenth-century Russia, a world of railway trains as distinct from *troikas*, of accepted European ways as distinct from the artificial culture of Russian provincial salons—bring it closer to our own age. But it must also be due to the anecdotal nature of the story itself, the casual form of the relationship between hero and heroine, the brevity of the episode, as compact and short-lived and devastating as a film story. The identification of author and hero, not in a pseudo-autobiographical manner but in a direct third-person observer-narrator relationship, contributes to the impression of modernity. It is also the most dramatic of Turgenev's novels in its unity of time, place and action. On the other hand, in its preoccupation with issues long since dead at the expense of the kind of elaborate portraiture at which Turgenev was so expert, this novel is incongruous and dated. The brilliant character sketches are disproportionately bitter; the dialogue is often too acid. The result is a novel of great interest, with all Turgenev's meticulous attention to significant and authentic detail, which nevertheless lacks the high artistic quality of his former work.

As a novel of ideas, *Smoke* is concerned with the future of Russia after the emancipation of the serfs. It offers three solutions—the future course of development as proposed by the left-wing intelligentsia, the desire for *status quo* at all costs as proposed by the representatives of officialdom, and the 'European' course advocated by Turgenev himself through the mouth of Potugin. What of the first two solutions? Turgenev does not conceal his contempt for the arguments advanced by the representatives of both the left and the right wing. The left-wing group, for instance, consisting of its leader, Gubaryov (a caricature of Ogaryov), its sycophantic enthusiasts such as Bambayev, its garrulous, self-opinionated students such as Voroshilov, its scandal-mongers like Madame Sukhanchikova, or its well-intentioned but misguided fellow travellers such as Pishchalkin and its opportunist henchmen like Tit Bindasov—this group is exposed as both ridiculous and dangerous (in Chapter IV). Turgenev represents such people as being spiteful, petty, stupid and ignorant. But chiefly they are woolly-minded in their ideas. Their interests are no longer centred, as they were in Bazarov's case, on the natural sciences. The natural sciences, as Gubaryov remarks, are useful as an education, but not as an aim. Their aims are now primarily political, concerned with the significance of the *artel'* and the peasant *obshchina* as a means of arousing the Russian people to some form of political action. For these people the *obshchina* has now acquired a mystical meaning. Gubaryov expresses it in the following way:

'Mm. . . . And the *obshchina*?' Gubaryov pontificated meaningfully, and biting a piece of his beard, stared at the table leg. 'The *obshchina*. . . . Do you understand me? It's a great word! And now, what's the meaning of these fires . . . these . . . these government measures against Sunday schools, reading-rooms, against the journals? And what's the meaning of the peasants' refusal to sign the settlement charters? And, finally, what's the meaning of what's happening in Poland? Don't you see where all this is leading? Don't you see that . . . mm . . . it's up to us . . . it's up to us now to unite with the people, so as to learn . . . to learn what the people think?'

The assumption behind these remarks is the assumption of the London emigrés: that the peasantry, or the Russian people, are a revolutionary potential and the left-wing intelligentsia must take advantage of the fact. In 1861, in fact, Herzen had called upon the Russian student youth to go to the people.[1] Gubaryov's remarks can therefore be seen as hinting at the beginnings of the *narodnik* or populist movement among the intelligentsia—a movement which Turgenev was to condemn, though in a sympathetic spirit, in his last novel, *Virgin Soil*. Here the idea, like Gubaryov himself, is caricatured, and the futilely romantic or Slavophil—for Turgenev generally uses the latter term in a pejorative sense—nature of the idea is to be emphasized by Potugin later.

The official set are introduced on the occasion of Litvinov's first meeting with Irina (Chapter X). Their political views veer between out-and-out reaction—the suppression of all freedom of expression in the press, the abrogation of the Emancipation edict, a return to the feudal past—and a right-wing official liberalism, which will pay lip-service to the idea of progress but will defend the aristocratic principle upon which the land-owners' authority was based and will counsel restraint in anything that smacks, however vaguely, of democracy. As one of the generals expresses it:

[1] See A. I. Herzen, *Poln. sobr. soch.* (P-grad, 1919), xi. 258 et seq.

'I am not an enemy of so-called progress; but all these universities and seminaries, these peasant schools, these students, these priests' sons, these *raznochintsy*, all that rabble, tout ce fond du sac, la petite propriété, pire que le prolétariat—' (the general spoke in a languishing, almost breaking voice), 'voilà ce qui m'effraie ... that's where we must stop ... and put an end to it.' (He again glanced sympathetically at Litvinov.) 'Yes, that's where we must stop. Don't forget that not one of us is making any demands, is asking for anything. Self-government, for instance, is anyone asking for it? Are *you* asking for it? Or you? Or you? Or you, mesdames? After all, you not only rule yourselves, you also rule us men as well.' The handsome face of the general brightened with an amused smile. 'My dear friends, why should we seek favours? Democracy is glad to see you, it is obsequious, it is ready to serve your aims ... and yet it's a two-edged sword. It's better to carry on in the old way ... it's much safer. Don't let the crowd think for itself too much, but have faith in the aristocracy which alone has any strength. . . . Yes, that'll be the better way. As for progress ... I personally haven't anything against progress. Only for heaven's sake don't let's have lawyers and juries and elected officials, —and at all costs don't let's interfere with the discipline, yes, the discipline, but you can build bridges and embankments and hospitals, if you want to, and why shouldn't you light the streets with gas?'

In other words, let there be as much progress as you like in improving certain social amenities, provided there is no harm done to the social prestige of the aristocracy. Litvinov's reaction to this point of view expresses the opinion of Turgenev. It is insulting to his 'plebeian' pride and to all the principles on which he had based his life. It is as dangerous, if not more dangerous, than the woolly-minded blatherings of the left wing. There is, however, an element of practical reasoning in the general's argument that has to be discredited. Turgenev achieves this not only by pushing home his attack through the mouth of Potugin but also by depicting the society of the official set a second time (Chapter XV). On this occasion its trivial pastimes and enjoyments make it appear as ridiculous as its left-wing opposite number. Both the solutions offered, therefore, by these two extremist groups are discredited and rejected in equal measure as being foolish and dangerous. If there is any bias in this censure, it is directed more against the official set than against the left-wing intelligentsia for the simple reason that Irina, through her marriage to Ratmirov, belongs to this set and is finally represented as being spiritually crippled through her obligatory adherence to it.

Between these two views there stands the figure of Potugin. His place in the novel is motivated so superficially by Turgenev that one is astonished at the lack of artistic sense which could have permitted such a violation of the novel's unity. Potugin is the friend whom Litvinov accepts on first acquaintance—this at once suggests that he is to be a 'positive' figure, since Litvinov has already been unfavourably impressed by the left-wing intelligentsia (the first meeting occurs in Chapter V)—and Potugin is also loosely associated with the relationship between Litvinov and Irina through his self-effacing love for her, so reminiscent of Turgenev's love for Pauline Viardot. But the story which Turgenev offers (in Chapter XIX) to explain the nature of the association is a piece of extravagant artifice which rings false. The dark hints of a tale best left untold merely serve to reinforce the impression that Potugin is a figure unessential to the fiction though essential to the novel as a political pamphlet. It is, in fact, the long passages of commentary spoken by Potugin (particularly in Chapters V and XIV) which hold up the development of the novel's action and turn this novel into a piece of public polemic, a political pamphlet designed to give expression to Turgenev's own views. And these views are often more personal than prescriptive, more idiosyncratic than ideological.

Potugin is 'classless' by social extraction, a *raznochinets*, one of the educated 'priests' sons' whom the general so deplored. Here Turgenev is again making a strong bid to gain the reader's sympathy for his own views, since a man of Potugin's type would presumably be of materialist persuasion, like Bazarov, believing above all in the efficacy of the natural sciences. Potugin, on the contrary, is represented as being a Westernist like Turgenev himself, endowed, moreover, with long experience of the Russian bureaucracy, with practical common sense, a realistic idealism and an insight into human nature which might be thought remarkable, were it not for the fact that Turgenev is speaking, like the apostolic dove, through his lips. It must be admitted that Potugin's views are largely critical, despite his protestations to the contrary. Yet it is in these criticisms that Turgenev offers us the most valuable insights into the Russian national character. These insights, political arguments apart, are the most interesting feature of the novel as a whole, valid not only for the mid-nineteenth century but for any century. They are the products of intimate knowledge and a lifetime's observation. They may be bitter, but they are no less true for all that. They are among the most candid pronouncements ever made by a Russian about his compatriots.

During the course of his first conversation with Litvinov, Potugin dwells on two interrelated problems which are important for an understanding of the Russian character. The first is the Russians' need to be led, to have a master or exemplar to look up to—in the case of the left-wing intelligentsia it is Gubaryov, who is acknowledged as leader for no other reason than his strength of will and his ability to plug away at one idea. 'Whoever has the stick is master,' sums up Potugin's argument. The second problem, closely related to the first, is the Russians' attitude to the West. There is in this attitude an element of *odi et amo*—a revulsion against the West as 'rotten' or 'depraved' (which, by the way, cannot be explained purely and simply by the tenets of Marxism-Leninism-Stalinism) and an admiration of the West, even in the very act of hating it, because the West is the source of the ideas which the Russians will ask to come and rule over them (as Soviet Russia became the wet-nurse to Marxism, that European changeling). Once these truths are accepted, Potugin's argument runs, then at least let the Russians' need to be led and their ambivalent attitude to the West be clarified and guided by sensible principles. If the Russians need to be led, spiritually as well as politically, let them look to their 'elder brothers', to Europe, of which they are—and this is always Turgenev's argument—an indivisible part, and not to the Russian peasantry, which is the source of salvation so incongruously advocated by the left-wing intelligentsia. Potugin offers a satirical picture of the likely relationship between the educated Russian and the peasant:

'If I were a painter, this is the picture I'd paint: an educated man stands in front of a peasant and bows low to him: "Cure me, my good man, I am faint from disease." While the peasant, in his turn, bows low to the educated man: "Teach me, good sir, I am faint from ignorance." Well, it goes without saying, neither budges an inch. While all that is needed is genuine humility—not in words only—in adopting from our elder brothers what they have invented, both better than we have and before us!'

If, in other words, the educated Russian desires to be humble, to be repentant, let him be humble and repentant before Europe, from which he has already derived, and is likely to derive in the future, so much benefit. There is no need, Potugin goes on, for any neurotic fear of Europe. The Russian must be selective in his borrowing, but he must realize that the Europe which he should respect is the Europe of *civilization*, not the Europe of gambling halls and prostitutes. Too often the Russian will see in Europe only the latter and will not appreciate the deeper roots of European civilization. As Potugin says towards the end of his first conversation:

I am not an optimist and all that is human, all human life, all this comedy with a tragic ending, does not appear to me in a rosy light; but why should one impute to the West what is, perhaps, rooted in human nature? This gambling hall is ugly, it's true; but is our homegrown gambling any more beautiful? No, my dear Grigory Mikhaylovych [Litvinov], let's be a little humbler and quieter: a good student sees the mistakes of his teacher, but keeps quiet about them out of respect, because these very mistakes are of use to him and serve to keep him on the right path.

Turgenev is clearly speaking here. Although he may be pessimistic about human life—it is now no more than 'all this comedy with a tragic ending'—he remains true to his youthful ideal of European civilization. But during the course of the second long conversation between Potugin and Litvinov (Chapter XIV) Turgenev gives his spokesman views of a more personal variety to utter. These again offer insights into the Russian character, although, being chiefly concerned with artistic matters, they are more spiteful in their critical tone. The bane of Turgenev is the Russian *samorodok* or 'born genius' who believes that he has no need to learn his craft or his art because he is instinctively endowed with qualities superior to those of his European counterpart. What in fact, Turgenev asks through the mouth of Potugin, has Russia to show for itself? In the sphere of the fine arts, nothing but a nonentity such as Bryullov. In the sphere of music Glinka is an exceptional talent, but his exception simply serves to prove the rule that the Russian musical heritage is insignificant. 'Oh, impoverished barbaric fools,' Potugin exclaims, 'for whom the traditional continuity of art does not exist. . . !' From this it is a short step to the total denunciation of Russia's heritage as worthless or, at best, a fake:

Last spring I visited the Crystal Palace near London; in this palace is housed, as you know, what is by way of being an exhibition of all that human ingenuity has achieved,—an encyclopedia of humanity, one might call it. Well, I walked round it, past all the machines and pieces of equipment, past the statues of great men; and I thought: if an order were to be issued that, together with the disappearance of a particular nation from the face of the earth, there should at once disappear from the Crystal Palace everything that that nation had invented,—our mother, Orthodox Russia, could disappear into the bowels of the earth, and not so much as a single nail, not so much as a single pin at the exhibition would be disturbed: everything would remain quietly in its place, because even the samovar, bast shoes, the shaft-bow, the knout—those famous products of ours—were not invented by us. . . . It's a slander! It's too much! you may say perhaps. . . . While I will say: firstly, that I don't know how to gild the pill when I'm condemning; and, secondly, that it's obviously not a question of being able to look the devil in the face, but people can't even look themselves in the face, and that it's not only children among us who like to be comforted with sweet words. Our old ideas came to us from the East, and the new ones we've managed for our sins to drag over from the West, and yet we still go on chattering about Russia's indigenous art! Some bold fellows have even discovered an indigenous Russian science: two and two still makes four, but somehow it seems more lively when it's Russian.

It is Russian inventiveness that is lacking, in Potugin's opinion. The Russian intelligentsia can pick up some old cast-off shoe from Saint-Simon or Fourier and, placing it on their heads, can walk about with it like a holy relic, but as for inventing anything so elementary as a machine for drying grain—that is beyond their powers. Yet, though they lack inventiveness, the Russians have a remarkable capacity for telling lies. The last thing the Russian wants to understand is facts. He can preoccupy himself with any number of theories and general conclusions, but a simple fact, such as the fact of monogamy commonly practised among predators in the animal kingdom—the illustration which Potugin offers—can upset a young champion of the natural sciences so much that he can fall into the heresy of idealism. But these are secondary matters. The essence of Potugin's argument is crystallized in his attack on the romantic idolatry which has been accorded to the only real indigenous culture of Russia, the culture of the Russian peasants. For Potugin, and of course for Turgenev, this makes nonsense.

'I, my dear sir, am of the opinion,' Potugin began again, 'that we are obliged to civilization not only for knowledge, art and law, but that even the sense of beauty itself and of poetry grows and enters into its own under the influence of that very same civilization and that the so-called people's, naïve, unconscious art is stuff and nonsense.'

To illustrate his point, he wonders why Russian epic literature—the folk-tales or *byliny*—had failed, unlike all other epic literatures, whether European or Asian, to produce a typical pair of lovers. Love had always been represented in the peasant *byliny* as magic or witchcraft; the relationship between man and woman, such as it was, had always been brutalized. And there had been, it seems, an innate lack of taste—a 'clumsy flamboyancy' (*meshkovatoye ukharstvo*), as Potugin puts it—about the artistic ideal of the common people. It is not much of a basis for art, he admits, but the Slavophils have to make themselves idolize it. On the other hand, it is always the virtues of civilization that he personally will reverence and admire. In his last conversation with Litvinov, before the latter's departure from Baden-Baden, he reiterates this basic principle of his life (Chapter XXV):

Each time that you start on something new, ask yourself: Are you serving civilization—in the strict and precise meaning of the word,—are you promoting one of its aims, does your work have that educative, European character, which alone is useful and fruitful among us in our time?

Again, these are Turgenev's own words. They comprise the essence of his point of view as a Westernist and the gist of the novel's message as a political pamphlet.

If this, in broad outline, summarizes Potugin's argument and the political message which Turgenev wished his novel to convey, then it also sheds light on a paradoxical element to be discerned in the relationship between Litvinov and Irina. *Smoke*, in fact, is a novel that may appear paradoxical in a variety of ways. The paradox of the un-heroic hero has already been examined. A further paradox is to be discerned in the way that Turgenev, formerly the champion of the serfs (in his *A Sportsman's Sketches*), here finally dissociates himself both from the peasant problem and from the most recent intellectual trends in Russia itself. Russia is represented in this novel, despite the in-sistence on the fact that Russia belongs to Europe, as being alien, far removed from the Baden-Baden world, as far removed, in some ways, as darkness is from light. This paradox complements yet another paradoxical feature of the novel: the fact that for the first time in Turgenev's novels the heroine is represented as being not only weaker than the hero (this was true, after all, of Odintsova in *Fathers and Children*), but actually unable to accept the hero's challenge. The in-compatibility of this relationship is thus directly the result of Irina's weakness. The wheel has now gone a full turn from the time when, in *Rudin*, the hero failed to live up to the heroine's challenge. The reasons for Irina's weakness may be socially motivated or the result of more obscure causes, but they are closely linked with that attitude to Russia as a source of darkness which is the basis of the political message of the novel.

One of Potugin's complaints against the 'born geniuses' is that they rely too much on their much-vaunted 'instinct'. His complaint springs directly from abhorrence of the kind of boastful nonsense which pro-claims—perhaps there are parallel manifestations in the Soviet Union today—that no one in Russia dies of hunger, that road travel is faster in Russia than anywhere else and that a Russian is any man's equal.

'Instinct!' he exclaims. 'What a thing to boast of! Take an ant in a forest and carry it a mile away from its ant-heap: he will find his way home; a man can do nothing of the kind. What's this mean? Does it mean he's lower than an ant? Instinct, no matter how exceptional, is unworthy of man: reason, simple, sound, commonsense reason—that's our true heritage, our pride.

This advocacy of reason as against instinct is the kernel of Potugin's, as of Turgenev's, argument for the Westernist cause. To proclaim Russia superior to Europe goes against reason; it can only appeal to the instinctive in man, or, specifically and only naturally, in the Russian man. But it is clear that for Turgenev this is not only a political question. During the sixties he dwelt on the problem of the instinctive or the irrational in human experience not only in *Phantoms*, as has already been mentioned, but also in *The Dog* (1866), and in both cases the irrational, manifested in a supernatural form, is closely linked with the problem of Russia as it presented itself to Turgenev. In *Phantoms* the supernatural is evident in the figure of the phantom lady, Ellis, a vampire, symbolic—or so one may assume—of the fact that love is only to be experienced once during a lifetime and also symbolic of love as possession by evil forces that overcome man's reason. Closely linked with this supernatural figure are Turgenev's misgivings about Russia, about the dark forces which have been unleashed in Russia after the Emancipation. His fear of the peasant *jacqueries*, for instance, might even be interpreted as a manifestation of his 'instinctive' antipathy, as a representative of the gentry, towards a lower class. Whatever the motives, his nocturnal travels in *Phantoms* are journeyings through the dark night of his own soul, revealing a Russia that is savage and cold, across which there marches the indescribable horror of death and annihilation. *The Dog*, not a personal statement like *Phantoms* but a 'mystery' story, nevertheless betrays a similar preoccupation with the problem of the supernatural in life, which harks back to *Faust* (1856) and forward to such stories of the seventies and early eighties as *The Dream*, *The Story of Father Aleksey*, *The Song of Triumphant Love* and *Klara Milich*; while it is also the most 'Russian' of Turgenev's stories. It is the story of how a poor Kaluga land-owner, Porfiry Kapitonych, became possessed by the spirit of a dog which haunted him during the night and had finally to be exorcized. Its 'Russian-ness' is to be seen in the use of a highly idiomatic narrative manner, reminiscent of Leskov's style in his tales and very unlike the 'pure' Russian which Turgenev normally used. The story is not very remarkable as Turgenev's stories go, but it opens and concludes with a question, put by one of Porfiry Kapitonych's audience, which touches not only on the problem of the dark forces that are abroad in Russia but also on the problem of the relationship between the supernatural and the reason. The question is: 'But if one admits the possibility of the supernatural, the possibility of its intrusion into real life, what part, after this, can ordinary reason be assumed to play?' No one can give an answer to such a question. Yet it is an important question so far as *Smoke* is concerned, for it is implied at the very basis of the relationship between Litvinov and Irina.

Originally Turgenev wished to call his novel *Two Lives*. Such a title would, firstly, have indicated the social contrast that he wished to present in depicting the two lives of Litvinov and Irina, separated by the different social worlds to which they belonged. But there is a further interpretation that may be put on this title—an interpretation which embraces the idea of the two lives that Litvinov experiences during his short stay in Baden-Baden. This idea seems to be grounded on the notion that the happiness of love may only be experienced once in a lifetime. On two occasions in the novel this idea is explicitly suggested. In Chapter VII, for instance, during the description of Litvinov's first passionate love for Irina while a student at Moscow university, it is stated:

Then followed the bright moments of first love, moments which are not ordained to be, and should not be, repeated in the same lifetime.

Later, in Chapter XVII, Litvinov thinks to himself, knowing that he is already in love with Irina for a second time:

Obviously one can't love twice; another life has entered into you, you have let it in—and you will never rid yourself of this poison, you will never break the bonds that bind you to it!

This notion of love as a poison, as a sickness, is a familiar idea in Turgenev, but less familiar is the idea of total possession by a passion which is destructive rather than ennobling. It is this that Litvinov experiences during his relationship with Irina. All the ideals and hopes of his former life are destroyed in his passion for Irina; he is possessed by this passion, which alters his character, divests him of the power to reason and leaves him finally with his life in ruins.

Such a conception of the power of love is, of course, latent in all Turgenev's previous studies, yet nowhere is it given quite the demonic force that it has in *Smoke*. Undoubtedly Turgenev's preoccupation with the supernatural and occult, increasingly apparent in his work after 1862, must have contributed to this change of emphasis. No doubt, also, in his relationship with Pauline Viardot he must have been made aware of the force of a love that could possess him for so many years. Indeed, it is also possible to suggest that Litvinov's carnal relationship with Irina—for there is a clear indication that it took a carnal form (Chapter XVII)—and his attempt to persuade her to leave her husband are a projection of Turgenev's relations with Pauline Viardot. But, personal issues apart, there is also a curious parallel between *Smoke* and Dostoyevsky's *Crime and Punishment*. Turgenev read *Crime and Punishment* when it appeared in *The Russian Messenger* in 1866 while he was engaged on writing his own novel and in several letters to friends he spoke of it with a mixture of admiration and censure.[1] Certain parallels between the novels are obvious: the concentrated, dramatic construction common to both, in which a day becomes a lifetime (as Irina remarks at the end of her last conversation with Litvinov in Chapter XXIII), the psychological analyses of character in the figure of the hero, common to both Litvinov and Raskolnikov, and the resultant preoccupation with the way in which a person can be obsessed by a passion or an idea. It is this notion of one 'possessed', so common to Dostoyevsky and yet so unusual in the relatively more lucid world of Turgenev's fiction, that distinguishes *Smoke* and suggests that the parallel between it and *Crime and Punishment* may be more than accidental. On the other hand, the supernatural and the occult had become popular subjects of discussion in the society salons during the sixties. Evidence of this is provided in Chapter XV of *Smoke*, when the American medium at Irina's evening party is being lionized. Spiritualism, the reading of Edgar Allan Poe, Schopenhauer's *Über das Geistersehen und das damit Verbundene* (1859) were all in vogue at the time. Moreover, this concern for the demonic is reflected in certain remarks which Potugin makes to Litvinov when he brings him a request from Irina (Chapter XI)—it is, indeed, the first time that an intimation is given of Potugin's connection with her—and these remarks hint fairly broadly both at an element of the supernatural in the novel itself and at an element of the demonic in Irina's character. The conversation runs as follows:

---

[1] To his friend, Fet, Turgenev wrote on 25 March/April 6 1866: 'The first part of *Crime and Punishment* is remarkable; the second part is redolent of fusty self-analysis.' *Sobr. soch.* (1958), xii. 360. For references to his letters to Borisov and Annenkov on *Crime and Punishment*, see M. K. Kleman, *Letopis' zhizni i tvorchestva I. S. Turgeneva* (1934), 157.

'Irina Pavlovna,' Potugin continued, 'suggests that that . . . how can I put it? . . . that set, in which you found her the day before yesterday, could not arouse any particular sympathy on your part; but she has asked me to say that the devil is not as black as he is painted.'

'Hmm. . . . Does this statement apply particularly to that . . . set?'

'Yes . . . and in general.'

'Hmm. . . . And you, Sozont Ivanych (Potugin), what opinion have you of the devil?'

'I think, Grigory Mikhaylych (Litvinov), that he is usually not the same as he is painted.'

'Is he better?'

'Better or worse, it's difficult to say, but not the same. Well, shall we go?'

A sentence or so later, Potugin quotes Shakespeare to the effect that 'there are more things in Heaven and earth, Horatio', which is again a hint of the problem that the practical, 'rational' man, Litvinov, has to face in his relationship with Irina. These, however, are only intimations. The real nature of the problem, and the extent to which it is connected with Turgenev's attitude to Russia at this time, has already been revealed in Chapter VI and the beginning of Chapter VII.

Chapter VI describes Litvinov's return to his room after his first conversation with Potugin. In his room he finds a letter from his father and not, as he had expected, from his fiancée. Among other things his father tells him of the evil power wielded over his coachman by a girl whom the coachman had deceived. The coachman was only saved from the demonic illness inflicted on him through the agency of a priest in Ryazan who performed an act of exorcism—and Litvinov's father encloses the priest's 'document' to prove the point. Litvinov, we are told,

reflected over this document; it conveyed to him a breath of the remote steppes, of the unenlightened darkness of their stagnant life, and it seemed remarkable to him that he should read it in Baden of all places.

This is the crux of the matter: Baden-Baden, Europe, the West is light, lucidity, reason; Russia is darkness, superstition, blind instinct. One scarcely needs to emphasize the parallel between the problem of the coachman in the letter from Litvinov's father and the problem of Porfiry Kapitonych in The Dog. The reason is imperilled in Russia; darkness reigns there. And at the beginning of Chapter VII Irina herself is associated with this idea of Russia as a source of darkness. The genealogy of her princely family, the Osinins, is briefly described:

they were pure-blooded and of the house of Ryurik, frequently mentioned in the early chronicles, rich and influential. But they fell into disfavour, so Turgenev tells us, through being accused of 'witchcraft and sorcery' and from that time their family influence had dwindled and declined. Obviously this cannot be regarded as a gratuitous piece of information. Irina, it seems, has been deliberately conceived of by Turgenev as one in whom there is vested a demonic power. Her influence over Litvinov, therefore, is to take the same form as the influence of the deceived girl over the coachman—a fact which is intimated in Chapter VI by the clearly symbolic meaning that can be read into Litvinov's discovery of the strange flowers in his room and of the letter from his father instead of the letter, as he had expected, from his fiancée. This is further emphasized by his subsequent nightmare and the sudden realization that the scent of the flowers reminds him of Irina. It may be remarked that it is only one of the curiosities in this novel that Potugin, the spokesman of Turgenev, should complain of the way love was always represented in the peasant *byliny* as a consequence of magic or witchcraft when just this very element of the occult is to play such a prominent part in the ensuing love-story.

As a result, the relationship between Litvinov and Irina in Baden-Baden is scarcely anything more than the story of an obsession. The love-story, in the typical Turgenevan manner, is presented in Chapters VII, VIII and IX, which comprise a background introduction to the story that is to occur ten years later in Baden-Baden. This is Litvinov's 'first love' for Irina. It is not surprising that, in this most paradoxical of Turgenev's novels, Irina should be Turgenev's most paradoxical heroine. By any standards she is the most striking figure in the novel. Unlike Litvinov, she is an unknown quantity in the fiction, presented always from Litvinov's point of view, so that her enigmatic characteristics are as much a source of mystery and fascination to the reader as they are to Litvinov. To him she is a 'bad angel', an evil genius, dressed so frequently in black, in contrast to his fiancée, Tat'yana, the 'good angel', and the challenge that these two women present to him is the choice between profane and sacred love. In lavishing so much artistry upon the characterization of Irina—for Tat'yana is a pale shadow, orthodox in her virtue to the point of dullness—Turgenev is here a kind of *advocatus diaboli*. This is not to suggest, on the other hand, that Irina does not have links with previous Turgenevan heroines. She has certain features in common with Odintsova, in the sense that, like Odintsova's, her social background was modest until she was patronised by a wealthy relative and married into the wealthy and influential official set. In this respect, Irina is a more elaborate study of the Odintsova-type, possessing many of the same characteristics of a feminine Hamlet.

In order, at the outset of the relationship, to supply the necessary information about Irina's life in the ten years since she last met Litvinov, Turgenev has to resort to the artifice (in Chapter XII) of making it appear that Irina wishes to know all about Litvinov. However, the information divulged during this first extended conversation between them almost exclusively concerns Irina—her connection with Potugin, her move to St. Petersburg and her four years of marriage to Ratmirov. The latter's biography is then introduced as a separate excerpt. So far Irina has only been able to offer the excuse of 'fate' as a means of condoning her conduct in rejecting Litvinov ten years earlier. But when they meet a day later (Chapter XIII), she has no wish to justify herself. She now claims his pity as one who has never experienced happiness since she knew him in Moscow, begs for his help and asks for his forgiveness. This he is ready to give, but by the end of Irina's evening party (and the conclusion of the polemical section of the novel), he is faced with a profound crisis of conscience. He is now, despite himself, involved in the 'tragic comedy' of life. He runs to Irina—the very fact that he runs is significant—to confess the 'unfortunate fact' of his love for her and declares that he must leave Baden at once (Chapter XVI). She agrees, but not before he has seen her for one last time. Yet he has little choice now (Chapter XVII):

He had never felt anything like it before: it was an unendurable, gnawing sensation of emptiness, emptiness in himself, round about him, everywhere. He was thinking neither of Irina nor Tat'yana. He had only one feeling: that the blow had fallen, and life was snapped in two like a rope, and he was seized and carried away by some cold and unknown force. Sometimes it seemed to him that a whirlwind had overtaken him, and he felt the rapid gyring and confused beating of its dark wings . . .

This image of beating wings, symbolic of the force of his love, harks back to the image of death in Section XXIV of *Phantoms*, reinforcing once more the close parallel between love and death. Clinging to the last vestiges of reason, he makes plans to leave for Heidelberg, but when he returns to say goodbye to Irina—for what he imagines is the last time—she confesses her own love for him, and this revelation makes him realize that his reason is no longer strong enough to overcome his emotions:

Everything in him was mixed up and confused; he was losing the thread of his own thoughts. He remembered Moscow, he remembered how *it* had over-taken him then like a sudden storm. He was gasping for breath: excitement, but a joyless and hopeless excitement, oppressed and tore at his heart.

When Irina finally comes to him, their profane love is consummated. She has committed herself to him entirely. By the morning of 18 August (Chapter XVIII) he is literally 'possessed' by this new love:

A strange change had taken place in him since the day before—in his appear-ance, in his movements, in the expression of his face; and indeed he felt himself to be another person. His self-confidence had vanished, and his peace of mind had vanished also, and his respect for himself; of his former state there remained nothing. The recent, unforgettable impressions had pushed all the rest into the background. A sensation he had never known before took possession of him, powerful, sweet—and evil; a mysterious guest had entered his sanctuary and taken possession of it, and lay down in it quietly at full length, like an owner in a new dwelling. Litvinov was not ashamed any more, he was frightened— and at the same time a frenzied courage burned within him: the captured, the conquered know this mixture of contradictory feelings; the burglar also knows it after his first robbery. And Litvinov had been conquered, conquered suddenly . . . and what had become of his honesty?

His fiancée's arrival precipitates the climax of his crisis of conscience. He admits that he has to make the inevitable confession to Tat'yana, but he delays until the following morning. He has already com-mitted himself to the point of realizing that he cannot turn back (Chapter XIX):

He had said farewell to his proper, well-ordered, respectable future: he knew that he was throwing himself head first into a whirlpool which was not even proper to look at . . . but this did not upset him. That was finished and done with, but how was he to stand before his judge? And if only it was a judge that came to meet him—an angel with a flaming sword, that would be easier for his guilty heart . . . but as things were he would have to plunge the knife in by himself. . . . It was horrible! But to turn back, to refuse the other one, to enjoy the freedom they promised him and acknowledged was his. . . . No! It would be better to die!

Potugin can sympathize with him in his predicament and can offer advice, but Litvinov is not content to love silently, as was Potugin, and he has, in any event, to make his confession to Tat'yana. When he finally does this, the climax has been reached and the moral of his predicament can be pointed (Chapter XX):

Litvinov came out on to the street as one stunned or dazed; something dark and heavy had settled into the very depths of his heart; a similar sensation must be experienced by a man who has cut another's throat; but meanwhile he felt easier, as if he had finally thrown off a hateful burden. The magnanimity of Tat'yana had overwhelmed him and he was keenly aware of everything that he was losing . . . and what did it matter? Annoyance was mixed with his repentance; he hurried to Irina as to the last remaining haven—and yet he was angry with her. For some while past, and increasingly each day, Litvinov's feelings had become more and more complex and confused; this confusion tormented him, annoyed him, and he was losing himself in its chaos. He thirsted for one thing alone: to find his way out finally on to a road, no matter what, so long as he did not have to go on circling round in this meaningless twilight. Positive people, of Litvinov's kind, should not be carried away by passion; it destroys the very meaning of their lives. . . . But nature takes no account of logic, our human logic; she has her own logic, which we do not understand and do not recognize, until it rides over us like a wheel.

The obsession of his love for Irina has thus produced its inevitable consequences. To Kapitolina Markovna, Tat'yana's aunt, it seems that he has been 'bewitched'. Whatever the truth, human logic has been powerless to overcome the force of the emotional attachment to Irina. He presents his challenge to her in his letter (Chapter XXIII). The past is smoke and dust, he claims; it is only his love for her that gives his life any meaning. At first, it seems that she may be able to accept the challenge, but in her last letter to him she admits that she has not the strength (Chapter XXV). She cannot go away with him, regardless of all her declarations about their freedom. The society which surrounds her has deprived her of the spiritual strength to make a new life—'It seems', she says, 'that there is no salvation for me; it seems that the poison has penetrated into me too deeply.' It is at this point that the political and personal issues in the novel unite. Turgenev's *odi et amo* relationship to Russia, his rejection of the Russia that has rejected him, is united with Litvinov's feeling that the smoke of the train carrying him away from Baden-Baden is as meaningless as life itself:

'Smoke, smoke,' he repeated to himself several times; and suddenly everything seemed to him to resemble smoke—everything, his own life, Russian life, everything human, especially everything Russian. Everything is smoke and steam, he thought everything is ceaselessly changing, everywhere there are new forms, events follow events, but in essence it is all the same; everything rushes, hurries somewhere—and everything vanishes without trace, without anything being achieved; another wind may blow—and everything rushes in

the other direction, and the same ceaseless, restless—and unnecessary—game
begins again.

Although three years later Litvinov makes amends for his conduct
in Baden-Baden, the fact remains that it is the pessimistic tone of his
thoughts as he travels in the train which epitomizes the mood of this
novel and gives it its title. *Smoke* sums up Turgenev's mood during the
sixties—pessimistic, irritable, caustic, and sombre. The strength of the
work resides very largely in the anger which informs both its polemical
passages and its view of life. Here Turgenev has committed himself to
particular opinions and particular views, and in committing himself he
has retained, notwithstanding the blemishes in the construction of the
work, much of the realistic vitality which was an outstanding feature
of his first four novels. The authenticity of the background scene, the
sense of place and character, the accidental nature of the relationship
between hero and heroine—these are the essence of Turgenev's
realism and they are all present in *Smoke*. One cannot regard *Smoke* as
an inferior novel by Russian or any other standards; it is only inferior
by Turgenevan standards. In this it betrays a diminution in his powers,
an indication that his touch is becoming less sure, but it is still an important work for what it has to tell us about Turgenev himself, his
view of Russia and his understanding of life.

7

THE FAILURE OF VIRGIN SOIL

TURGENEV anticipated that *Smoke* would give rise to adverse, and possibly inept, criticism, and he was not unduly disturbed when, as he informed Herzen, he was criticized by 'both reds and whites and from above and below and from the side—particularly from the side' for his novel.[1] He had given public expression to his opinions, both political and personal, and he had thus vindicated his silence in the earlier years of the sixties. He felt in the circumstances that he had no need to defend himself against the criticism directed at his novel by the conservative right wing—in fact, he took pride in such criticism—but he took exception to the critical interpretation put upon Litvinov by the young radical critic, Pisarev. The latter had complained that Turgenev had played traitor to the spirit of the sixties by abandoning the type of Bazarov, typical of the sixties in his dedication to the natural sciences, in favour of the practical mediocrity, Litvinov. It was a false accusation and Turgenev had little trouble in disposing of it.[2] Even though the criticism might be adverse, Turgenev had the compensation of knowing both that he had spoken his own mind in *Smoke* and that this fact did not prevent the novel from enjoying a great popular success among the reading public. With the appearance of a separate edition of the novel in November 1867, he reinstated several passages which Katkov, the editor of *The Russian Messenger*, had asked him to expunge when the novel was first published in that journal. Subsequently French, German and English editions of the novel appeared and the success which it had enjoyed in Russia was finally repeated throughout Europe. Turgenev had now achieved international fame.

For ten years, from 1867 to 1877, Turgenev was to publish no major work, though many minor works of great beauty—*A Lear of the Steppes* (1870), *The Torrents of Spring* (1871), *Punin and Baburin* (1874), *Living Relics* (1874), along with several other lesser works—were to come from his pen. Practically all of them were nostalgic, evoking

[1] Letter to Herzen, 4 June/23 May 1867. *Sobr. soch.* (1958), xii. 378.
[2] Letter to Pisarev of same date as letter to Herzen. Ibid, 376-7.

experiences from his own past, or from earlier periods in the century, with a clarity and perception of detail that immediately related them to the present. It is in these years that past and present seem to fuse in Turgenev's work. His pessimistic philosophy, founded on the assertion that nothing ever changes, acquired a personal and a universal meaning in the delicate blend of private reminiscence and historical objectivity which pervade these stories. They were also related to the present in their concern with particular themes which held implications for the social developments of the late sixties and seventies. *A Lear of the Steppes*, *Living Relics*, *The End of Chertopkhanov* and others refer back to the period, and the themes, of *A Sportsman's Sketches*, while at the same time reflecting the growing concern of the younger intelligentsia for the peasantry; *Punin and Baburin* and *The Watch* (1875), though set in the past, reflect the increasing importance of a new type of *raznochinets* who was to be typified by Turgenev in the figure of Solomin; *Knock* . . . *Knock* . . . *Knock* in its study of suicide and *The Unfortunate Girl* in its study of the heroine, Susanna, driven to desperation by her life in an alien household reflect issues that Turgenev is to elaborate in depicting Nezhdanov and Marianna in *Virgin Soil*. Consequently, these stories, though set in the past, reflect the implications of the present—of the sixties and seventies, that is—and foreshadow the intentions of the future. Similarly, writing his *Literary Reminiscences* in 1868, Turgenev was both crystallizing his memories and thoughts on the past and reassessing his aims for the future. Nowhere is this more evident than in his brilliant characterization of Belinsky as a man who, though believing in the values of the West, understood and loved Russia with an insight that was keener and an instinctive compassion that was deeper than any equivalent emotion shown by the Slavophils. After turning his back on the Russian scene in *Smoke*, Turgenev was once more feeling his way back to the understanding of Russia and its destiny which he had inherited, as an article of faith, from Belinsky. *Virgin Soil* was to be the climax of this process.

Turgenev's attitude to Russia was dependent very largely on the degree to which events in Europe affected his belief in the West. The disturbances of 1848 had led him to a reappraisal of the Russian scene which was accompanied by a deeper understanding of the peasant problem and the problem of the type of intellectual 'superfluous man'. The outcome of this new emphasis in Turgenev's thinking was his work during the fifties, his short stories and his novels, climaxed by *Fathers and Children* at the beginning of the following decade. The next event to rekindle his interest in the Russian scene was the Franco-Prussian war of 1870-71. This served to put an end to the personal idyll of his years at Baden-Baden in the company of Pauline Viardot, who, as a French citizen, was obliged with her family to take refuge in London during the hostilities. For Turgenev it was also an event that was politically distressing since, though he was not at all dismayed by the downfall of Napoleon III in France, he felt that his belief in the West had been betrayed by the Prussian aggressiveness of Bismarck. The bombardment of Strasbourg and the destruction of its library seemed in the nature of crimes against Western civilization. As one might expect, he soon followed the Viardots to London and, when conditions permitted, accompanied them to Paris where he was to spend, either in his apartment in the Rue de Douai or at Bougival, the remaining years of his life. In Paris, though poorer as a result of the Emancipation and obliged to sell possessions, such as land from his Spasskoye-Lutovinovo estates and his collection of paintings, he was to enjoy a wealth of friendships with such prominent literary figures as Flaubert, the Goncourt brothers, Daudet, Zola, Maupassant and, from America, the young Henry James. Instead of being, as he had been during the sixties, the Russian who called upon his compatriots to look to Europe for enlightenment, he was now the Russian to whom Europe looked for enlightenment about things Russian. The difference was important. He could forget his hurt feelings at the reception accorded to his work in Russia because his reputation in Europe gave him every right to feel that he had performed a service to his country. His Westernist beliefs were justified during these last years of his life, even though he always insisted on being, among his European friends and acquaintances, a Russian first and only secondly the writer with a European reputation. Thus there was no need for him to adopt the pose of disliking Russia which had been a feature of his life in Baden-Baden. Turgenev had only two loves in his life, but they ran deep: his love for Russia and his love for Pauline Viardot. During the Baden years he had abandoned Russia in favour of Pauline Viardot. In Paris he could indulge both loves with equanimity, but without the passion that is youth's prerogative. It is ironic—part of the irony of his life as a whole —that Turgenev should have achieved in old age what he craved for so passionately in his youth, when it was always youth itself that he reverenced and made the corner-stone of his art.

The failure of *Virgin Soil* must be ascribed to a lack of passion. It is an old man's novel. He first made plans for it in 1870 and elaborated the preliminary sketches of the main characters in 1872. But five years were still to pass before the novel was to appear. In 1876 he finally started work on it in earnest and completed the writing of it in three months—an unusually short period by any standard and remarkable even for Turgenev, who was not a slow writer once the idea and the characters had been fixed—and it was to be the longest and structurally most complex of his novels. It appeared in two parts—a precaution against the censorship proposed by the editor, Stasyulevich—in Nos. I and II of *The Messenger of Europe* for 1877. Immediately upon its appearance it was attacked from all sides. On this occasion, because it was an avowedly political work, the criticism was largely justified. Turgenev was quick to realize the fact. Whereas in the case of *Smoke* he had remained almost indifferent to the hostility of the reception, his reaction to the criticism of *Virgin Soil* was instantaneous. To one correspondent he wrote on 17 March of that year:

> ... as a result of my absenteeism I could not *know how* to write it as it should have been written: truthfully and realistically ... I am myself dissatisfied with my work—and in the depths of my heart I agree with the greater part of the criticism (and never has it been so unanimous) ...[1]

Two days later he wrote to Stasyulevich:

> I have had my eyes opened with regard to *Virgin Soil*; it is an unsuccessful work. I am not referring to the unanimous condemnation of all organs of the press, which, by the way, cannot be suspected of being in league against me; but a voice has awoken in me—and cannot be silenced. No, it is impossible to attempt to unearth the very essence of Russia when one lives almost constantly far away from it. I had taken upon myself a work that was beyond my strength. ... In the destiny of all outstanding Russian writers there has been a tragic side; mine was my absenteeism, the reasons for which it would take a long time to divulge, but the influence of which has found profound expression in this last work—and it is to be my last work.[2]

And on the same day that he wrote to Stasyulevich, he also wrote to his elder brother:

> There is no doubt that, as you say, *Virgin Soil* has failed; and I am beginning to think that such a fate is deserved. One cannot suggest that all the journals have entered into some kind of league against me; rather it must be admitted that I made a mistake: I took upon myself a labour that was beyond my

[1] Letter to A. M. Zhemchuzhnikov, Saturday, 17/5 March 1877. Ibid, 513.
[2] Letter to M. M. Stasyulevich, Monday, 19/7 March 1877. *Sobr. soch.* (1949), xi. 321.

powers and I fell down under its weight. In fact, it's impossible to write about Russia without living there.[1]

The refrain of all these letters is the same: *Virgin Soil*, unanimously condemned in the press, has proved a failure. It has failed because Turgenev had been absent from Russia for too long and had in consequence taken upon himself a task that was beyond his powers. The truth of these remarks is, unfortunately, borne out by the novel itself. All the outstanding Russian writers of the nineteenth century had a tragic side to their destinies, and Turgenev's tragedy was, as he puts it, his 'absenteeism'. Being absent from Russia for so long, he could not *feel* the atmosphere of Russia, even though he wrote the greater part of his novel at Spasskoye, and this absence of feeling was to be a tragic flaw in the kind of topical, realistic novel which he had chosen for himself. It is the absence of verisimilitude, of authentic knowledge of, and feeling for, so many aspects of character and situation, which is the most significant blemish in *Virgin Soil*. Turgenev, always so sensitive to new currents in the social scene, could appreciate at once that he had failed to embody the current of populist feeling in a work of authentic realism, pertinent to the time and redolent of its atmosphere.

Virgin Soil, when it appeared in 1877, was simply not pertinent to the time. With its action set in the summer of 1868 and its conclusion in 1870, it dealt with the modest beginnings of the populist movement which had, by 1877, already fizzled out into political terrorism, resulting for the intelligentsia in a period of disorderly drifting that was to lead it eventually to Marxist Social Democracy and Bolshevism. 'Populism' (*narodnichestvo*) was a composite name given to a movement which, like the Russian intelligentsia itself, had as many different specific aims as it had adherents. While, however, admitting the diversity of opinion and feeling which existed within the loosely defined boundaries of the movement, it must be stressed that it was a 'movement'. It had no broad strategy and it lacked conscious leadership, yet it was the first deliberate attempt on the part of the Russian intelligentsia to achieve practical expression of a common purpose in some form of concerted action. It received its impetus from the Emancipation and its common purpose from the social and economic unrest in the countryside which was consequent upon the Emancipation. The peasants, once they were emancipated, found themselves more defenceless than they had been formerly under serfdom. They were now open to exploitation by avaricious industrialists as well as

[1] Letter to N. S. Turgenev (same date as on previous page). Ibid, 321.

by unscrupulous land-owners. Emancipated in little more than name, they appeared to the intelligentsia as the one force in the land which could threaten the authority of the autocracy. The intelligentsia had therefore only to take the initiative in revealing to the peasantry the true nature of their plight and the latent power which resided in their hands for them to unite with the intelligentsia in effecting, if not a political, then at least a moral revolution in Russian society. Yet in many ways the common aim of the populists was scarcely even as specific as this. Socialists, salvationists, anarchists, repentant noblemen, revolutionaries and students of all ages were seized by the ideal of 'going into the people', as it was called. Populism was a mystique or religion of the people (*narod*), in which a feeling of guilt towards the peasantry who had been enslaved for so long was combined with a desire to achieve a moral regeneration of society upon Russian, as distinct from Western, lines. Its appeal was more emotional than rational, and for this reason its moral ideals were humanistic but lacking in cogency, while its sociological ideals were 'subjective' and utopian. In political terms, its aim was enlightenment rather than incitement.

As a movement it began modestly in the late sixties, precipitated by the Smolensk famine of the winter of 1867-68 (mentioned by Nezhdanov in Chapter II of *Virgin Soil*), when young students decided to 'simplify' themselves by arraying themselves in peasant costumes and encouraging the peasants to listen to their populist tracts. It gained momentum in the seventies and reached its climax in the summer of 1874, when between two and three thousand students and members of the younger intelligentsia—the small scale of this movement by contemporary standards is one of its tragic and appealing aspects—went 'into the people', to the villages and fields and taverns, in order to enlighten the peasantry. Despite all the enthusiasm and self-sacrifice, the results were pitiful. The peasant mentality, always suspicious of strangers, and especially of strangers who have only the authority of their own voices, resisted all attempts at enlightenment, except in one or two cases where the energy and strength of will of the individual populist gained the peasants' approval. In the majority of cases the populists achieved nothing, and in many cases the peasants turned them over to the police. The result was mass arrests, imprisonment for several years, the delayed trials of 1877, persecution and despair.

Turgenev visited Russia during the seventies, both meeting personally and corresponding with several of those who participated in the populist movement, but for the greater part of the time he resided in Paris and viewed the activities of the younger intelligentsia from afar. The revolutionary aspirations of certain sections of the intelligentsia were repugnant to him. In his novel he made a particular point of censuring the activities of Nechayev, the documents on whose trial in 1871 were known to him, by introducing references to him as the shadowy Vasily Nikolayevich who gives the orders to the populists and who is discussed, in unfavourable terms, by Nezhdanov and Marianna in Chapter XXII. On the other hand, for the ardour and self-sacrifice of the populists, who were the pawns in the revolutionary game played by Nechayev, Turgenev could feel nothing but admiration, although he disapproved of their ideas. In analysing the cause of the lifelessness and lack of authentic feeling in *Virgin Soil*, it is here that one must look first of all. Turgenev's attitude towards the young populists was ostensibly objective, calm and reasoned; yet it was also non-committal. As he wrote to Stasyulevich shortly before the publication of the first part of the novel, after the demonstration outside the Kazan Cathedral in St. Petersburg:

You will tell me that that foolish street scene was no more than the dirty froth which comes to the surface of any society from time to time; I agree; yet I still do not consider it superfluous to remind you in a few words of those considerations which guided me during the composition of *Virgin Soil*—and which, as you may remember, I outlined to you by word of mouth during our meeting in Bougival last autumn. The younger generation has so far been represented in our literature either as a pack of rogues and scoundrels—which, in the first place, is unjust and, secondly, can only offend the younger generation of readers as being libellous and false—or this generation has, so far as is possible, been made into an ideal, which is again unjust and—what is more—harmful. I decided to choose a middle course—to get closer to the truth—by taking the young people, for the most part good and honest people, and showing that, notwithstanding their honesty, their very cause itself was false and lifeless and that it could not fail to lead them to a complete fiasco. Whether I have succeeded, it is not for me to judge; but that was my idea, and you can see how eminently *censorable* and well-intentioned it is. At least, the young people cannot say that it is an enemy who has decided to depict them; on the contrary, they must feel the sympathy which lives within me—a sympathy if not for their aims, then for their persons. And it is only in this way that a novel, written for them and about them, can be of use to them.[1]

[1] Letter to M. M. Stasyulevich, 22 December 1876/3 January 1877. *Sobr. soch.* (1958), xii. 502. On 6 December 1876 there was a demonstration of the revolutionary organization 'Land and Will' (*Zemlya i volya*) outside Kazan Cathedral in St. Petersburg. Turgenev feared that a demonstration of this kind might prejudice the chances of his novel being accepted by the censorship. The demonstration was notable for the first public speech of Plekhanov.

By choosing a middle course of the kind he suggests, Turgenev was admitting that he could feel sympathy, but it was the sympathy of one who was not committed to one attitude or another. Although ostensibly objective, in the last analysis it was no more than a lukewarm admiration which concealed a dangerous paradox. The distinction which he makes between the aims of the populists and their persons was artificial, especially for a writer like Turgenev who had been used to accepting both the man and his ideas. That he could sympathize with them as people, but not with their ideas, that he could regard them as honest, but claim that their cause was false, was simply to admit that he could not conceive of them 'in the round'. It is as a result of his refusal to accept the ideas of the young populists in his novel that their characterization is pallid and lifeless by comparison with the characterization in his previous novels. Turgenev's characters live as artistic creations because their ideas have a living meaning for them. In the case of the younger generation as represented in *Virgin Soil* this is not so.

In discussing *Virgin Soil* one is more or less obliged to use terminology appropriate to a work of Socialist Realism. It is, in the first place, a novel comprehensible only in political terms. It sets out to contrast the old and the new in the shape of the pseudo-liberal, conservative, landed aristocracy of the older generation and the populist *raznochintsy* of the younger generation. This inevitably leads, in the second place, to a clear-cut division of the characters into black and white: the liberals and conservatives are all bad characters, while the populists are all good characters. In this respect *Virgin Soil* is singularly prophetic of the type of Socialist Realist novel so common in Soviet literature. It contains its 'positive' hero from among the people (Solomin) and its positive message for the future; it has its industrial background and its 'typical' characters; it offers a story as the fictional skeleton upon which to hang the political matter of the work; it gives the impression of being consciously planned to serve a political end. Having, therefore, lowered the sights of one's criticism to the level required for this type of novel, one is bound to admit that it is successful within its own terms of reference, a literary ancestor of Gorky's *Mother* and innumerable subsequent Socialist Realist works. But it is a denial of art to lower one's standards in this way. The political novel appears to substitute for considerations of artistic form a scheme— which in the best cases is symmetrical, but which can be no more than an arid formula—in the exposition of different political points of view.

In the case of *Virgin Soil* it is this scheme that is evident and not the form. As in everything Turgenev wrote, there is a sense of proportion even about this scheme, and it has a satisfying symmetry, but it is a scheme which relies for its effect upon the story element rather than upon the force of characterization.

The 'story' of *Virgin Soil* is the most complex 'story' in Turgenev's novels, the result of a multiplication of subsidiary characters and subsidiary themes. Briefly, it relates how the hero, Nezhdanov, a member of a populist organization, is invited by Sipyagin, a wealthy liberal land-owner, to be tutor to his son. Nezhdanov travels with Sipyagin to the latter's estate in the country and there meets the heroine, Marianna, with whom he falls in love. Marianna, more in love with the cause for which Nezhdanov is working than with Nezhdanov himself, joins him in a plan to 'simplify' themselves with the object of working among the peasants of the district. They are aided in this by the manager of a local textile factory, Solomin. Marianna and Nezhdanov leave the Sipyagin house, take up residence in the factory and set about the business of spreading propaganda. Nezhdanov has long been aware of the fact that he cannot believe in the cause for which he is working and his experiences among the peasants force him to the conclusion that he cannot continue with the pretence. In the end, he shoots himself. Meanwhile, Markelov, Sipyagin's brother-in-law, a dedicated worker for the populist cause, is arrested and turned over to the authorities by his own peasants. Sipyagin, casting aside his liberal principles, arraigns Markelov before the governor of the province and demands that Marianna, Nezhdanov and Solomin should be arrested as well. However, by the time the police reach the factory, Nezhdanov is dead, and Marianna and Solomin have already left, shortly to be married. The attempt at enlightening the peasantry has thus proved abortive. It remains for Paklin, Turgenev's spokesman in the novel, to point the moral in the last chapter, which is by way of being an Epilogue.

Paklin may be the figure who gives direct expression to Turgenev's personal opinions, but it is really in the figure of the hero, Nezhdanov, that Turgenev's ambiguous attitude, both towards the populists and towards the fiction itself, is best expressed. The paradox of the unheroic hero is here seen at its greatest. Although Turgenev intended Solomin to be regarded as the hero of the work, it is Nezhdanov who occupies the centre of the fiction, unifies, in a formal sense, the different themes and carries the burden of the story on his shoulders. There are, however, suggestions of parody about his portrait which tend to exaggerate the paradoxically unheroic features of his character. As a result, he appears as a kind of *reductio ad absurdum* of the type of unheroic hero so familiar from Turgenev's previous studies—a paradoxically young 'superfluous man', as if Turgenev were recreating at the end of his life and for the last time the figure of Steno with which he had begun his literary career. In the detailed character sketches of the main figures, which Turgenev drew up in 1872, Nezhdanov is described as being 'a tragic nature with a tragic destiny'.[1] It was obviously Turgenev's intention to make Nezhdanov a figure whose tragic destiny would emphasize the tragically misguided aims of the younger generation of populists. But Nezhdanov can scarcely be regarded as typifying a generation. His tragic destiny is all too plainly the outcome of the tragic division within himself. He is, in Paklin's phrase (Chapter XXXVIII), 'the romantic of realism', the Hamlet aspiring to be a Don Quixote, the bastard aristocrat aspiring to be a peasant-loving democrat, the poet *manqué* aspiring equally ineffectually to be a practical revolutionary. These contrary elements in his character make him an interesting figure —indeed, the most interesting figure in the novel—but one whose tragedy is not so much representative of a generation as of that conflict between artistic form and political purpose which was at the root of Turgenev's art. In the last resort, Nezhdanov's divided character seems to reflect the division within Turgenev himself, which he had analysed so frequently in previous studies but which is nowhere more obvious than in this, his last major figure in his last major work; and it is necessarily Nezhdanov's weaknesses that are exaggerated in this weakest and most 'architectural'[2] of Turgenev's novels.

Just as there is a lack of unity in the character of Nezhdanov, so there is a lack of unity within the novel itself, which must be attributed to the fact that Nezhdanov, as hero, is never in any sense a dominating or commanding figure. It has the appearance of a novel which is divided against itself. In the case of the characters, this division is obvious, as has already been suggested. On the one hand, there are the populists: Ostrodumov, Mashurina, Markelov, Nezhdanov, Marianna and Solomin; on the other hand, the liberals and conservatives: Sipyagin, his wife, Valentina, and Kallomeytsev. The novel is con-

---

[1] André Mazon, 'L'Élaboration d'un roman de Turgenev: Terres Vierges', *Revue des Études Slaves*, v (1925), 92.

[2] Henry James records Turgenev as speaking about the danger of having too much 'architecture' in a novel. Henry James, *The Portrait of a Lady* (1921), pp. viii-ix.

structed so that in Part I all these characters are presented in their respective 'places' in the fiction and the differences between them are as yet only implied. Only at the beginning of Part II (particularly during the scene at Sipyagin's house in Chapter XXIV) are the representatives of both attitudes—Sipyagin, his wife, Kallomeytsev, Solomin, Marianna and Nezhdanov—brought together, and all the subsequent action is designed to illustrate both the differences between the two attitudes and their falseness: the false aims of the populists, on the one hand, in attempting to bridge the gap between the educated classes and the peasant masses, and the false liberalism of Sipyagin, on the other hand, which is revealed by his hostile attitude to Markelov and the younger generation of populists once the true nature of the latter's aims has become apparent. Among the representatives of the two points of view, however, certain differences in type are discernible. Of the populists, Ostrodumov and Mashurina are plainly the most typical, uninspiring but devoted figures whose destinies are linked with that 'anonymous Russia' which is evoked at the end of the novel. Markelov and Nezhdanov fall into a category of their own. Exceptional people, they are nevertheless 'unfortunates' who can never enjoy success in life. Marianna and Solomin are again different. They have the zeal of the Don Quixotes and a practical ability which enables them to overcome the obstacles of temperament that condemn the 'unfortunates' to failure. Of the liberals and conservatives, Sipyagin is the man who professes a tolerant liberal attitude but is quick to change his mind when his career is threatened. His wife, Valentina, is a 'poseuse'—almost another version of Turgenev's mother in her odd mixture of pretensions to culture and tyrannical disregard for those weaker than herself. Kallomeytsev is the typical conservative, satirized, but none the less convincing for all that, with a social background that is not quite as aristocratic as he might have wished.

Just as there are these two groups and two points of view in the fiction, so the novel depicts two worlds that are mutually incompatible: the world of the landed gentry and the world of industry. It is the latter which is the most novel feature of *Virgin Soil*. The noise of satanic mills had had no place in Turgenev's fiction previously, and here its jarring note resounds only too clearly, as is to be seen in his description of the textile mill of which Solomin is the manager (Chapter XVI):

The mill was obviously in full production and overloaded with work: from all around there came the lively bustle and hum of ceaseless activity: the machines puffed and rattled; the looms creaked, wheels buzzed, straps whirled and flapped, trolleys, barrels and loaded carts were wheeled in and out; shouted orders were heard, bells and whistles, workmen in belted shirts, their hair tied with straps, and work-girls in print cotton dresses hurried to and fro; harnessed horses moved their loads. . . . It was the energy of a thousand human beings that resounded, long drawn-out, like the throbbing of a violin string. Everything went correctly, sensibly and at full speed; but not only was there no smartness or neatness, there was not even a trace of cleanliness anywhere; on the contrary, everywhere one was struck by the neglect, the dirt and the grime; there a window-pane was broken, here the plaster had peeled from the wall, the boards had loosened, a door yawned wide open; a large puddle, black, coated with a rainbow-coloured slime, stood in the middle of the main courtyard; further on rose heaps of discarded bricks and lying about on the ground were scraps of matting, mats, boxes and lengths of rope; unkempt dogs with distended stomachs strayed in silence among this rubbish; in a corner, under a fence, there sat a small boy of about four years of age, with an enormous belly and a tousled head, entirely covered in soot—he sat and cried hopelessly, just as if he had been abandoned by the whole world; near him a sow, covered with the same soot and surrounded by various of her young, was devouring cabbage stalks; ragged washing bobbed on a stretch of line—and such a stench, such oppressive heat everywhere! It was just as a Russian factory should be—not like a German or a French textile mill.

For Turgenev the mill itself seems to be an alien scene, observed as a concatenation of acts and sounds, with no authentic understanding of its processes and purpose, and in no sense intimately experienced. Yet the human tragedy of this industrial scene is touchingly conveyed in the brief glimpse of the four-year-old boy who 'cried hopelessly, just as if he had been abandoned by the whole world'. The 'humanity' of Turgenev remains, but one cannot fail to detect his revulsion at this manifestation of nineteenth-century industrialism. It is in this respect that he reveals not only the extent to which his absence from Russia had impaired his understanding of the most recent changes that had occurred there, but also the extent to which he was always the cultured nobleman, with roots in the eighteenth century,—the epitome of an age in which factories had no place. The world he reveals here, as in the scene of the provincial town through which Markelov and Nezhdanov drive in Chapter X, is prophetic of the world of Gorky's fiction or the Five-Year-Plan novels. It is incongruous, ugly, and ignoble, though it is a testament to Turgenev's integrity as a realistic writer that he should not shrink from depicting this new —and to him—strange world. Yet it is strange and alien to him, and to the extent that he fails to understand it, as is clear from his description of the factory, so he fails to portray with any convincingness the 'industrial' figure, Solomin.

Solomin, according to the character sketches of 1872, was intended to be 'a real Russian practical man on the American pattern'.[1] The original conception of Solomin as a revolutionary is toned down in the novel. He is represented as a man of 'gradualist' views, sympathetic to the populists but unwilling to accept their belief in the peasantry. Although a *raznochinets* or classless by social extraction, his allegiance is clearly to the new class of the proletariat and he is solicitous in defence of this class. He defends the rights of the factory worker both against the gentry, who are too bureaucratic in their methods of factory management, and against the merchant class, who are more efficient in exploiting the workers for purposes of profit. As a fictional character, however, Solomin is a failure. He is given words to speak and actions to perform, but there is no attempt at characterization in depth. His failure is comparable with the failure of Insarov in *On the Eve*. Both are theoretical characters who have not been portrayed 'in the round' and in both cases this seems to be due to the fact that their respective backgrounds—the Bulgarian background of Insarov and the industrial background of Solomin—have not been fully understood by Turgenev.

Between the world of the landed gentry and the world of industry there lie two other worlds, those of the eighteenth century and the twentieth. Nothing reveals more clearly Turgenev's allegiance to the past and to an age which is already on the point of disappearing than his tender, sentimental portrayal of the figures of Fomushka and Fimushka (Chapter XIX). Islanded in their quaint eighteenth-century world, they possess a culture and a tranquillity of mind which offer an idyllic contrast to the political rancour, the feverish desire for progress, the industrial clangour and the false values of the nineteenth century. The epigraph to *Virgin Soil*—'To turn virgin soil one should use not a plough which glides over the surface of the earth, but a plough which cuts deep'—is apposite here. The activities of the populists will merely scratch the surface of Russia, whereas to unearth Russia's true heritage one has to realize—as Turgenev insisted so often towards the end of his life—the way in which the present is related to the past (represented here by Fomushka and Fimushka) and to the future which is represented, or so Paklin thinks (Chapter XX), by

[1] André Mazon, op. cit., 96.

the merchant, Golushkin. Golushkin, opportunist supporter of the populist cause, epitomizes Turgenev's misgivings about the future. It is here that *Virgin Soil* becomes more than an exposure of the falsity of the populist and liberal attitudes; it is a lament over a past way of life that ended with the Emancipation and a future in which the merchant class, as personified by Golushkin, will soon usurp the social authority which had previously been enjoyed by the gentry. Moreover, it is a future in which the old values of culture and enlightenment, the eighteenth-century heritage so dear to Turgenev himself, will have no meaning.

The only aspect of the fiction which has any of the vitality customarily to be found in Turgenev's novels is the world of the landed gentry, that world of country estates and provincial salons which had been the background to all Turgenev's novels before *Smoke*. The figures of Sipyagin, his wife and Kallomeytsev have a vitality, despite the obviously satirical intent with which they are drawn, that reveals at once Turgenev's mastery of portraiture in circumstances which are familiar to him. Sipyagin is a more grandiose version of Pavel Petrovich Kirsanov, just as his estate of Arzhanoye is more grandiose than the Kirsanovs' Mar'ino. This background is known and felt, and consequently Sipyagin's grandiloquent speeches, his wife's flirting with Nezhdanov—so reminiscent of the relationship between mistress and tutor in *A Month in the Country*—and Kallomeytsev's perpetual conservative ill temper ring true in their pretentiousness and absurdity. Again, Marianna and Nezhdanov, so long as they are presented against this familiar background, have an appealing freshness, but as soon as the scene shifts away from the world of Arzhanoye, and the study of contrasting types gives way to the story element (as it does in Part II of the novel), something of the vitality in their characterization is lost. They tend to become puppet figures acting in a prescribed manner to suit the purposes of the story. Their psychological integrity as characters seems to evaporate, Marianna in sacrificing herself to the cause and Nezhdanov in abandoning himself to despair and suicide.

This novel, like all Turgenev's novels, has its love-story, in the relationship between Nezhdanov and Marianna—complicated by Markelov's fruitless love for Marianna and Marianna's increasing love for Solomin—but it never gives the impression of being a paramount issue in the fiction. Its purpose is more obviously functional than in any previous Turgenevan novel: to reveal the extent to which the idealist, Nezhdanov, is superfluous in the new Russia where only practical men of Solomin's calibre are required to plough deep into the 'virgin soil'. In this relationship Marianna is represented as being much the superior figure, endowed with those Quixotic virtues of self-sacrifice and enthusiasm which naturally draw her away from Nezhdanov towards the supposedly superior, though frankly less interesting, personality of Solomin. It is in the relationship between Marianna and Solomin that, for the first and only time in Turgenev's work, love must be assumed to unite the ideological and personal aspirations of hero and heroine without fear of mutual incompatibility. This is the optimistic conclusion of the novel, but it is artificial and shallow for all that.

The schematic form, albeit symmetrical, the division of the characters into good and bad, the diminution of the importance of the central figure all contribute to the weakness of this novel. The result is a lack of organic unity between its various parts and a consequent lowering of the artistic temperature of the work as a whole. Turgenev had always to choose between being an artist or a political spokesman. It is this conflict, embodied with such tragic consequences in the figure of Nezhdanov, that makes the novel neither an artistic unity, in the sense of being unified by the presence of one dominant figure (whose characterization absorbs the interest of the fiction and unifies the personal and ideological issues), nor a successful political pamphlet, since Turgenev's absence from Russia, his uncommitted attitude towards the populists and his condemnation of their ideas give it neither the profound 'objectivity' of *Fathers and Children* nor the passionate bias of *Smoke*. It has to be remembered, also, that *Virgin Soil* is a work curiously lacking in 'philosophical' content; everything is subordinated to the socio-political function of the novel. It appeared, moreover, at a time when the Russian literary scene was dominated by Tolstoy and Dostoyevsky, whose large canvases dealt with human problems in magnified perspective and on a scale that set Turgenev's more delicate and sensitive manner in the shade. By comparison with *Anna Karenina*, for instance, or *The Brothers Karamazov*, *Virgin Soil* was out of date not only in its lack of topical reference, but also in its form and its manner. With pretensions to epic form, it nevertheless fell far short of the epic manner which Tolstoy had brought to the novel; while its story interest could never rival the intricate and dramatic plots of Dostoyevsky. It was simply Turgenev's attempt to regain the favour of the younger generation—a deliberate concession to the spirit of the seventies in its treatment of populism; but it was

written by a man whose heart remained in the forties, faithful to
Westernist ideals and European principles.

Yet, even if Turgenev was not consciously in search of a religious
panacea, as were Tolstoy and Dostoyevsky in their investigation of
God's ways to man, nor even successful in making his novel a committed work in the political sense, he offered in *Virgin Soil*—perhaps
unintentionally—a prototype of the political novel of the future and,
allied to this, a prophetic portrait of a type of hero who has much
relevance to the present day. It is, in fact, the prophetic element in the
novel, as expressed in what Paklin has to say, that is so disturbing and
revealing. Paklin, the talkative cripple, who inadvertently reveals to
Sipyagin the whereabouts of Nezhdanov and Marianna, thus con-
tributing directly to the failure of their work for the populist cause,
is an embodiment of Turgenev's uncommitted attitude. It is he who
insists at the beginning of the novel (Chapter IV) that the peasantry
is like a Juggernaut which will crush and destroy those who sacrifice
themselves to it. Indeed, this was to be the destiny not only of Nezhdanov, but of the younger generation of the Russian intelligentsia as a
whole in the years before Marxism took root in Russia. If this has
relevance to Russia in the last years of the nineteenth century, then
more revealing still is the note of prophecy in Paklin's words at the
end of the novel (Chapter XXXVIII), when he is speaking to Mashurina
about Solomin as the man of the future:

'Men like him—they are the real men! They can't be understood all at once,
but they are the real men, believe me, and the future belongs to them. They're
not heroes. They're not even the "heroes of labour" about whom some fool
—an American or an Englishman—wrote a book for the edification of us
heathens. They're strong, colourless, dull men of the people. But now they're
the only kind that's needed! You look at Solomin—he's clever as the day is
long and healthy as a fish in water. . . . That's something to wonder at, isn't it!
Among us in Russia it used to be the case that if you were a living man with
sensitivity and intelligence—then you were bound to be diseased! But Solomin
has a heart that aches just like ours—and he hates the same things that we hate
—but his nerves don't trouble him and his body functions as it should, which
means: he's the right type! Consider now, here's a man with an ideal and
yet sensible, an educated man and yet from the people, a man who's
unsophisticated and yet in his right mind—What more do you want?'

It is just such men as Solomin—the 'strong, colourless, dull men of the
people', not the Platon Karatayevs of Tolstoy or the Alyoshas of
Dostoyevsky—who were to inherit the future. Turgenev perceive

this more clearly than any of his contemporaries. In this respect, Solomin is a twentieth-century figure, unreal in the novel for the simple reason that he is like a ghost from the future technocracy of the Soviet Union. Turgenev could admire such men and offer a prophetic vision of them, but they would always be as remote from him as the Soviet Union is from his own age.

* * * * *

During the remaining years of his life his fame, based on his *A Sportsman's Sketches* and his earlier novels, was finally acknowledged by friends and enemies alike. In 1878, a year after the publication of *Virgin Soil*, he was chosen to be vice-president of the international literary congress in Paris, with a seat of honour next to Victor Hugo. In 1879 his friendship with Tolstoy was renewed after seventeen years of rift between them and his visit to Russia in that year became a triumphal progress, ovations and receptions being accorded to him by supporters and political enemies, by the older and the younger generation. In June of the same year he was honoured by Oxford University with the degree of Doctor of Civil Law; and in August he was made an *officier d'instruction publique* by the French Government. Returning to Russia in 1880 for the unveiling of the Pushkin monument in Moscow, he was once more acclaimed, though on this occasion his refusal to commit himself on the subject of Pushkin's genius, in a speech of interest but too guarded for it to have mass appeal, was not to arouse the same fervour as was accorded to Dostoyevsky's more emotional and less scholarly oration. His last visit to Russia was in the spring and summer of 1881. For the last two years of his life, until his death at Bougival on 22 August, 1883, he was to be little more than a semi-invalid. Yet Turgenev had had his triumph. He had become a great figure in his own age. His *Poems in Prose*, written at the end of his life, summarize his many themes and distil the essence of his magical style. It is in his work as a novelist, however, that his fame will endure.

8

THE NOVELIST'S NOVELIST:
THE BEAUTIFUL GENIUS

IT was Henry James who described Turgenev as the novelist's novelist ('Turgenev is in a peculiar degree what I may call the novelist's novelist, an artistic influence extraordinarily valuable, and ineradicably established')[1] and it was the highest compliment that he could pay. For Henry James such a definition had a meaning that was at once both personal and professional. In the personal sense, Henry James could say of Turgenev that 'no one could desire more than he that art should be art; always, ever, incorruptibly, art',[2] while of Turgenev the novelist he could say, with an equal measure of sincerity and admiration:

> If his manner is that of a searching realist, his temper is that of a devoutly attentive observer, and the result of this temper is to make him take a view of the great spectacle of human life more general, more impartial, more un-reservedly intelligent, than that of any novelist we know.[3]

But to understand the honour that he wished to bestow on Turgenev by describing him in this way, one must also remember that he was for Henry James a 'beautiful genius'. Turgenev touched James's heart and the charm remained there all his life. Of all the writers in the last hundred years who have felt the charm and succumbed to it in varying degrees, Henry James was by far the most sensitive as an artist and the *cri du cœur* attributed to him by Ford Madox Ford—'Ah, he was the real, but a thousand times the only—the only real beautiful genius!'[4] —is therefore the most valuable single description that can be applied to Turgenev.

When a writer is called a novelist's novelist by another writer, it must mean that the one has learned something of inestimable value about his art from the other. It naturally also means that the writer

[1] Henry James, *The House of Fiction: Essays on the Novel* (1957), 170.

[2] Henry James, *The Art of Fiction and other essays* (1948), 104. Originally in 'Ivan Turgénieff', *Partial Portraits* (1888).

[3] Henry James, *French Poets and Novelists* (1878), 275.

[4] Quoted from Ford Madox Ford, *Mightier than the Sword* (1938), 190.

in question has made some significant personal and unique contribution to the art of the novel which the other writer could not overlook and might wish in turn to acquire for himself. From this it follows that the writer in question must also have enlarged the novel's scope or lent it some special distinction which the novel, as a genre, had not possessed previously. In the final resort, of course, it must mean that one learns something new from this writer and his work—something new, that is to say, about the human condition, about human relationships, about life and the way people live it. In all these respects Turgenev can be said to have made his contribution.

The initial impact of Turgenev on European literature and the European reading public obviously owed much to the fact that he was Russian. His 'Russian-ness' exercised the attraction of anything a little strange, unusual or exotic, but his mastery of his medium meant that there was no need to make allowances. It was not the strangeness or exoticism of his 'Russian-ness' that made Henry James exclaim with admiration at Turgenev; it was the inherent distinction of his work and the equally surprising fact that his work not only stood comparison with European standards of the novel but transcended those standards. It was not because he was writing in Russian or writing 'Russian' novels, but because his novels were 'Turgenevan', unmistakably distinctive and individual, that Europe had to sit up and take notice. Probably Europe will never cease to be surprised by the fact that Russians are capable of taking examples from Europe and improving on them. In the case of Turgenev the initial surprise is understandable. He made previous vogues and manners in the novel appear to be out of date. No sensitive European writer—and, even more to the point, no sensitive American writer, such as was Henry James—could afford to overlook the importance of Turgenev once that importance had been recognized and established. Although Tolstoy and Dostoyevsky were to achieve greater eminence later—partly, of course, as a result of Turgenev's activity on their behalf in promoting translation of their works, especially in Tolstoy's case,—Turgenev was the first of the great Russian novelists to make an indelible mark on European and American literature. This was largely due to the fact that Turgenev's attitude to his art and *ipso facto* his attitude to life were generally more acceptable, and comprehensible, to European sensibilities than the Jehovah-like omniscience characteristic of Tolstoy's attitude ('A mixture of poet, Calvinist, fanatic, and aristocrat—in some ways reminding one of Rousseau, though more honest than Rousseau—of high moral intent but at the same time an unsympathetic being'[1]—Turgenev wrote of him) or the deliberate preoccupation with the abnormal and the ideological dichotomies, symptomatic of man's moral dilemma, which permeate Dostoyevsky's work. It was the sense of artistic proportion, the classical restraint combined with the realistic idiom, the pictorial brilliance balanced by the insights into human nature, which had the greatest appeal. In Turgenev's extremely personal view of life there was the same realism—unyielding in its agnosticism and its refusal to offer any solutions to man's problems that contravened the reality of his being. But inseparable from this realistic view was a pessimism that could not be so readily accepted. Beyond the lucid world of Turgenev's fiction, sometimes on its very fringes, sometimes penetrating the fiction itself, was the menacing darkness which proclaimed that man had no choice. In a nineteenth century of ebullient capitalism, or in a twentieth century of ebullient communism, such pessimism may seem misplaced, but Turgenev did not look at the world through the spy-glass of a system or a faith. His method was that of realistic observation, indicating the truth as it was there to be observed, pointing to the reality as it existed, and man can have his ideas and his ideals, his loves and his passions, but the truth and the reality will always remain the same. It is the sharpness of Turgenev's sight—as a writer, as an artist, as a recorder of the social and political scene, as one who understood the human condition—which must always draw readers to him. Europe can understand Russia much better through a reading of Turgenev than through a reading of any other Russian writer. The content of the fiction itself may have aged, but the universal attributes of Turgenev himself as they are expressed in his work have the perennial vitality that is inseparable from greatness.

We may like to think of him nowadays as a novelist's novelist, though during his own lifetime Turgenev never regarded himself as being anything more than a writer of stories. He always had high hopes for the success of his works when they first appeared, but his sensitivity to criticism and his modesty about his own talent—not a false modesty, simply the result of being aware of his limitations as a writer—never led him to overestimate the worth of his achievement. In his correspondence, which has so far not been collected for publication in a uniform edition, in his *Literary Reminiscences* and elsewhere Turgenev has revealed much about himself that is of value in determining his own attitude to his art. It is his correspondence which is

[1] Letter to P. V. Annenkov, 15/3 April 1857. *Sobr. soch.* (1958), xii. 273.

especially rich in such statements. Indeed, he was a brilliant and prolific writer of letters—there are about 6,000 extant letters of his[1]— and many of them, chiefly those written to aspiring authors who had sent him their manuscripts, are full of sensitive, witty and thoughtful observations on matters, both particular and general, relating to problems of literary craftsmanship. On his own attitude to the novel, however, he displays an understandable diffidence. Writing to Goncharov, who was in many respects Turgenev's antithesis as a writer and who harboured a malevolent suspicion of Turgenev's integrity, he says, speaking of his own kind of novel:

It remains for me to write stories [*povesti*] in which, without pretending to offer a roundness or a strength in my characters and without pretending to offer a profound and comprehensive penetration of life, I would be able to express what came into my head. There will be rents in my work which will have to be sewn up, and so on. How can one help that? Whoever is in need of a novel in the epic sense, that person will not need me; I would as soon think of creating a novel [*roman*] as of walking on my head: no matter what I write, my work will always take the form of a series of sketches. *E sempre bene!*[2]

E sempre bene! one may repeat after him. His novels are not burgeoning epics. When they aspire to epic form, as in *Virgin Soil*, they are failures, but when they have pretensions to be no more than elaborate sketches or portraits etched in with the lightest of touches, they are perfect works, models of craftsmanship and form. This was the kind of novel that he could write, and he could write no other. Similarly, he could never aspire to be a writer dominated by a 'tendency'—his Westernism excepted—which went against the grain of his writer's instinct. To be successful in his own kind of novel he had to be true to his class feelings and his artistic temperament. Writing to his friend, Countess Lambert, a year after the publication of *Fathers and Children*, he offers an explanation of his position:

You blame me as a man (in the sense that I am a political figure, a citizen) and as a writer. In the first instance you are correct, in the second—no, or so it seems to me. You are right in saying that I am not a politician and in asserting that the government has nothing to fear from me; my convictions have not changed since my youth, but I have never occupied myself, and will never occupy myself, with politics: it is foreign and uninteresting to me, and I pay attention to it only to the extent that I have to as a writer whose vocation it is to paint pictures of the contemporary scene. But you are wrong when you

---

[1] *Sobr. soch.* (1958), xii. 5.
[2] Letter to I. A. Goncharov, 7 April 1859. Ibid, 304-5.

demand from me in my *literary* work what I cannot give, fruits that do not grow on my tree. I have never *written for the people*—I have written only for that class of public to which I belong, beginning with *A Sportsman's Sketches* and ending with *Fathers and Children*; I do not know what use I have been, but I know that I have kept unswervingly to the same aim—and in this respect I do not deserve to be censured. It seems to you that it is only out of idleness that I do not write, as you say, a simple and moral story for the people; but how do you know that I haven't tried twenty times to do something of this kind and abandoned it finally because I had been convinced that it was not in my line, that I *did not know how* to do it? It is here that the weak side of the most intelligent people who are *not* artists betrays itself: having accustomed themselves all their lives to arrange matters in accordance with their own wishes, they cannot understand that the artist is frequently not a free man in his own creations—and so they are ready to accuse him of idleness, of epicurean behaviour and so on. Believe me, every one of us does only what he's given to do, and to force oneself to do something else is worthless and fruitless. That's why I shall never write a story for the people. A quite different cast of mind and character is needed for that.[1]

This is Turgenev speaking as only a true writer can speak. He could not change himself, just as he could not be 'a free man in his own creations'—they are words which acknowledge an important truth that every writer has to face. For Turgenev this feeling of inevitable constraint had a special meaning, partially mirrored in the pessimism of his view of life but particularly evident in the aim which he had set himself—the aim of portraying life truthfully, impassively, with an artistic detachment that, without abandoning artistic proportions, recreated life in realistic terms.

His method was objective. Writing to a correspondent in 1876, he says:

. . . if the study of human physiognomy, of the lives of others, interests you *more* than the statement of your own feelings and thoughts; if it is, for example, *pleasanter* for you to describe truthfully and precisely the outward appearance not only of a man but of a simple object rather than to express eloquently and glowingly what you feel upon seeing this object or this man, then it means that you're an objective writer and you can start writing a story or a novel. So far as the labour of it is concerned, without constant application any artist will inevitably remain a dilettante: there's no use in waiting for the so-called noble moments of inspiration; if inspiration comes, all the better: but you must

<hr>

[1] Letter to E. E. Lambert, 9 May/27 April 1863. Ibid, 352-3. It must be remembered that he wrote this letter at a time when he was implicated in the 'affair of the thirty-two' and politically isolated after the rupture with Herzen.

work all the same. And you must apply yourself not only to your work, to seeing that it expresses precisely what you wanted to express, to the degree and in the form that you wanted to express it; but you must also read, learn unceasingly, study everything around you, strive not only to capture life in all its aspects, but also to understand it, to understand the laws by which it moves and which do not always appear on the surface; you must through the play of circumstances aspire to create types—and at the same time remain faithful to the truth, not be satisfied with a superficial study, beware of effects and falsehood. An objective writer takes upon himself a heavy burden: he should have strong muscles . . .[1]

It was part of his method in achieving such an objectivity to make use of living models as a basis for his fictional portraits. His notes on *Virgin Soil* and, to a lesser degree, on *Smoke* are especially revealing in the way they enumerate the personages upon whom the fictional characters in the novels were to be modelled.[2] 'I have never started from *ideas*, but always from *images*,'[3] he wrote to Polonsky, and writing to one of his English translators, in the last year of his life, he insisted that 'in general in my works I have constantly relied on living experience, striving, to the extent I was able, to raise only incidental phenomena into types'.[4] Henry James himself records Turgenev as saying words to the same effect.[5] There is undoubtedly much in Turgenev's work that is simply fictionalized autobiography, but this cannot alter the fact that it is always presented as if it were seen or experienced for the first time and objectively transmuted into art. The intimate knowledge of what he was writing about merely served to clarify and deepen his vision of it. It is only where the intimate knowledge is lacking—in such cases as Insarov and Solomin— that the objectivity of his method fails to reveal the living reality beneath the surface appearance. Turgenev knew that this was his weakness and admitted it on several occasions. *Scribitur ad narrandum, non ad probandum* he quoted to one of his correspondents,[6] and it was in general his motto. When he is simply narrating what he knows, as distinct from trying to prove an argument—which is the weakness of *Smoke* and *Virgin Soil*—his method is exemplary. It is here that his

1 Letter to V. L. Kign, 16 June (O.S.) 1876. Ibid, 492-3. This letter must have been written while Turgenev was busy with *Virgin Soil*.
2 See André Mazon, op. cit.
3 Letter to Ya. P. Polonsky, 27 February/March 11 1869. *Sobr. soch.* (1958), xii. 408.
4 Letter to Sidney Jerrold, 2 December 1882. Ibid, 568.
5 Henry James, *The Portrait of a Lady* (1921), p. viii.
6 Letter to E. V. A., 26/14 December 1878. *Sobr. soch.* (1958), xii. 532-33.

light touch, his faculty for saying just the right amount, is seen at its best, for he possessed the knack of never being a bore ('car le secret d'ennuyer est celui de tout dire', he warned another correspondent[1]). There have been many objective writers, but not so many who have learned to avoid the tedium which comes of labouring their objectivity to the exclusion of artistic sense. Turgenev was prevented from succumbing to this weakness through his own unique artistic sense—that indefinable characteristic of his genius which gives him the greatest claim to be 'the novelist's novelist'—although his attitude to the novel was supremely professional. Once the image had fired his imagination, he did not create 'spontaneously': he made careful, preliminary sketches for each character in his fiction, emphasizing significant features of personality and appearance, and then proceeded to outline, chapter by chapter and often in remarkable detail, the course of the narrative. On the evidence available, it seems that he remained astonishingly faithful to this preliminary plan of the characters and the narrative during the actual composition of his novels. His objectivity and his artistry, therefore, depended for their ultimate success upon his mastery of the language. To those who have access to his work only in translation the magic of the original can still be felt, depending of course upon the expertise of the translator; but for Russians, and those who have a knowledge of Russian, Turgenev's prose can only be read with admiration. Its virtues have been so widely acknowledged and so often described that there is no need to dwell on them, except to say that for anyone learning the language there is no better or more rewarding way of cultivating his knowledge than through reading the prose of Turgenev. All too often translations have captured only glimmerings of the subtlety and beauty of the original or, in being too accurate, have failed to convey the emotive shorthand which runs through the delicate rhythms and cadences of his sentences.[2]

But, though he was an artist in the noblest sense of that word, he wrote for a particular public and was always sensitive to the fact that his work had to be good enough to deserve that public's favour. Writing to Konstantin Leont'yev in 1853, he expressed his view on the matter by saying:

Know this: you can't dupe the public one iota—the public is wiser than any of us; you should also know that in offering it all of yourself, your flesh and

[1] Letter to L. Ya. Stech'kina, 7 May/25 April 1878. Ibid, 525.
[2] To my knowledge, the most successful English translation of a work by Turgenev is Sir Isaiah Berlin's translation of *First Love* in *First Love and Rudin* (1950).

blood, you must still be grateful to it if it so much as accepts or values your sacrifice, if it so much as pays any attention to you. This is understandable, and I will say more: this is only just. The public does not need you, but you need the public.[1]

In addition, of course, to the favour of the public Turgenev had also to win the favour of the censorship. To be a writer of the kind of socio-political novel which he had chosen for himself he had to accommodate himself both to the tastes, often so very diverse and fiery, of his reading public and to the demands of the censorship. These were a Scylla and a Charybdis which it required great skill to negotiate, and Turgenev was not always successful in overcoming the prejudices of the one without offending the susceptibilities of the other. But in his novels Turgenev was always a 'committed' writer—not 'tendentious', but committed to life itself, its political as well as its human reality. He knew that he had responsibilities as a writer and that such responsibilities entailed restrictions upon his total freedom of expression. Thus, when Turgenev spoke of freedom, he spoke of it primarily as something of great personal value, regardless of the fact that he enjoyed relatively considerable freedom from economic worries, for he was always struggling against impositions upon his own freedom, whether artistic or ideological, political or social, which were both products of the age in which he lived and manifestations of the predilection for tyranny in the human soul.

Freedom for Turgenev began within man himself. Man had to free himself first of all from enslavement to systems and habits of thought. His advice to Tolstoy was:

You are growing calmer, improving and—what is most important—you are becoming free, free from your own views and prejudices. . . . God grant that your mental horizon may grow wider every day! Systems are only dear to those who cannot take the whole truth into their hands, who want to catch it by the tail; a system is just like the tail of truth, but truth is like a lizard; it will leave its tail in your hand and then escape you; it knows that within a short time it will grow another.[2]

Tolstoy was not the sort of man to heed this kind of advice. He believed that truth could be rationalized and systematized to suit his purposes. Turgenev found all such systems abhorrent, particularly those systems of political thought, such as Socialism, which were only

---

[1] Letter to K. N. Leont'yev, 9 June (O.S.) 1853. *Sobr. soch.* (1958), xii. 160.
[2] Letter to L. N. Tolstoy, 3/15 January 1857. Ibid, 261.

the tail of truth. In his opinion, the true yardstick of political freedom was the freedom of the individual. It was for this reason that he finally came to admire, as superior to all other political systems, the liberal democracies of France and England. But he also thought of freedom as one of the great ideals bequeathed to the world by the revolution of 1789, as one of the rights of man, for which none the less man had to dedicate and sacrifice himself, obliterating his ego and his personal feelings, in the manner of a Don Quixote. It was inseparable from those other ideals which he proclaimed in his novels, such as Fatherland, Science, Art, Justice, Love (love-the sacrifice and not love-the pleasure) —ideals which could unite mankind. More important still, however, was the freedom of the individual as it affected the artist. In his *Literary Reminiscences* he quotes from Goethe who, like the ideals of 1789, represented for Turgenev the essence of the European spirit, and he addresses himself with Goethe's words to the younger generation of writers:

Greift nur hinein in's volle Menschenleben!—I would say to you in the words of the teacher whom we have in common, Goethe—
> Ein jeder lebt's—nicht vielen ist's bekannt,
> Und wo ihr's packt—da ist's interessant!

Talent alone gives the strength required for this 'seizing hold of', this 'capturing of life', and you cannot give yourself talent; but even talent alone is not sufficient. You must be in constant touch with the milieu that you have chosen to write about; you must have truthfulness, an inexorable truthfulness in regard to your own sensations; you must have freedom, complete freedom of outlook and ideas—and, finally, you must have education, you must have knowledge. ... Nothing emancipates man so much as knowledge—and nowhere is freedom more essential than in the sphere of art, of poetry: it is not without reason that even in the language of officialdom the arts are called 'free'. ... No! without truthfulness, without education, without freedom in the very broadest sense— in regard to oneself, to one's preconceived ideas and systems, even to one's people, one's history—a true artist is unthinkable; without this atmosphere around one one cannot breathe.[1]

Again, in the Preface to the 1880 edition of his novels, he insists upon the freedom of the artist, and addresses himself on this occasion, in

[1] Turgenev offers the following translation of Goethe's lines: 'That is to say: Put your hand down (I don't know how to translate this better) inside, into the depths of human life! Everyone lives by it, though it is not familiar to many—and where you seize hold of it, that's where it'll be interesting!' *Sobr. soch.* (1956), x. 354-5. I have omitted one or two sentences from this passage in the *Literary Reminiscences*, especially one about the absence of true freedom in Tolstoy's *War and Peace*, because these, though interesting, were superfluous to Turgenev's main argument.

words that have an unmistakably prophetic ring, to the literary critics who had so often misinterpreted his work:

Any writer, *not devoid of talent* (that is, of course, a first essential)—any writer, I say, strives first of all to reproduce faithfully and realistically the impressions received from his own life or from the lives of other people, and every reader has the right to judge the extent to which he has succeeded and where he has gone wrong; but who has the right to point out to him precisely which impressions are suitable for literature and which are not? If he has been truthful, then it means that he's right; but if he hasn't any talent, no amount of 'objectivity' can help him. Recently there have sprung up among us writers who regard themselves as being 'unconscious creators'—and they always take their subjects 'from life'; but at the same time they are permeated through and through by their unfortunate 'tendencies'. Everyone knows the saying: *a poet thinks in images*; this saying is completely incontrovertible and true; but on what grounds do you, his critic and judge, permit him to reproduce in artistic form a picture of nature or—if you like—of life among the people or the portrait of an integrated character (there's another *miserable* word for you!); but let him put his hand to something disturbing, psychologically complex, even morbid—particularly if this is not a fact of a personal nature, but one drawn from the depths of his own soul by that same life of the people and of society —you cry: 'Stop! That won't do! That's a reflexion on it, a preconceived idea, that's politics, publicism!' You maintain that the publicist and the poet have different tasks. . . . No! They can be exactly the same for both; except that the publicist looks at them with the eyes of a publicist, and the poet—with the eyes of a poet. In the sphere of art the question: how? is more important than the question: what? If everything that is rejected by you settles into the soul of a writer like an *image*—note that I say *like an image*—then on what grounds do you suspect his intentions, why do you drive him out of that temple where on decorated altars there sit the high priests of 'unconscious' art—on altars before which there burns the incense so often lighted by the hands of these very same high priests? Believe me, a real talent never serves aims outside itself and always finds its satisfactions within itself. The life surrounding a writer gives him his content—he is its *concentrated reflection*; but he is just as incapable of writing a panegyric as he is of writing a lampoon. In the last resort, it is beneath him. To submit to a given theme or to promote a particular programme is for those who can do no better.[1]

It is in these words that Turgenev is speaking as the real novelist's novelist. He not only knew the art of writing a novel, but he also knew the dangers that beset the novelist who sets out to portray life in realistic terms. Apart from considerations of talent, objectivity,

[1] *Sobr. soch.* (1956), xi. 409-10.

education, and knowledge, Turgenev knew that the greatest danger
for the novelist was the threat to his freedom of expression. Novelists
in the West have never had to experience this danger in the way that
Turgenev himself and his fellow writers, at every period in Russian
history though more particularly in the Soviet Union, have had to
experience it. This fact alone must enhance Turgenev's achievement.
During his career as a writer he may have discovered and perfected
the art of writing a novel; he may have made the single most important contribution to the establishment of a tradition of the realistic
novel in Russian literature; he may have earned the admiration of his
contemporaries, both in Russia and in Europe, as a novelist supreme in
his own field; yet he probably deserves the title of 'novelist's novelist'
chiefly because he understood the responsibility which devolves upon
a writer who strives to make his novels not only a mirror of life, but a
mirror of man's conscience. It is in this sense that Henry James's
definition will always apply to Turgenev, regardless of changes in
fashion or the passage of years.

It is impossible, on the other hand, to define the exact nature of
Turgenev's genius. His work will always have a different appeal to
different people. To Henry James it was the beauty that appealed most,
and there is no denying that Turgenev's work conveys a sense of the
beautiful which is not to be found in any other Russian novelist.
Turgenev himself regarded beauty as the only imperishable thing in
life. In one of the most interesting letters that he wrote, to Pauline
Viardot, in the period of his 'first love' for her, he revealed both the
cause of his love for her and, linked with it, his idea of beauty:

. . . You ask me what 'The Beautiful' is. It is, despite the action of time, which
destroys the form in which it is expressed, always here . . . because Beauty is
the only imperishable thing, and so long as even the smallest remnant of its
material form exists, its immortality is ensured. 'The Beautiful' is evident
everywhere, it manifests itself even in death. But nowhere does it shine with
such power as in the human personality; it is here that it speaks most clearly
to the mind, and that is why I always prefer a great musical talent served by
an imperfect voice to a good voice which is stupid, the beauty of which is
only material.[1]

Yet this can only be an aid to the definition of his genius. Whether it
be the artistic form of his novels, the poetic atmosphere, the brilliance
of the natural scene, the feeling of life—these elusive qualities which

[1] Letter to Pauline Viardot, 12 September 1850. *Sobr. soch.* (1949), xi. 88-9.

add up to the term 'Turgenevan'—it is impossible to say. His work is beautiful because it makes us aware of the meaning of beauty: probably there is no other definition. But it is Turgenev's treatment of two of the commonest themes in literature—the themes of youth and love— which is at the very centre of his appeal as a novelist. In Turgenev's hands, youth and love have a special beauty because it is their very impermanence which makes them valuable, to be perpetually sought for and perpetually regretted.

It is difficult to pinpoint the causes of this nostalgia for youth which is such a common theme in Turgenev. It may have its roots in the un- pleasantness of his own youth. Certainly he inherited it as part of the romantic tradition which had such a strong influence upon him when he began writing. During his career as a writer, however, it lost much of its romantic colouring and became assimilated into his realistic view of life, forming a *leit-motif* that runs throughout his work. It was an antidote to the pessimism that so often threatened to overwhelm him and make him abandon literature forever. It was also part of his pose—a cruel word to use, but he justified the use of it on many occasions—of premature senility at an age when most men would regard themselves as being in their prime. Yet for Turgenev youth meant not only freshness and vitality, it also meant hope, idealism, the willingness to sacrifice, enthusiasm and love. It was associated very closely with his admiration for the emotional spontaneity of the heart, which con- trasted so strongly, in his belief, with the rational failings of the head. All his heroines are young, though it is the youngest of all—Natal'ya, Liza, Yelena, Marianna—who have the greatest emotional spontaneity. It was always the feminine heart which possessed this 'naturalness' for Turgenev, and he admired it because he was himself, without being in the least effeminate, curiously feminine in his sensitivity and emo- tional response. The masculinity of the head and the femininity of the heart blended in him to a remarkable degree. But youth was a time of the heart, and when youth had gone the heart atrophied. Turgenev's pose of old age was partly an attempt to hide his fear of age which killed the freshness of the heart. As he wrote to Polonsky in 1873:

The cold of old age penetrates more deeply into my soul each day and seizes hold on it more firmly; an indifference to everything which I note in myself now begins to frighten me! Now I can say with Hamlet:

'How stale, flat and unprofitable
Seems me that life!'

. . . For one or two weeks of youth—the most foolish, wild, corrupt youth, but youth nevertheless—I would forgo not only my reputation, but the fame of real genius, if I was such a genius.[1]

Bound up with this nostalgia for youth were his feelings about love and death. Turgenev will always be recognized as a master of the love-story, but for him love was always an accidental emotion beyond the control of those who experienced it. It was an accident of life that ennobled man, though it was also a tragic emotion which made man conscious of his human frailty. In elevating the importance of love Turgenev was, it seems, attempting to create a balance between it and death. There were only these two alternatives for man, in his view. For in his calm, intelligent scrutiny of the world he saw that life and nature had a logic which was not amenable to rational interpretation. Yet in all his greatest work he compensates for this by achieving a subtle balance between the poles of human experience, between love and death, joy and sadness, youth and age, innocence and maturity. From this balance there emerges the momentary harmony, the momentary unity between hero and heroine, the momentary promise of happiness; though happiness itself merely served to underline the fact of life's tragi-comic impermanence.

In a letter to the famous satirist, Saltykov-Shchedrin, within a year of his death, Turgenev wrote:

. . . I offer as consolation to you (albeit rather poor consolation) what Goethe said shortly before his death. He was, it would seem, surfeited with all the happiness that only life can give—he was famous, loved by women, despised by fools, and his works were being translated into Chinese, and the whole of Europe journeyed to pay homage to him, and Napoleon himself said of him: C'est un homme! . . . but nevertheless he said, at the age of eighty-two, that during all those long years he had only been happy for *a quarter of an hour*! It's the same for us and God himself has ordained it so.[2]

The consolation of the sick Turgenev to the unhappy Saltykov is an ironic epitaph. Ironic because, though Turgenev's life obviously had more than a quarter of an hour's worth of happiness, in Turgenev's attitude to the world and in the way he transmitted the pageant of life in his fiction there is always this 'quarter of an hour' quality: of happiness and life itself as infinitely fleeting, scarcely begun before it is finished. This was his conception of life, and it was a conception both

---

[1] Letter to Ya. P. Polonsky, 21 February (O.S.) 1873. *Pervoye sobraniye pisem I. S. Turgeneva* (SPB., 1884), 213.

[2] Letter to M. E. Saltykov, 31 October 1882. *Sobr. soch.* (1958), xii. 563.

born of his experience in living and, in part, moulding the pattern of his life to suit it. At the end of his life the hypochondria, the pessimism, the fear of death were all abnormally heightened, but the ironic sentiment in the words of consolation to Saltykov was always present in varying degrees in what Turgenev has to tell us about the human condition.

BIBLIOGRAPHY

This bibliography makes no claim to be comprehensive. It includes all works mentioned in the text and in the notes and some of the more important works consulted in connexion with this study. The most recent bibliographical introduction to Turgenev, which gives details of standard bibliographies but excludes non-Russian material, is E. M. Yefimova's *I. S. Turgenev: Seminariy* (Leningrad, 1958). For a critical survey of works on Turgenev published in Russia since the revolution, attention is drawn to P. Brang, 'I. S. Turgenev in der russischen Literaturwissenschaft 1917-1954', *Zeitschrift für Slavische Philologie*, xxiv (1956), 182-215, 358-410; while for Turgenev criticism published in England and America, including some mention of Turgenev translations, Royal A. Gettmann's *Turgenev in England and America* (Urbana, 1941) is important. The bibliography in Henri Granjard's excellent study, *Ivan Tourguénev et les courants politiques et sociaux de son temps* (Paris, 1954), is extremely useful, especially for details of non-Russian studies; it also provides the best bibliography of Turgenev's published letters.

Places of publication of English, French and Russian works are London, Paris and Moscow respectively unless otherwise indicated.

WORKS OF TURGENEV

Sobraniye sochineniy, izd. Glazunov, 10 vols. (1883). (The last edition of his works to be prepared by Turgenev in person.)

Pervoye sobraniye pisem (SPB., 1884).

Sochineniya, pod red. K. Khalabayeva i B. Eykhenbauma, 12 vols. (1928-1934). (The first Soviet edition, with commentaries by L. V. Pumpyansky and very comprehensive notes; despite criticism of the anti-Marxist bias in the commentaries, this remains the fullest edition of Turgenev's works.)

Sobraniye sochineniy, pod red. N. L. Brodskogo, 11 vols. (1949). (Important only for its last volume, which contains a selection of Turgenev's letters—mostly, however, in shortened form.)

Sobraniye sochineniy, 12 vols. (1953-1958). (The commentaries are not as extensive in this edition as in the Khalabayev-Eykhenbaum edition of 1928-1934, but the texts have been carefully verified and the final volume contains a useful selection of Turgenev's letters.)

Literary Reminiscences, trans. David Magarshack, with an essay by Edmund Wilson (1959).

MEMOIRS, BIOGRAPHIES, CRITICAL STUDIES, ETC.

ANNENKOV, P. V., *Vospominaniya i kriticheskiye ocherki* (SPB., 1881).
Literaturniye vospominaniya (SPB., 1909).

ANTONOVICH, M. A., 'Asmodey nashego vremeni', *Sovremennik*, 1862, No. 3.

BELINSKY, V. G., *Sobraniye sochineniy*, 3 vols. (1948).

BOYESEN, HJALMAR, 'A Visit to Turgenev', *The Galaxy*, xvii (1874).
'Ivan Turgenev', *Scribner's Monthly*, xiv (1877).
'K biografii I. S. Turgeneva', *Minuvshiye gody*, 1908, No. 8.

DOBROLYUBOV, N. A., *Pervoye polnoye sobraniye sochineniy*, pod red. M. K. Lemke, 4 vols. (SPB., 1911).

DOSTOYEVSKY, F. M., *The Diary of a Writer*, trans. Boris Brasol, 2 vols. (1949).

FORD, FORD MADOX, *Mightier than the Sword* (1938).

GARNETT, EDWARD, *Turgenev, A Study* (1917).

GERSHENZON, M., *Mechta i mysl' I.S. Turgeneva* (1919).

GOLOVIN, K. F., *Russky roman i russkoye obshchestvo* (SPB., 1904).

GRANJARD, HENRI, *Ivan Tourguénev et les courants politiques et sociaux de son temps* (1954).

GUT'YAR, N. M., *Ivan Sergeyevich Turgenev* (Yur'yev, 1907).

HAUMANT, ÉMILE, *Ivan Tourguénief: la vie et l'œuvre* (1905).

HERZEN, A. I., *Polnoye sobraniye sochineniy*, pod red. M. K. Lemke, 22 vols. (P-grad, 1914-1925).

HIRSCHKOWITZ, HARRY, *Democratic Ideas in Turgenev's Novels* (New York, 1932).

Istoriya russkoy literatury 19-ogo veka, pod red. D. N. Ovsyaniko-Kulikovskogo. 5 vols. (1908-1910).

Istoriya russkoy literatury, pod red. M. P. Alekseyeva, viii (1956).

JAMES, HENRY, *French Poets and Novelists* (1878).
Partial Portraits (1888).
The Portrait of a Lady, 2 vols. (1921).
The Art of Fiction and other essays (1948).
The House of Fiction: Essays on the Novel (1957).

KLEMAN, M. K., *Rudin. Dvoryanskoye Gnezdo*, pod red. M. K. Klemana (1933).
Letopis' zhizni i tvorchestva I. S. Turgeneva (1934).
I. S. Turgenev. Ocherk zhizni i tvorchestva (1936).

LEONHARDI, WOLDEMAR, *Turgenjeffs Romane* (Leipzig, 1909).

LUBBOCK, PERCY, *The Craft of Fiction* (1921).

Lukacs, Georg, *Der Russische Realismus in der Weltliteratur* (Berlin, 1949).

Magarshack, David, *Turgenev, A Life* (1954).

Maurois, André, *Tourguéniev* (1952).

Mazon, André, 'L'Élaboration d'un roman de Turgenev: À la Veille, Premier Amour, Fumée', *Revue des Études Slaves*, v (1925).
'L'Élaboration d'un roman de Turgenev: Terres Vierges', *Revue des Études Slaves*, v (1925).

Mirsky, D. S., *A History of Russian Literature* (1949).

Ovsyaniko-Kulikovsky, D. N., *Sobraniye sochineniy*, ii (SPB., 1913).
Istoriya russkoy intelligentsii, 2 vols. (SPB., 1914).

Phelps, Gilbert, *The Russian Novel in English Fiction* (1956).

Pustovoyt P. G., *Ivan Sergeyevich Turgenev* (1957).

Salonen, Hugo Tauno, *Die Landschaft bei I. S. Turgenev* (Helsingfors, 1915).

Schütz, Dr. Katharina, *Das Goethebild Turgeniews* (Bern, 1952).

Trautmann, Reinhold, *Turgenjew als Novelist* (Leipzig, 1948).

Tseytlin, A. G., *Masterstvo Turgeneva-romanista* (1958).

Turgenevsky sbornik, pod red. N. K. Piksanova (P-grad, 1915).

Tvorchesky put' Turgeneva: sbornik statey, pod red. N. L. Brodskogo (P-grad, 1923).

Venok Turgenevu, 1818-1918: sbornik statey (Odessa, 1918).

Vogüé, Vicomte E.-M. de, *The Russian Novel* [1886], trans. Col. H. A. Sawyer (1913).

Yarmolinsky, Avrahm, *Turgenev, The Man, His Art and His Age* (1960).
Road to Revolution (1957).

Zaytsev, Boris, *Zhizn' Turgeneva* (Paris, 1949).

Zelinsky, V., *Sobraniye kriticheskikh materialov dlya izucheniya proizvedeniy Turgeneva*, 3 vols. (1884-1917).

Zhitova, V., *The Turgenev Family* (1947).

INDEX

This Index includes all surnames, important place names and titles contained in the text and notes. It does not include fictional names.